MY LIFE IN LOYALISM

MY LIFE IN LOYALISM

BILLY HUTCHINSON

With GARETH MULVENNA

First published in 2020 by
Merrion Press
10 George's Street
Newbridge
Co. Kildare
Ireland
www.merrionpress.ie

9781785373459 (Paper)
9781785373466 (Kindle)
9781785373473 (Epub)

A CIP catalogue record for this book is available from the British Library.

Typeset in Sabon LT Std 11.5/16.5 pt

Front cover image: Peter Muhly/AFP via Getty Images.
Back cover image courtesy of Eddie Kinner.
Unless otherwise stated, all images are taken from the author's private collection.

Merrion Press is a member of Publishing Ireland.

CONTENTS

List of Abbreviations

ACT	Action for Community Transformation
CLMC	Combined Loyalist Military Command
CLPA	Combined Loyalist Political Alliance
DUP	Democratic Unionist Party
IICD	Independent International Commission on Decommissioning
INLA	Irish National Liberation Army
IRA	Irish Republican Army
MLA	Member of the Legislative Assembly
NICRA	Northern Ireland Civil Rights Association
NILP	Northern Ireland Labour Party
NIO	Northern Ireland Office
PSNI	Police Service of Northern Ireland
PROPP	Progressive Release of Political Prisoners
PUP	Progressive Unionist Party
PIRA	Provisional Irish Republican Army
RHC	Red Hand Commando
RMP	Royal Military Police
RUC	Royal Ulster Constabulary
SYT	Shankill Young Tartan
SDLP	Social Democratic and Labour Party
SPG	Special Patrol Group
UDA	Ulster Defence Association
UUP	Ulster Unionist Party

UVF	Ulster Volunteer Force
UWC	Ulster Workers' Council
UUAC	United Unionist Action Council
VPP	Volunteer Political Party
YCV	Young Citizen Volunteers

Preface

After an event in the Shankill Road Library in October 2016, which had been organised by the Action for Community Transformation initiative to promote my book *Tartan Gangs and Paramilitaries: The Loyalist Backlash*, Billy asked could he have a private word with me. He had been on a panel earlier in the evening with me, Eddie Kinner and Dr William Mitchell, during which he had talked candidly about his experiences as a member of the Young Citizen Volunteers in the early 1970s; experiences which he had shared with me for my book. 'I think it's time I told my life story, Gareth, and I'd like you to help me.'

I'd known of Billy since the late 1990s when, alongside David Ervine, he had come to the fore as an impressive advocate for progressive loyalism and an inclusive Northern Ireland for all people. He was also a Member of the Legislative Assembly (MLA) for the area I lived in, North Belfast, as I moved from Methodist College to Queen's University to continue studying politics. With my ongoing research interests in political and paramilitary loyalism in Northern Ireland, it was inevitable that I would at some stage come to meet Billy, and I did so some time after completing my Ph.D. at Queen's University. He agreed to speak on the record for my oral history of the emergence of Tartan Gangs and loyalist paramilitaries in the early 1970s, and ever since we have remained in close contact.

This book is the fruits of that relationship and friendship, whereby Billy placed his trust in me to assist in writing his story.

I don't and can't agree with everything that Billy has done in his life, and he wouldn't want me to. Thus, without being so heavy-handed as to write a 'disclaimer', there are many events in this book which I do not endorse or support.

However, I do feel honoured to have been asked by Billy to assist in writing his life story. I took this project on because I feel that his story – an incredible journey from young paramilitary through to politician – is an honest and insightful account that will add to a better understanding of loyalism during the Troubles in Northern Ireland.

Dr Gareth Mulvenna,
June 2020

Introduction

> My so-called public image does not reflect my true self at all and so few people really know me outside of sensational newspaper headlines.
>
> **Gusty Spence, excerpt from resignation letter to UVF Belfast Brigade HQ (1978)**

This book is my story. It is not an attempt to rewrite history. I want to take responsibility for my actions; actions I took because of the circumstances I and other young men found ourselves in during the violent early 1970s in Northern Ireland. I made choices in my life and I want to be honest about how I came to make those choices. I want to show that the story of working-class loyalism during the Northern Ireland conflict is not a one-dimensional story. The tabloids have filled plenty of column inches about me, and thus people perceive me in a certain way which is based on what they read or hear, but this book is my perspective and I aim to show that my story, and the stories of other young men of my generation, is more complex and nuanced than the way journalists and propagandists have tried to portray it.

By being able to tell my story, I understand that I am in a privileged position. Many of the people who I grew up with died during the conflict or are injured and unable to tell their stories. I hope that some people reading this book will recognise their experiences reflected in mine.

It is a story in three parts: growing up at the beginning of the Northern Ireland Troubles, becoming involved in loyalist paramilitarism and being incarcerated in Long Kesh for my actions; my years in prison, where I gained an education and decided that upon my release I would seek to help the community from which I hailed without resorting to the gun, and finally, how, through politics and the Progressive Unionist Party, I sought to make Northern Ireland a better place for everybody.

This is my life in loyalism.

Billy Hutchinson,
June 2020

CHAPTER 1

Shankill Born

I was born on Saturday, 17 December 1955 in a small two-up, two-down red-brick house at 98 Matchett Street off the Shankill Road. My parents William and Elizabeth greeted me into the world as everyone around them was eagerly anticipating Christmas, rushing around and making all their traditional festive preparations. In the midst of all this, it seems that I didn't make much of an impression; indeed, after the local doctor had helped to deliver me, he turned to my mother and said, 'Mrs Matchett, you're the best mother on Hutchinson Street.' It would be fair to say that my life hasn't exactly run in a straight line since.

Parts of the Shankill are in North Belfast and other parts are in West. Matchett Street is on the North side, between the main Shankill and Crumlin roads. The whole area has been redeveloped, and many of the old streets have disappeared. In those days, however, those streets were tightly packed with red-brick terraced houses where extended families lived in strong networks of kinship. Our house was near the end of the street, and where numbers 94 and 96 should have been there stood wasteland which had apparently been created by a Luftwaffe bomb during the Blitz. It sounded like a good story when we were young, but it wasn't true. Our house had an outside toilet which rarely worked and a yard that flooded in the winter. The roof leaked continuously, and the house was always full of damp. Such were the living conditions for thousands of families in the

Greater Shankill area. Like many other children born to working-class parents in Belfast at this time, I was a 'drawer-baby'. Despite what it might sound like, the term doesn't mean that I was an art prodigy, it just meant that I slept in the only cot that was available – the bottom drawer of the dressing table.

My parents had only moved into 98 Matchett Street two and a half years before I was born. They were hard-working people and well known and well liked in their respective circles. My father, who I am named after, was a bookie's clerk. He was also a prolific and skilful gambler, affectionately known as 'Big Hutchie'. In 1955 gambling wasn't the mainstream pursuit that it is now, and my father had to move from bookie to bookie across Belfast to set up games. He was 'well-got' in both the Protestant and Catholic working-class areas of the city and would spend a lot of time with friends in Clonard, off the Falls Road. Indeed, my father often took me to Dunville Park on the Falls Road to play and to the cinema at Clonard to watch the latest films. I remember spending a lot of time on the Falls rather than the Shankill as a small boy. During these sojourns he would often bring me to his friend's house at the Falls end of Cupar Street for a visit. I remember the family had a holy water font in their hallway and religious statues and pictures of figures such as the Virgin Mary in their living room. I had never seen these on the Shankill, and it was seemed very mysterious. As a child these pictures and statues were quite frightening to me if I am honest. Fear often came from a point of ignorance, but it was infectious and thrilling. One of the games that we would play as young lads was running up and down the steps of the Holy Cross Catholic church at Ardoyne. The whole idea was that if you were caught by the priest, people said you would be put in cells in the catacombs below the church and driven off to the south of Ireland. Absolute rubbish of course, but we didn't know that at the time. The fear of 'Rome Rule' and the 'priest-ridden' Republic of Ireland was enough to frighten even those on the Shankill who didn't subscribe to evangelical Protestantism. Although I was never taught bigotry at home, it was obvious to me that there were invisible and often unspoken-of barricades that separated people on the Shankill and the Falls roads. A few years later these would become real physical barricades, erected to try and stop people from killing each other.

My mother, known to most people as Lily, had been married previously. I had a brother, George, and a sister, Elinor.

I often think I was the product of a mixed marriage. My parents were both Protestants, but their political views were quite different. My dad was a socialist and had friends in the Catholic community through his work, while my mother was a strong unionist who believed we were in the heart of the British Empire. Her maiden name was Grant, and her father William was one of hundreds of thousands of men who had signed the Solemn League and Covenant on Ulster Day, 28 September 1912. Like those hundreds of thousands of others, he was adamantly opposed to Home Rule. Nevertheless, politics did not rule my mother's life. For her, like many others, it was just a part of who she was. Sadly, however, those deeply ingrained fears of Ireland being a 'priest-ridden' state meant that she blocked my early ambition to travel South to train to be a jockey. My father was all for it, but fear of the unknown ruled my mother. Despite this, she was better known for being the life and soul of the party who enjoyed singing and laughing. She was also confident in speaking her own mind. She was a cleaner and worked for several Jewish families who lived in the big houses up the Antrim Road. She toiled hard for her employers, who thought fondly of her, and she took on extra work at night in a local bar. In between these shifts she would come home and attend to her children and husband.

I remember the first day I went to Glenwood Primary as a 4-year-old in 1960. I knew the building, as I'd been past it before, but nothing prepared me for the inside. It reminded me of a big treasure chest, and to my young eyes the corridors and windows seemed to sparkle in the sun. In the first years at primary school, my mother met me at the gate every day after classes had finished and took me across the road to the library. Shankill library appeared imposing to me as a child, with its tall white pillars standing on either side of a large door that had to be approached by walking up four steps. Mother was a great reader and she would set me down in front of the children's books in the library. She always said that it didn't matter what was in the book, it just mattered that you read; that reading broadened your horizons and worldview. Years later, when I was in Long Kesh, this advice would become extremely relevant. Often you found yourself reading something to pass the time, but it meant that you were keeping your brain occupied and absorbing information. I kept up the visits to the library until I was about 14, before things changed dramatically in Northern Ireland.

My granny lived in the Hammer district of the Lower Shankill. I would often go and visit her before she died in 1966, and on many of those visits I would accompany her to Downing Street. I would help her by carrying big heavy bags of straw or hay from her house, and at Downing Street there was a gateway where we would go and get clean hay and straw in exchange for the old bags. You might wonder why I was helping my granny shift big bags of hay around Belfast in the 1960s – it was to fill the mattress in her bedroom. She would stuff the mattress with this fresh hay and sew it up with a big darning needle. We didn't have a bath in our house either. There was a tin bath which hung on a nail in the back yard; if I wanted to wash myself, it had to be brought into the house and filled with water heated in a pot on the stove. On Fridays I would go down to the bathing cubicles in Malvern Street with everyone else to get a proper wash. We were poor, and so was everybody else in the Shankill area. I remember an old lady, probably about my granny's age, who lived near us on Matchett Street. Every now and then she would have asked me to go and get her stuff from the local shops, as she was unable to get out herself. I vividly recall her, sitting in her house with a shawl around her with gas mantles on the walls. The house had no electricity. This was in the mid-1960s, when Prime Minister Terence O'Neill was making big noises about new industries investing in Northern Ireland and the whole idea of 'go-ahead Ulster'. I could see first-hand that not everybody was able to share in the economic dividend that O'Neill was promising.

When I think of that old lady and others like her, I am always reminded of William Conor. Conor was a local artist who was born in Fortingale Street in 1881 in the Old Lodge area behind Crumlin Road courthouse. He captured the 'shawlies', mill girls and cloth-cap wearing shipyard men in his sympathetic portraits of working-class life in Belfast. It was Gusty Spence who introduced me and others to his work when we were in Compound 21 of Long Kesh. Gusty's notion of cultural expression in art was rooted in the inspiration he had drawn from Conor's paintings. Consequently, he had murals painted on the cubicle walls inside the huts in each of the UVF/RHC compounds as a matter of pride in our heritage, not just for decoration. The murals were designed to represent our past, present and future. Many depicted the reality of life within the loyalist community: the poverty; the smudge-faced labourers in their cloth caps, who trudged home from the factories; a pawn shop on the Old Lodge Road. An article published in 1925, in London's *The Studio* magazine, stated that

> Conor is a painter of genius and ... he is a painter of Belfast. There are notes in his work which suggest he could not have painted anywhere else. If a modern manufacturing town could have folk songs and if those folk songs could be translated into pictures, or if the feelings which inspired

them could be pictorially represented, they would take the form of the art of William Conor.

In September 2015 I was absolutely delighted to speak at the unveiling of Conor's Corner at the top of Northumberland Street on the Shankill. It is a lasting tribute from the people of the Shankill to one of their own. I was joined on the day by the renowned local journalist and art lover Eamonn Mallie, who spoke fondly of Conor's work.

Despite the poverty that was depicted by Conor in some of his paintings, people in the Shankill were proud of where they came from. We didn't know any different and our pride was often underpinned by the military service history of the area. One of my neighbours and friends was Robert McQuitty. Robert and I spent many hours on the street playing football. Ball games weren't allowed on the streets, and in the days before the Troubles the police must have had very little to do because the minute that they saw you kicking a ball they would be on top of you. So, every time we saw a 'peeler' we would pick the ball up and run as fast as we could. We called one of the policemen 'the Durango Kid' because on his motorcycle, chasing us up and down the narrow alleyways, he reminded us of the antihero on horseback from the popular Western films starring Charles Starrett.

The McQuitty family fascinated me. Robert's father was an ex-soldier who had served all across the world with the Signal Corps. Each of the children had been born in outposts across the globe such as Cyprus, Singapore and Malta. These were all places that I knew from the map in our geography class in school and which seemed exotic and exciting from the less-than-glamorous vantage point of the backstreets of Belfast. I heard all about British military campaigns in far-flung places such as Aden and Korea. Veterans of these campaigns and others, like Mr McQuitty, lived throughout the Shankill. The Empire and the

Shankill's contribution to it was something that people such as my mother were fiercely proud of. While my father might have had a more cynical perspective of the whole thing, he would have been very much in the minority. Military service was something to be proud of – it elevated men in the Shankill to folk-hero status and became woven into the complex tapestry of Britishness, loyalism and unionism that made up our community's DNA.

Gusty Spence would become a huge part of my life later in the early 1970s. As a member of the Royal Ulster Rifles, he was stationed in Cyprus from 1957 and fought for the British against the EOKA guerrillas led by Georgios Grivas. While proud of his military service, Gusty was, like many of his comrades, disillusioned by what he came home to. It became obvious to him and other men on 'Civvy Street' that the rich and powerful in the ruling class had used them and others in previous generations as cannon fodder for their empire-building pursuits. While the National Health Service was an outstanding legacy for those men who had fought in the Second World War, there was little else of material benefit for people like Gusty who returned back to slums in cities such as Belfast, London, Cardiff, Liverpool, Sheffield, Manchester, Nottingham, Glasgow and Leeds. Gusty always told this story about being in a betting shop on the Shankill in the early 1960s after he had left the army due to ill health. There were two fellas standing near him and they were loudly arguing over 'who owned Australia', so one of them turned to Gusty and said, 'Gusty, you're an educated man – you've been around the world ... tell him, don't we own Australia?' To which Gusty replied, 'Of course we own Australia, but you haven't the arse in your trousers!'

When the Empire declined in the 1960s, our sense of 'Empire Britishness' all but died out with it. People on the Shankill could no longer comfort themselves with the perception that they were at the centre of a much bigger project. Looking back, the 1960s should have been a turning point for working-class Protestants in Northern Ireland. With the collapse of the British Empire and demands for civil rights emerging from the Catholic community, it was obvious that changes were afoot. Instead of being resistant to this zeitgeist, people in the Shankill and other Protestant areas should have demanded better from those unionists who took their seats in Stormont. We were portrayed as the Protestant ascendancy, but that was a falsehood. It was the landowners and factory owners who were the ascendancy. We were merely the people who made them rich and kept them in furs and diamonds.

Although the electorate in the Greater Shankill did vote for independents and Northern Ireland Labour Party (NILP) candidates, they were broadly nervous about protesting against the government too much. To do this would have played into the hands of republicans, or at least that is what people were told. We were kept in our place, but we were no better off than people on the Falls Road. Billy Mitchell, a future Ulster Volunteer Force (UVF) comrade and Progressive Unionist Party (PUP) colleague of mine, was always quoting my dad on this issue: 'Hutchie's da was right. We may have got a slum quicker than a Catholic, but it was still a slum.'

Although the Empire was in decline, the people of the Shankill still retained a Britishness that was rooted in a sense of belonging to the wider British working class and its struggles. This common working-class identity was forged in the struggles of Belfast's industrial working class, which linked them to workers on the Clyde and in Liverpool's docks as well as the other great industrial centres of Britain, rather than to the mainly agricultural south of Ireland. Like many other men of his generation, my uncle Billy Grant had to travel to England for work when there was none available in Belfast. The working-class political consciousness that existed on the Shankill had a stronger East–West dimension than a North–South one.

As a child, however, such things didn't really bother me because I didn't know any different. We were poor, and that was it. For most of the 1960s I was more interested in boyish pursuits. The Shankill was the centre of my world, and for young boys like me it was a playground as well as a home. I was always playing sports in Woodvale Park with my friends. Football, cricket, pitch and putt. Like many other boys my age, I became fanatical about football more than any other sport. The local team was Linfield – 'the Blues' – and I supported them passionately, being brought up in the Linfield tradition. They were and still are followed largely by people from the unionist and loyalist community, but they are one of the most successful club sides in world football. In the years shortly after I was born, from 1957 to 1960, the legendary former Newcastle United centre forward Jackie Milburn played for the Blues, scoring 68 goals in 54 appearances. His shot was so hard that Gusty's nephew Edward, who was a young ball boy at Windsor Park at the time, later told me that he was knocked out by a wayward Milburn strike that hit him square in the chest. The statistics don't lie however, and Milburn found the back of net more times than he struck an unfortunate ball boy.

My mother was from a Linfield-obsessed family and she was forever singing all the songs, most memorably 'Head, heel or toe ... slip it to Joe', in tribute to Joe Bambrick, the legendary centre forward who had scored 286 goals in 183 appearances for the club between 1927 and 1935, when she was a young girl. My uncle Billy and my maternal granda ran the Hammer Linfield supporters' club, and it was Billy and my aunt Isobel who started taking me to Windsor Park in the 1961/62 season. Though I have absolutely no memories of it, I was later told that my first game was Linfield versus Distillery. It was a glorious first season of watching the Blues that I was treated to: 1961/62 has quite rightly gone down in club lore as the most successful and exciting season in its history. Linfield won seven trophies, something they had done once before, forty years previously, but never again since. My aunt and uncle used to say that I must have been a lucky charm that first season. Bluemen of my generation still talk excitedly like the schoolboys we were about that magical season. To top it off, one of the players, Isaac Andrews, lived near us, and when he made his way up the street every day, my friends and I would run after him, saluting and cheering the hero in our midst. When we kicked the ball to him, he would playfully kick it back.

I started going to away games as well. The supporters' bus would pick us up in the Hammer. It was one of those old Northern Ireland Transport buses and was, ironically, coloured green. Imagine, a load of hardcore Linfield supporters travelling on a green bus! One early trip to Coleraine stands out. It took absolutely ages to get there, and the bus felt all jittery like one of those old charabancs. Despite this, I loved it and enjoyed watching the older lads in their twenties sitting around playing cards. I didn't feel out of place in their company.

For a good part of the 1960s Linfield supporters from the Shankill could safely walk across to the Falls Road, down the side of the Royal Victoria Hospital crossing the Grosvenor Road into Roden Street past Kelvin School, and then across the Donegall Road into Donegall Avenue past the railway bridge and into Windsor Park while wearing our red, white and blue scarves and rosettes. That's the route Uncle Billy, Aunt Isobel and I took when we were walking to home games. As the decade wore on and people became more polarised, this would become impossible.

Linfield were my local team, but I also became passionate about Leeds United. In Belfast it seemed like everyone had an English team such as Liverpool or Manchester United, while many people supported Rangers or Celtic in Scotland. For me, Don Revie's side were just the best. When I started supporting Leeds, they were still in the old Second Division, so I could hardly be accused of being a glory-hunter when they had their golden years shortly after I became a fan. People often ask me why I support Leeds and not Liverpool, Arsenal or Manchester United. My mother gave perhaps the best response to that question. When she was up at Long Kesh once for a visit, someone asked her, 'What's your Billy at? He supports Leeds and thinks Chris Tavaré is the best opener for England even though it takes him four hours to score fifteen runs! Is he just an awkward bugger?' She replied, 'Well, you'll always need to remember, my son likes to be controversial. He'll never go with the flow.' My mother knew I was stubborn and hard-headed, a bit like herself.

In the early 1970s I would eventually get to see Leeds in the flesh. Harvey, Reaney, Madeley, Bremner, Charlton, Hunter, Lorimer, Clarke, Jordan, Giles, Gray. I was over in Liverpool on UVF business as a 17-year-old and stood in the famous paddock at Anfield with some Liverpool-supporting friends. The view was pitch-level, just like the terracing in front of the South Stand at Windsor Park, and if memory serves me right, Leeds lost the game. For once the result didn't matter a jot to me. Just getting to see the legendary Revie team in real life rather than on the television in black and white was exciting. I didn't go to a game at Elland Road, Leeds United's home ground, until I got out of prison. Now I've been more often than the bins are collected. I've enjoyed the highs of Howard Wilkinson's side lifting the League Championship in 1992 and suffered the lows of relegation to League One (English football's third tier). Leeds are my team, and I'll follow them through good times and bad. 'Marching on Together', as the Leeds fans so passionately sing.

While marching after Leeds United was my passion, marching with the Orange Order was never my thing. Every spring the Shankill would begin to come alive after the long Northern Irish winter, and around Easter people would begin practising their flutes, drums and accordions for the annual marching season. These instruments soundtracked the stretching of the evenings. I did enjoy all the colours and sounds of the Orange, but I was never into the religious aspect of it. I respected the people who were involved in it, and a lot of my friends carried the string in the parade, but I was content to watch. Like most kids in the Shankill community, what I really loved was helping to build and keep guard of the local bonfire; it was a matter of pride. You wanted your street's bonfire to be the best. Come the Twelfth morning, however, I could usually be found in bed, enjoying a long lie-in after being up very late on the Eleventh night. On the Eleventh night each street in Protestant areas would light a bonfire to remember the fires that were lit along the coast in 1690 to guide King William of Orange into Carrickfergus. My friends and I would watch the flames from the bonfire crackle and burn into the night sky while the whole street, from the youngest baby to the oldest grandparent, revelled in the jovial party atmosphere.

Outside its poorer areas, like the Shankill, Northern Ireland in the 1960s was beginning to blossom with a sense of positivity. Young people, who in previous generations might never have met each other, were now mixing more freely and enjoying the showbands at local dances and touring bands such as the Beatles and the Rolling Stones. This upbeat mood would be stopped abruptly in its tracks, and the Shankill, my home, would become the epicentre of a bad news story. In late June 1966 a local ex-soldier named Gusty Spence and a group of men who were involved in an organisation called the UVF were arrested and charged with murder in what became known as the 'Malvern Street shooting'. A young Catholic barman, Peter Ward, was shot dead after enjoying a late-night drink with friends from the International Hotel. They had gone to Watson's of Malvern Street in the Hammer, near my granny's house. Watson's was one of the few pubs that served alcohol afterhours and the young men quite innocently decided to visit after work in search of a pint.

Very few people would have known it at the time, but the UVF had been formed in secret in 1965. The men who joined in 1965 firmly believed that they were carrying on the same kind of anti-Home Rule struggle of their forefathers some fifty years previously. Politicians and preachers had been proclaiming dire warnings about an Irish Republican Army (IRA) uprising in 1966, on the fiftieth anniversary of the Easter Rising. This was just a few short years after Operation Harvest, the IRA's border campaign of bombings and shootings, had ended in surrender. There were fears among right-wing unionists that this type of campaign could be easily resurrected as the Rising commemoration approached. These same unionists were opposed to the Prime Minister of Northern Ireland, Captain Terence O'Neill; they felt that he was too ecumenical and liberal in his outlook and that he had taken rapprochement with his counterparts in the Republic of Ireland too far too quickly.

In March 1966 Gerry Fitt of the Republican Labour Party won the West Belfast seat from the sitting Ulster Unionist Party (UUP) member of parliament, James Kilfedder. When Celtic won their first league title in twelve years a couple of months later, finishing two points above Rangers, Fitt appeared at a victory parade of local fans in Raglan Street off the Falls Road. 'We beat them in politics, now we've beaten them in football,' he told the assembled crowd. Presumably 'them' meant people like me: Protestants, unionists and loyalists from the Shankill Road who were all presumed to be Rangers supporters. This was supposed to be our MP. Although Fitt didn't often let sectarianism cloud his working-class political outlook, this sort of proclamation didn't fill people on the Shankill with confidence. If we were to be beat, then surely there had to be a 'winner'? Would that mean our way of life would be under threat by people like Fitt who wanted a reunified Ireland? With hindsight, it's easy to say that Fitt was merely 'flag-waving' in an attempt to appeal to his electorate with lowest common denominator identity politics, but in the febrile streets of working-class West Belfast, every perceived threat to the constitutional aspirations of either community was like a painful welt that quickly scarred and remained part of the collective psyche.

The fear of sell-out and surrender was contagious in the spring of 1966. This all came to a head on 21 May when the UVF issued a press release that was signed off by 'Captain William Johnston', a moniker that I would later become very familiar with. It stated:

> From this day, we declare war against the Irish Republican Army and its splinter groups. Known IRA men will be executed mercilessly and without hesitation. Less extreme measures will be taken against anyone sheltering or helping them, but if they persist in giving them aid, then more extreme methods will be adopted ... we solemnly warn the authorities to make no more speeches of appeasement. We are heavily armed Protestants dedicated to this cause.

Days later an active service unit of the UVF killed a young Catholic named John Scullion in the Falls Road area when their efforts to track down and assassinate IRA leader Leo Martin had been frustrated. After the shooting of Peter Ward at Malvern Street, the republican MP Harry Diamond claimed that he had received a telephone call from a Captain Marshall of the Shankill Volunteer Division, threatening him. Diamond also referred to the recent outlawing of the UVF by Terence O'Neill but warned that he had heard of other organisations willing to take up their mantle, such as the Sandy Row Revenge Squad and a group named after the Peep o' Day Boys from the late 1700s. The 1966 version of the Peep o' Day Boys, according to Diamond, were 'taking an oath to deal with Catholics and with Protestants who associate or mix or in any way deal with Catholics'.

As a boy of 10, I have to be honest and say that these events and the subsequent fear and rumours had no impact on my little world. I remember hearing the adults talking about what had happened, but football, cricket and reading were my main pursuits. Gusty Spence and his comrades were in Crumlin Road Gaol,* and as far as I was concerned, life on my street just went on as normal. As the 1960s came to an end, however, it soon became apparent that childish things would have to be put to the side. In a couple of years Northern Ireland would change dramatically and I would be set on a path that I could never have imagined when I was a young boy kicking my football on Matchett Street. Rather than being a vague name in the newspapers, Gusty Spence would become a mentor to me, and I, as a teenager, would become a leader of men under his guidance.

* HM Prison Belfast, better known as Crumlin Road Gaol, was opened in 1846 and designed by the English architect Sir Charles Lanyon. Based on HM Prison Pentonville, the 'Crum', as it was colloquially known, was five-sided with four storeys and four wings and a circular landing in the middle. By the 1960s it had become run-down and was badly infested with rats and mould.

CHAPTER 2

THE WIND OF CHANGE

In September 1967 I started secondary school at Ballygomartin Boys'. For most of the young lads in the Greater Shankill area, the three main schools that provided their education were 'Ballygo', Somerdale on the Crumlin Road and the Boys' Model on the Ballysillan Road. I had to get either the No. 73 or No. 74 bus to and from Ballygomartin, as it was quite a distance on foot up the Shankill and past Woodvale to get there. I focused on my studies, as my parents expected me to, and I also continued my visits to the library and enjoyed playing and watching football. Around the time I was in second year at school, I started going to Linfield matches with my friends rather than my aunt and uncle. Going to Windsor Park and other grounds around Northern Ireland and following the Blues in a larger group led to me meeting other lads my age from different parts of Belfast and further afield. Little did I know it then, but some of these lads would become good friends of mine and would later, in the early 1970s, become the nucleus of a group formed to fight the IRA.

It became increasingly obvious as the months went by in 1967 and 1968, when we were travelling across the country in support of Linfield, that the mood in Northern Ireland was beginning to change. There was a strong feeling of tension in the air. Things had been relatively uneventful in the aftermath of the arrest of Gusty Spence and his comrades, but there was a wind of change that was tangible. Nationalists complained about their civil rights being denied and the Northern Ireland Civil Rights Association (NICRA) was set up to highlight these issues. Visiting different towns around the province with my fellow Blues supporters, we also began to hear more about an evangelical preacher called Ian Paisley who was warning of the dire consequences for the Protestant community if NICRA got its way. He and other like-minded preachers and politicians pushed the message that NICRA was an IRA Trojan horse. Protestants were being told that if Ireland was reunified then Protestants would be persecuted and forced to live in a state controlled by priests; 'Rome Rule' was used as a scare tactic, as it had been in the days of the anti-Home Rule movement at the start of the twentieth century.

Paisley had been in and out of the Shankill over the years and had a small support base among those who had the same evangelical beliefs. The Shankill had a proud history of supporting political independents, but Paisley was regarded as a bit of a curiosity who, if he had stood in the area, most likely wouldn't have won a seat in parliament. In 1967 and 1968, as he drove toward his goal of political power, a significant number of working-class Protestants began to listen more closely to what he was saying. His synthesis of religious and political rhetoric touched a nerve with people who were increasingly feeling under attack in a rapidly changing situation.

My dad had no time for Paisley. One time when I was a young boy, he was due to open the Orange arch on Paris Street off the Shankill. My dad warned me to stay away, telling me that Paisley 'would fight to the last drop of everyone else's blood'. How prophetic.

***

The late 1960s was a strange time to be a young teenager; it was both exciting and unnerving. At Easter 1969 the Junior

Orangemen were attacked on their way back from a parade in Bangor by residents of Unity Flats just before their return to the Shankill. This was crazy: the Junior Orange consisted of kids and young teenagers. It was pure sectarianism by people who didn't want a Protestant or loyalist about the place.

Rumours began, people were glued to their radios and some even tuned into police radio frequencies to hear what was going on. Some self-starters set up their own pirate radio stations which broadcast propaganda and community messages and played loyalist and Orange party music. Alongside all of this, there was global unrest. There were student riots in Paris, civil rights campaigns by African Americans in the United States and the madness of the Vietnam War. All of this was being broadcast straight onto the television in the corner of the living room when I was sitting down to my tea. With the Vietnam situation in particular, you were constantly seeing death. It may have been in black and white, but you knew it was blood you were looking at. Civil rights, unrest, death. All these things were being brought into the house while at the same time the streets outside were beginning to descend into the same kind of turmoil and destruction.

***

The new decade started off relatively quietly, and although I was disappointed that Linfield were lagging in a league which would eventually be won at a canter by our bitter rivals Glentoran, there was plenty to keep a young man like myself entertained. It was a landmark year for the hard rock music that I enjoyed listening to, with Black Sabbath and Led Zeppelin releasing seminal albums. I was also an avid reader of the *New Musical Express*. Reading the *NME* led me to discover the legendary American blues artist Robert Johnson. Johnson had died in 1938, but with the Rolling

Stones covering his song 'Love in Vain' on 1969's *Let It Bleed*, his work was undergoing a renaissance in 1970. Once I bought my first Robert Johnson record, I never looked back, and blues has been my favourite genre ever since.

Despite the political turmoil rumbling on in the background, life for us young ones was lived at a much slower pace than teenagers experience nowadays. I was spending time with my friends, doing the things that a 14-year-old boy does like playing football and chasing girls. We used to go camping in Millisle, a small seaside town on the Co. Down coast. Anywhere else, life would have been great for a young man, but Northern Ireland in 1970 wasn't a normal place, and it was only going to get more and more abnormal. It didn't take long for the political situation to deteriorate. The previous summer had been one of conflagration, the like of which Belfast had not witnessed since the early 1920s. We thought that it was a one-off, and something we would never see the like of again. In actual fact, it turned out that the trouble of August 1969, where the Falls and Shankill clashed while Londonderry descended into a war zone, was merely a precursor to what would be an extremely long, violent and bloody decade that would change a lot of people's lives and see so many other lives lost. Little did I know it then, but I would be at the forefront of the UVF's war against the IRA for almost three years.

As the end of the 1969/70 football season came into view, we had the Irish Cup final to look forward to, even if the Blues were trailing way behind in the league in fourth place. The Irish Cup final was played at Cliftonville's North Belfast ground, Solitude, on 4 April. Linfield faced off against Ballymena and lifted the cup after a 2–1 win, the first time since 1963. Despite our joy at seeing the Blues victorious, there was a toxic backdrop to the period in which the final took place. On the morning of the cup final, the IRA had planted a bomb in an estate agent's in

Lower Donegall Street. The explosion occurred just as women and children were making their way into town to do their Saturday shop. Four people were injured, and the Minister for Home Affairs, Robert Porter, stated that 'The people who did this have no right to call themselves human beings.' There had been trouble at New Barnsley the previous week when republicans had forced Protestants – many of whom were Bluemen – out of their houses in the new estate. Loyalists were beginning to feel extremely angry. Although the streets surrounding Solitude were still primarily Protestant in 1970, the lower part of the Cliftonville Road stood opposite the republican New Lodge. As we made our way out of Solitude after the celebrations had died down, most of us from the Shankill walked across Manor Street or Cliftonpark Avenue and over to Agnes Street or Silvio Street and back to our homes. Those Linfield supporters who lived in East and South Belfast were obliged to walk down to the Antrim Road and past the New Lodge, where republican mobs were waiting on them. Intense fighting occurred and the army used CS gas to disperse the crowds. This type of spontaneous and sporadic rioting would become the norm in the coming months, and I would often be in the thick of it, leading and directing other young loyalists from the front.

The Tartan gangs began to emerge in 1970. The Tartans were the latest in a long line of street gangs in Belfast. My friends and I were always kitted out in Wrangler jackets and jeans and Doc Martens boots. Long hair was beginning to replace the skinhead look, and we were just like young lads in other parts of the UK. What set the Shankill Young Tartan (SYT) apart from other gangs across the UK was that, like the other Tartan gangs of the time, we adopted a unique tartan that would identify us. For the SYT it was the Stewart Royal tartan, made from fabric we bought from the Spinning Wheel near the City Hall. The tartan could be worn around our wrists, like the way football supporters at the time sometimes wore their scarves; or it could be worn as a scarf or cravat or tucked into our jacket pocket. If we had the Stewart Royal showing, we were identifiable as the SYT. We were notorious. Along with the Woodstock Tartan from East Belfast, we became a formidable force and were always out in numbers at riots, parades or football matches.

After the summer, the SYT really took off. The gang became a big deal just as the first whistle blew for the 1970/71 Irish League football season. Trouble had also started to increase around the situation at Unity Flats due to the intensification of trouble there since August 1969. There came a stage when loyalists couldn't pass Unity Flats without getting harassed or provoking residents into a riot of some sort. At the end of August two youths aged 17 and 18 from Rathlin Street were arrested and charged with hurling sectarian abuse at residents of the flats when they were returning home from a dance. They received six-month prison sentences, which was completely over the top for the offence. Most of the disturbances at North Street approaching Unity Flats occurred, however, as us Bluemen were making our way back from Linfield's home fixtures at Windsor Park. We were often drawn into confrontations, which meant that we had to fight to defend ourselves, but sometimes people were getting arrested for next to nothing. On 5 September a father and son from Urney Street, an area which had been at the interface of the trouble with the Falls in August 1969, were arrested for singing a sectarian song outside Unity Flats to the tune of 'She'll Be Coming Round the Mountain'. The son was sentenced to six months imprisonment while charges against the father were dropped. Inspector Cahal Ramsey warned that 'people should not interfere with police or army'. This was ironic, because it looked very much as though the police, who had recently been disarmed following the Hunt Report, and the army were not prepared to interfere with republicans but were eager to give loyalists a hard time.

The previous evening, a 35-year-old IRA man named Michael Kane had blown himself up while attempting to bomb an electricity transformer off the Malone Road. The following Tuesday, Kane's funeral procession left St Patrick's Church in nearby Donegall Street, making its way past Unity Flats and the bottom of the Shankill through Millfield. There were over a thousand people following the hearse, which was flanked by a number of IRA men wearing black berets and gloves. Hundreds of women and children watched from the pavements. There was a lot of anger on the Shankill that IRA men in full military uniform should be allowed to walk openly in a supposedly mixed area, and a small crowd of loyalists congregated at the junction of Boyd Street and Brown Street, where they started singing songs and waving the Union flag. The loyalists were brought under control by the police and army, but nothing was done about the uniformed republican paramilitaries following the hearse. The Royal Ulster Constabulary (RUC) and troops just looked on. As the procession reached the Whiterock area of the Falls Road, four shots were fired into the air. This was all allowed to occur while young lads from the Shankill were being given jail time for supposedly shouting sectarian slogans. It didn't seem fair, and the disparity between the way in which republicans were appearing to be given a free hand while Protestants were being punished only added to the anger and frustration among people in the area toward the authorities.

This air of discontentment began to intensify and increase each time we made our way home to the Shankill, past Unity Flats, after the match. Once we turned off Royal Avenue and into North Street and then up toward the bottom of the Shankill, the police would begin to round us up. In modern terminology it would be called 'kettling'. While we were getting all sorts of abuse from the residents of the flats and bystanders, the Special Patrol Group (SPG) of the RUC and the Royal Military Police (RMP) were busy working us over. We were reaching the stage where we had had enough of this physical maltreatment. As is often the case, it was the local women who intervened to try and stop the trouble intensifying. In the middle of the month a number of women from the Shankill who were clearly exasperated by the situation started to come down the road to the flashpoint with the intention of leading their sons, brothers or husbands past the crowds that regularly assembled outside the flats on match days. Despite these peace-making efforts, it was only a matter of time before something cataclysmic happened in the area. The blood was up, and the young Shankill loyalists were spoiling for action.

***

The week of Monday, 21 September began like any other week for me. I got up, washed, put on my school uniform, ate my breakfast, picked up my haversack and made my way to Ballygomartin for another week of lessons. Six days later I would be on the army and police 'most wanted' list. I would remain on it for over four years.

On Saturday, 26 September at 4.50 p.m., I joined the usual throng of Blues supporters leaving Windsor Park. Myself and my friends were chatting away about our plans to meet again for a big match on the following Wednesday. Linfield had drawn Manchester City in the UEFA Cup Winners' Cup and we were really looking forward to seeing some of the English league's best players in Belfast. City had a great side at the time and were defending the Cup Winners' Cup with star players such as Corrigan, Lee, Summerbee, Bell, Young and Pardoe. Even though I was Leeds through and through, it was thrilling to think that these top division players would be gracing the Windsor turf in a matter of days. There were rumours that City's skinhead hooligans would be looking for revenge after some young loyalists went on the rampage before the first leg at Maine Road. We didn't care and were confident we could handle whatever came our way. What we didn't realise was that a major and more immediate conflagration was on the horizon as hundreds of us made our way along Royal Avenue after the match, toward the bottom of the Shankill where Unity Flats was located. We were buzzing at the prospect of the Man City visit in a few days, and as usual we were chanting Linfield songs and loyalist songs with some gusto.

When we got to the junction of North Street and Carrick Hill, we attempted to do the 'hula', a sort of chant we shouted as we stamped our feet and pushed forward as a large crowd – I think it was influenced by 'Zulu' or something similar. It seemed that on this weekend the SPG and RMP had decided to make an example of some of us. The atmosphere was more febrile than usual, and we could tell they were spoiling for a confrontation. They started lashing into the crowd and snatching people to arrest them. Billy Carlisle, known in those days as 'Billy the dummy', was a deaf mute who lived off the Shankill. He was pulled out of the crowd and arrested. Word spread that Billy had been arrested for singing 'God Save the Queen', which would be some feat for someone who couldn't even speak. Later, Inspector Thomas McIlwaine stated, in an article in the *Belfast Telegraph*, that 'Contrary to Press reports the Army never claimed that they heard Carlisle shouting. The charge had been brought because of Carlisle's "physical conduct".' In the heat of the moment it didn't matter. We saw this as a step too far. The authorities were content to allow the IRA to march in uniform through this area, but now they were rough-handling and arresting Linfield supporters – including the deaf and dumb – for misbehaving or having the temerity to sing the national anthem; the fuse had been well and truly lit.

What happened next was two days and nights of sustained rioting in the Shankill that has gone down in local folklore. It didn't take much to spark a riot in those early days of the conflict, and often people went out and threw a few bricks to let off some steam, but this was different. We were absolutely fed up with the harassment that men, both young and old, had been on the receiving end of on the Shankill. Republicans were being treated with kid gloves while loyalists were being beaten up and down the areas in which they lived by forces that we had always thought were supposed to be on the same side as us. So it was that over the last weekend of September 1970, hundreds of people, mainly young men like me, came out and decided to give the army a taste of their own medicine.

As the rioting continued up the Shankill from Unity Flats, people kept passing new stories of supposed treachery by the police or army back to those at the back of the scrum: so-and-so has been hit with a baton, that kind of thing. As news spread, people from the Upper Shankill – Woodvale, Ballygomartin and Highfield – began to make their way down the road to offer their support. On this weekend, the King's Own Royal Regiment were stationed in the old Milanda bakery building on Snugville Street, right in the heart of the Shankill. The group coming up from the city centre converged with those coming down the road and congregated at the top of Conway Street. Across the road was Snugville Street. The network of interconnecting streets behind 'Fort Milanda' that stretched back to the Crumlin Road were loyalist. The soldiers were penned in. Whoever had designated the old bakery building as a barracks had obviously never considered that people from the Shankill would turn on the army. By its very nature, urban warfare is fought on streets, down alleyways, from inside houses and backyards. There are no conventional battlefields, so we had to make up our own. We did our best to make sure that there was no level playing field and used our intimate knowledge of our own community to create a rat race where the army couldn't beat us.

The beleaguered men of the King's Own drew up the barricades and must have contented themselves that their siege would not be a long one. Nevertheless, we were young and angry, and our energies were far from spent. Hundreds of us pushed each other to get into Snugville Street, and we began throwing anything we could get our hands on at Fort Milanda. The situation settled down a bit as people went home to get changed for Saturday night, but as the evening wore on more and more people descended onto the Shankill. Snugville Street became the epicentre as chaos ensued. It was a surreal atmosphere. At one point in the evening, Frankie Curry was driving around in a blazing double-decker bus that he had hijacked and petrol-bombed on the Crumlin Road. Frankie was a young man from my age group and the nephew of Gusty Spence; he became a prominent member of the Red Hand Commando (RHC), and he was later killed on 17 March 1999.

A large post was pushed down and pulled from the pavement. This became a battering ram that was used to eventually break down the gates of the Milanda base. Dozens of us ran into the grounds of the old bakery, not entirely sure what we were going to do next. We were venting our frustrations at the brutality of the army's actions against Linfield supporters at Unity Flats, but how could we make a point that they would remember?

There was another reason why I was so enthusiastic to get noticed. Although I was only 14, a lot of the local men who I subsequently discovered were involved with the UVF thought that I was much older. This was most likely due to my tall, wiry frame and long hair swinging about, obscuring my face. It was also undoubtedly down to my ability to coherently articulate what I thought about the declining security situation in the province. I wanted to make a positive impression on the organisation, because even at that young age I knew that I wanted to be in the

UVF. As I rioted along with numerous other young men outside the Milanda, I saw an opportunity to do something that would get me, and my friends, noticed and make this by-now typical riot worthwhile. The regimental flag of the King's Own was flying atop the sangar. I assessed the situation before I jumped up against the wall and clambered onto a drainpipe. A massive cheer went up from the crowd below me. Adrenaline surged through my body. I knew I couldn't back down now. I climbed up onto the top of the sangar, where I snatched the regimental flag and stuffed it in my jacket. A massive cheer and stomping feet now filled the street below me. I descended from my lofty position very quickly and re-joined my friends.

Capturing the flag like this was a victory for us, but it was a burning humiliation for the King's Own; in military terms, they had been disgraced. It was a battle, and one we felt that we had won.

To be honest, when I was snatching the flag from the sangar, I never for one minute thought about how serious it could become; later, the army would shoot people for a lot less. For me and the other young Linfield fans in my group we certainly didn't feel like we were doing all of this for fun. It might be called 'recreational rioting' nowadays, but in 1970 we saw ourselves as street soldiers of a kind. This wasn't just thuggery or troublemaking. We were defenders of the community, and when we were involved in these riots we employed the tactics of urban warfare. On this occasion my friends created a diversion to ensure that I could get to the flag unharmed. I would come to rely on this comradeship and the implicit trust we all had for one another in the years ahead. On that September weekend we took on the army because they were carrying out acts of aggression against people from the Shankill just for being loyalists.

The rioting continued as I made my way back onto the Shankill, and through the night and into the following morning people continued to sporadically attack Milanda. On the Sunday evening a crowd tried again, but by this stage the army had become fed up. Although no shots had been fired, plenty of CS gas had been used to try and disperse the crowds over the previous 24 hours. This wasn't the first riot I had been involved in, and by now I had learned that no matter how much of our youthful energy we expended, the army could also keep replenishing itself. Now it was time for a new tactic – a changing of the guards. The King's Own retreated as reinforcements were dispatched in the form of a squad of well-rested members of the Parachute Regiment, or 'Paras'. We didn't have the same resources. We got tired and inevitably made mistakes, and in our naivety, we didn't think that the Paras would ever get stuck into us. They did – with a vengeance. They beat the hell out of us. For most of us, this was finally the sign to get offside and disperse before somebody got killed. We were exhausted and taking on the Paras would have resulted in a bloodbath.

People might wonder why we, as loyalists, were attacking the army of a state we professed an allegiance to. The answer is simple. The army was being heavy-handed with young men on the Shankill, and we saw them as an obstacle to getting our hands on the republicans while the authorities dithered. No matter where we went after that long September weekend, the Paras would come driving up alongside us in their Land Rovers and start whistling and shouting at us about our long hair. We weren't the only long-haired lads in the UK at the time, but the soldiers with their close-cut military hairstyle obviously saw us as a bit of a joke.

> 'There's a big sissy! There's no virgins on the Shankill, we've seen to that you Orange bastards!'
>
> 'Catch yourself on mister. You haven't fixed us. We'll be back! You'll be sorry!'
>
> 'Irish bastards!'

All of this was calculated by the army and was clearly designed to goad us into confrontations. Due to our youthful bravado, we never once rejected their offers for a fight.

***

In the wake of the Milanda riot, some of the older loyalists in the area decided to form a so-called 'peace committee' to deter young Linfield supporters from going near Milanda after matches. Davey Payne, later to become a notorious member of the Ulster Defence Association (UDA), along with Ken Hagan of the UVF were two of the men who marshalled the crowds. Like the soldiers who were getting in our way, we were probably an obstacle to Ken and another UVF man who shall remain anonymous, both of whom were trying to harness our aggression into something more regimented. This sort of rioting was becoming par for the course in Ulster at the time, and we were never far from the action if things kicked off on or near the Shankill. Over the penultimate weekend of January 1971, the Shankill erupted into violence once again. And once more it was in the hours following a Linfield match. A large group of us decided to block off the Shankill at Brown Square. When the police got stuck into us, we moved on up the Lower Shankill toward Boundary Street, where we set up a makeshift barricade with whatever we could lay our hands on. The SPG soon rolled into action, driving their vehicles through the debris, which was acting as a very weak barrier. In no time, snatch squads had arrested around four Bluemen and the RUC had pushed most of us back up the road toward our homes.

As news got around about the arrests, and people had more than likely had a few post-match drinks, a large crowd of about 200 made its way to Tennent Street at 9.00 p.m. to protest. The large group then moved onto the Crumlin Road and back through Disraeli Street. Stones were thrown toward the Ardoyne before the army dispersed everyone. Undeterred, another group of around 200 appeared on the Shankill near Northumberland Street at 11.00 p.m. before making their way down to an army unit at Townsend Street, where they began attacking the soldiers. Water cannons were deployed and rubber bullets were fired. It was obvious that the army were not going to use defensive tactics as they had done at Snugville Street the previous September. The crowd then moved down to Boundary Street, where hijacked cars were turned into another barricade. There followed a period of quite vicious rioting, which lasted into the early hours of Sunday. Most of the trouble was in the area between Crimea Street and Townsend Street. By 2 a.m. things had settled down, but fourteen people had been arrested while eleven soldiers and eight police were injured.

The following evening, at around 7 p.m., the blood was still up, and a large group of Shankill loyalists converged on Percy Street and moved down Northumberland Street toward Divis Street and the Falls Road. Before they reached the peace line, they were stopped by the army. Tensions appeared to be calmed by Johnny McQuade, a member of the UUP, who addressed the crowd, appealing for people to go home. Although they moved back to the Shankill and potential confrontation with people on the Falls and Divis had been avoided, the group grew to around 400 and Tennent Street police station was once again the target of people's ire. Rubber bullets were fired by the army during sporadic outbreaks of rioting. One of the army's sorties brought them into Matchett Street, where I lived. Twenty people were arrested. Luckily, I wasn't one of them. I could breathe a sigh of relief, but not for long; that wasn't the end of the matter, and I was now a wanted 'man'.

***

On the following Monday, 25 January, I was on the bus, returning from Ballygomartin School. The journey took me down the Woodvale Road and into the Upper Shankill area. I usually got off the bus at Tennent Street, where I walked the short distance to my home. On this particular Monday, as the bus stopped opposite the Four Step Inn, my mate Jakey Kane jumped on, knowing that the next stop would be the one where I usually got off. He also knew where I nearly always sat and he came racing up the stairs to the back, breathlessly shouting, 'You better get off the bus Hutchie 'cos the army is waiting on you!' I was a bit taken aback and asked how he knew that they were waiting for me, to which Jakey cried, 'Just trust me, mate! I tell you – they're waiting on you with the police!' I realised pretty quickly that he wasn't having me on, so I didn't get off at my usual stop. A crowd of pupils from Ballygomartin jumped off the bus at Tennent Street, where, sure enough, there was a group of soldiers and policemen from the local station standing around waiting. By now I was crouching beside my seat, looking out the upper deck rear window. I breathed a sigh of relief as I watched the uniformed figures disappear into the distance and the bus made its way toward Crimea Street, where I decided it would be safe to get out.

I was on my own walking along Crimea Street, taking a longer route home, and although the fuss had died down and I was well away from the army and police, I was still full of nervous energy. I began to think about the situation that had just occurred. *This is crazy. I'm 15, still at school and the police and army are waiting for me.* I was trying to think through what I was doing and where I was at. *I've got the responsibilities of somebody ten years older than me.* I finally got up to the house and got my school uniform off. I tried to settle down and watch the television; I think *Blue Peter* would have been on. I couldn't settle, and I kept thinking about what had happened, my mind replaying the scene on a loop. *I'm no longer one of the kids. I'm something different now.*

Later on, after I'd had my tea, I ventured back out onto the Shankill Road, where I soon encountered some of my friends. They were full of it – 'Fuck me! Did you see those ones earlier waiting for you?!' I was curious as to how they were sure it had been me that the army were waiting on seeing as they hadn't pursued me back to the house. My pals assured me that they had been asking all about me and where I was. The army hadn't told anyone what it was all about, but I was sure they still had my cards marked after the escapade at Fort Milanda and the rioting of the weekend that had just finished.

Later on, that evening, when I was making my way home down a side street, I was suddenly surrounded by a convoy of Land Rovers. One of the police officers jumped out and ran over to me with a pair of cuffs. I ducked out of his way and said, 'Here, you can't arrest me, I'm too young! My parents aren't here.' He was well prepared and said, 'Well, we'll have to go and get them then, won't we?' I was brought to the police station at Tennent Street, where I was soon joined by my dad, who was absolutely enraged. 'What are youse doing?' he asked. 'We're charging William for rioting and disorderly behaviour.' Although my dad didn't condone the fights we got into after Linfield games, he was prepared to defend his son: 'Where's the evidence? Why didn't you arrest William at the time? There's always snatch squads in these situations, isn't there? Why'd you not snatch him?' It almost seemed like dad was the one doing the questioning; he would have made a good interrogator, I thought to myself. 'Oh, we didn't get a chance,' said one of the police officers, who was by now looking very pleased with himself. I soon realised why he was so smug. From a big brown envelope he produced a series of black and white army photographs of me amid the chaos at Milanda. I had a hankie wrapped around the lower half of my face, but there was no mistaking who the lanky, long-haired 14-year-old in the picture was. I thought the game was surely up, but my dad kept challenging the police, asking them how they could know who it was in the photograph if the person had a hankie obscuring their face. In his heart he must have known it was me, but his protestations worked because the charge was eventually thrown out and I didn't have to face the juvenile court.

When we got a good bit away from the police station, my dad turned to me and said, 'Are you stupid, William? Why are you getting involved in this nonsense?' I kept up the pretence that it definitely wasn't me, but my dad just said, 'If it is you or it isn't you, I don't care. That's not the issue, I just want you to pack it in now.' Parents *know*; they have a sense about things, and my dad obviously sensed that I was on a path leading toward conflict. It was a conversation I am sure many mothers and fathers had with their sons on the Shankill at the time. I kept protesting, but he just said, 'Other people will get you to do things, but you'll be the one that'll end up in the jail. William, if you're ever seen doing anything, you'll be recognised. Other people blend in, but you stand out with your long hair and your clothes.'

I was a bit impetuous and arrogant, and just brushed off everything that my dad said to me. After all, a lot of my friends had been involved in the rioting in late 1970 and over the previous weekend so why were the army and police so particularly interested in me? Over the next few days, I thought long and hard, and asked myself some pretty tough questions. *What is this all about and where is it taking me?* Obviously, the security forces had identified me as a ringleader, as someone who was controlling some of the rioting and trouble that had been occurring after Linfield games. *The police and the army aren't going to let me be anything other than this.* Having to live on my wits at such a young age was definitely a strange way to exist. Everyone seemed to think I was 'the lad' and a big leader. *No matter what I do, it'll never change. They'll always believe that I control what's happening on the streets.* That's fine if people perceive you that way, but how does a 15-year-old cope with that? In my head I did often feel older than I was, or maybe I had convinced myself that I did. I definitely thought I was a bit more mature than most others my age, so maybe I was thinking a bit more deeply about the situation than people might have expected me to. The more I was treated like a man, the more I tried to act like one.

I thought once or twice that maybe I should just pack it all in, get offside and concentrate on school; but how could I? *The police, the army. They want to put enough pressure on me to make me crack.* People around me were constantly talking about the fears they had around the increasing violence and political instability. There and then, I decided I was never going to crack. From that moment I became determined that I would never give in. As a result, I experienced nothing but harassment, particularly from the army. Chased. Beaten up. Challenged in the streets. Never allowed to move without them dogging me. I steeled myself and became hardened. And I was all of 15. Much older people were looking to me and my friends as defenders of the community. We weren't just a group of teenagers anymore; we were considered to be men, and increasingly we were in the company of people older than us who were involved in paramilitarism. The old fellas often stood at the street corners and talked about the gunmen of 1921 and the previous Belfast 'Troubles', with its loyalist icons such as Buck Alec. The constant message was that the IRA was bad, the IRA was the enemy, the IRA must be put down. So, it seemed strange to me that the police had been disarmed while the IRA was being given a free hand at running around planting bombs and murdering people. There was always talk that the IRA wouldn't back down and that they would keep re-emerging, generation after generation, until they succeeded in their goal of reunifying Ireland and getting rid of the 'Brits'. When republicans talked about the 'Brits', people on the Shankill and other loyalist areas could only read that as including us. We were British and proud, so what would happen to us if the IRA won? It didn't bear thinking about.

CHAPTER 3

A Dreadful and Bloody Period

On 6 February 1971 the IRA shot dead a young soldier named Gunner Robert Curtis in the New Lodge area of North Belfast. Curtis, who was a few weeks away from turning 21, had only been in Northern Ireland since the start of January when his regiment was deployed as part of the response to deal with the growing unrest. He had been married for little over a year, and his wife had just informed him that she was expecting their first child. Curtis should have been full of happiness, but instead his young life was about to be cut tragically short. Republicans in the New Lodge and Duncairn area had started rioting when the army arrived to search for IRA weapons. Gunner Curtis was the first British military casualty, and although we on the Shankill had given as good as we got with the army, to see a young soldier killed during a riot in a republican area sickened people in the Protestant community. Worse was to come as the conflict exploded in 1971.

On 10 March the Ardoyne Provisional Irish Republican Army (PIRA) struck in an operation that disgusted the large majority of people in Northern Ireland and beyond. Three off-duty and unarmed young Scottish soldiers with the 1st Battalion Royal Highland Fusiliers were drinking in Mooney's, a popular bar in the centre of Belfast. Two of the soldiers were brothers from Ayr – John and Joseph McCaig, aged only 17 and 18 – while the third was Dougald McCaughey from Glasgow, aged 23. According to reports, the three young men were invited to a party by women they had met while drinking. They were driven to White Brae, Squire's Hill, off the Ligoniel Road on the northern outskirts of the city. The three soldiers were each shot in the head by members of the PIRA from Ardoyne when they stopped to urinate at the roadside. Their bodies were discovered by local children who were playing nearby.

The killings intensified anger in the Protestant community and led to a march by a huge number of Belfast's shipyard workers on Friday, 12 March, which was designed to highlight an increasing desire for the reintroduction of internment for republicans. The march was led by Billy Hull, convenor of the engineering shop stewards at Harland and Wolff. Up until this stage, I and other loyalist activists felt that the police and the army had an outside chance of getting to grips with the IRA. These murders demonstrated just how ruthless and callous the IRA could be, and consequently any hope we previously held slowly began to evaporate. Around this time, I remember loyalist entertainers and singers such as Sylvia Pavis, who appeared in clubs around the Shankill, singing a song about the soldiers to the tune of 'Silent Night'. It was mournful and aptly reflected the depression felt among people from my community during the first few months of 1971. After the killings of the soldiers, the mood among working-class loyalists nosedived into an abyss of negativity and anger. I'm sure that I wasn't alone in thinking far more about what was happening on the streets of Belfast than what I was being taught in the classroom at Ballygomartin.

As I had turned 15 before Christmas, I was able to walk out of school that Easter and seek employment. I knew that my days of studying were over for the time being. Even though I was beginning to dedicate more of my time to the emerging paramilitary scene on the Shankill, I still had ambitions to get a good job. I was keen to follow in the footsteps of Robert McQuitty's cousin and become a continental fitter with Mackies. To me, as a 15-year-old, having a job like this sounded like the best thing ever with its promise of travel, good clothing and attractive women in different countries. Given everything that was going on around me, I was destined to stay closer to home, and during my initial job search before leaving Ballygomartin, I paid visits to foundries, factories and shops. For a young Protestant male, it wasn't hard to get a basic job in 1971. I ended up calling into Belfast Tubular Furniture on Sydney Street West, only yards from my mother's front door. The company made tubular furniture such as bar fittings, tables, stools and school desks. I was delighted when the owner decided to give me an immediate start. The wages were £5 a week; hardly a fortune, but not bad for a 15-year-old who had walked out of school with no formal qualifications. I was immediately put to work on a bending machine, where I was responsible for shaping chair legs and table frames. After a less than glorious start, I became quite proficient at the job and it's likely that if you sat in a tubular seat in Belfast in 1971 or 1972, then it was probably one of my 'works of art'.

It was around this time, just after I had left school, that the Tartans made the front of the local newspapers for the very first time. The SYT and the Rats from the Black Pad became household names overnight. On 27 April, the *News Letter* ran a sensationalistic front-page story declaring that 'Shankill Gang War is New Threat to Belfast Peace'. One angry resident told the paper that we were just young hooligans:

> Last week I saw members of the two gangs fighting in a vicious and cruel manner. They used belts and knuckle-dusters and I saw one young boy knocked to the ground and about three other youths started kicking him in the face. Just then a couple of men arrived on the scene and went to the boy's aid. When they asked him who was responsible he

> refused to answer. From what I can gather they have a code of silence and you must not squeal.

There is no doubt that the Tartans were vicious fighters, not unlike the football hooligans you would have seen in England at the time, but the SYT, the Rats, the Woodstock Tartan and Catholic gangs such as the Nurks from Newington were just the latest in a long line of similar groups that had fought on the streets of Belfast for decades. We all loved to get stuck in and have a fight, and at this time, as the newspaper article rightly suggested, most of the fighting was between rival Protestant gangs. It was all about territory and a sense of belonging. In those very early days of the Troubles there were still around 70,000 people living in the Greater Shankill area, and people found a strong sense of belonging, identity and kinship in being from the Hammer, the Nick, the Black Pad, the Woodvale and so on. Despite the infamy and notoriety that the Tartans had gained, a significant number of us were drifting away from the gang scene at this stage and continuing to develop ideas about how we would respond to the IRA if an armed reaction was required. Fighting after Linfield matches at Unity Flats allowed us to feel like we were defending our community, but throughout 1971 republicans were increasingly directing a campaign of terror against the Protestant community.

The sheer ruthlessness of the IRA was again demonstrated on Tuesday, 25 May, when a man casually walked into the reception hall of Springfield Road police station carrying a briefcase. As he walked in, he would have seen that there was a man, a woman and two children, as well as several police officers standing around. Although he carried a briefcase, the man wasn't a lawyer or legal representative; he was a republican, and the case he held in his hand had a smoking fuse protruding from it. As quickly as he entered the station, the terrorist dropped the briefcase into the hall and fled on foot. One of the police officers hastily organised an evacuation procedure, ushering those in the hall outside through the reception office. Sgt Michael Willetts, a 27-year-old soldier with the Parachute Regiment, was on duty in the inner hall and sent an NCO upstairs to raise the alarm. Sgt Willetts assisted in the evacuation, standing in the doorway to shield those taking cover. The bomb exploded and Sgt Willetts was killed. An official memorial states that

> His duty did not require him to enter the threatened area. All those people who were approaching the door from the far side agreed that if they had had to check to open the door, they would have perished. Sgt Willetts waited, placing his body as a screen to shelter them. By this act of bravery, he risked and lost his life for those of the adults and children.

When all the details emerged, I was moved by the bravery of this soldier. The Paras were not well liked on the Shankill, but Sgt Willetts had shown extreme courage in protecting innocent people from terrorists.

A song in memory of him entitled 'Soldier' was released by the English singer-songwriter Harvey Andrews in 1972. It sold hundreds of copies on the Shankill, where a local record shop played it regularly through a loudspeaker. There was a feeling of disgust among the loyalist community when we found out that as the innocent people and the mortally injured Willetts were being moved from the scene, local republicans congregated outside the station and started celebrating and jeering. I just couldn't comprehend the mental process of the person who planted the bomb. Surely, he saw the children. Did he not think that they may also be Catholics? Members of the community from which he came. Hearing about the people who were shouting and celebrating outside afterwards made me feel angry. The republican rhetoric of complaints about hundreds of years of supposed oppression paled into insignificance when republicans were quite content to blow up kids just to say that they had struck a blow to the local police, who they considered as combatants. Could the IRA not see that despite all their complaints about the 'Brits' and the soldiers, here was one of those very people going beyond the call of duty to save local Catholics from being killed by the IRA?

By the time June 1971 came around, there were fears among loyalists that the Provos (a term for the Provisional IRA) would attempt to replicate the devastation they had caused a year earlier. As the marching season got underway, the Tartans were intent on ensuring that there would be no repeat of the events of June 1970, when the IRA opened up on Protestants around the Lower Newtownards Road and Crumlin Road. The SYT accompanied members of the Orange Order and the bands that were taking part in the annual Whiterock Parade that made its way through North and West Belfast. The parade passed off relatively peacefully and we were content that we had done our bit. The following week in Stormont, the Ulster Unionist Minister for Home Affairs, John Taylor, in an attempt to deflect nationalist criticism away from the Orange Order, referred to us as 'young hooligans who sometimes attach themselves to a parade'. Taylor just didn't get it, or else he was trying to kid himself. We saw ourselves as defenders of the community, and we were prepared to do whatever we could to ensure that the IRA didn't enjoy a repeat performance of their carefully choreographed attacks on loyalists the previous year. In a response to Taylor, Austin Currie, a nationalist MP, didn't have any qualms about describing the situation as he saw it:

> I listened with interest to the Minister's reference to what he described as the young hooligans who accompanied the

> Orange parade on this occasion ... I wonder if it is absolutely correct to describe these people as young hooligans.
>
> Accompanying this parade was a large number of young men in blue denims ... I am told that ... these young men numbering hundreds attempted to goosestep and behave in a disciplined military way.
>
> I presume they could be called true blues. These are militants on the Unionist side, and they accompanied this march for the express purpose of ensuring that if there was any trouble they would be able to go into action as a type of military force ... there is more than young hooliganism involved in this.

The so-called respectable unionist politicians were always quick to deny that any kind of organising was going on within the loyalist community at this time, though they were quite content to whip us up when they wanted to bare their teeth at the British or Irish governments. This was mirrored in their attitudes toward the loyalist paramilitaries, who they publicly condemned but privately encouraged.

***

That summer there was a strange feeling on the streets of Belfast. It was like a heaviness or a feeling of expectation, the uneasy calm before the storm. Everyone did their best to get on with their normal everyday lives, and I was no different. I was beginning to get fed up where I was working, so in August I decided to quit making tubular furniture and took up a job in Mackies, where I became an apprentice machinist. As always seemed to be the case in Northern Ireland at the time, turbulent events in society overtook any sense of achievement you got from things that were happening in your personal life.

On 9 August the people who had been campaigning for the reintroduction of internment finally had their wish granted. Men, young and old, were lifted from Catholic areas on suspicion of being involved in the IRA. There was a palpable tension in the whole of the community, but particularly in interface areas where Protestants and Catholics lived in such close proximity. In the wake of the IRA campaign of the preceding months, there was an increased fear among Protestants that they would suffer at the hands of frustrated republicans. Chaos ensued across Belfast as things exploded. In Protestant areas, the rumour mill went into overdrive. Pirate radio stations were broadcasting constant bad news, and intercepted police radio frequencies confirmed people's worst fears as loyalists prepared for all-out civil war.

On the night of Sunday, 8 August, a van full of IRA men toured the Ardoyne, and over a loudspeaker they warned Protestant families that if they did not leave, then they would be burned out of their homes. On 9 August, after a weekend of republican violence that was described by one newspaper as being 'worse than the worst of the Blitz' (which had destroyed parts of Belfast during the Second World War) tensions were inevitably running high. A 40-year-old Protestant security guard was killed by a nail bomb that had been thrown by republicans into Mackies, where I had just started work. During a gun battle with the IRA, a middle-aged Protestant widow named Sarah Worthington was shot dead by a soldier inside her home at Velsheda Park, near Farringdon Gardens in the Ardoyne area of North Belfast. Mrs Worthington's family were helping her move from the area, which was in the process of being destroyed by republican arsonists. The following day a local newspaper reported that 'Protestant families in Alliance Avenue began leaving their homes this afternoon. Men hijacked lorries and vans on the main Shankill Road to carry away furniture and other belongings. First estimates said that 50 families were involved.' Loyalists on the fringes of paramilitary groups were involved in hijacking those lorries and vans used to ferry Protestants and their belongings to safe areas. People were acting irrationally and out of a sense of fear and anger, as indicated in another newspaper report: 'A Protestant man, who also lost all his possession [*sic*], including a television set, a radiogram and records, seemed to think the burning of the houses was the right thing to do. Mr Basil Houston said that if Catholics wanted houses they should build them and pay a proper rent, and not get cheap rents in the area.'

Many Protestants were setting fire to the gas mains of houses that had been vacated in Ardoyne. This was done to ensure that Catholics would not take up residence in those houses that had been owned by Protestants. Actions that might have been regarded as criminal behaviour in previous decades by working-class Protestants in this area were now regarded as a just, rational act under the prevailing circumstances. A report estimated that 70 per cent of the out-bound movement from Ardoyne and its surrounding area was by Protestant families, eighty of whom sought sanctuary in the Ballysillan estates of Silverstream, Benview and Tyndale, with another fifty-six families moving to Glencairn; further Protestants migrated to areas such as Woodvale and Shankill, along the Shore Road, out to Glengormley, Rathcoole and Monkstown, and across to East Belfast, in particular to Dundonald. In redoubts such as Torrens and Heathfield between the Oldpark and Crumlin roads, armed active service units of loyalists were successful in ensuring that republican incursions were unsuccessful. Ironically, I would again be drawn into the conflict around this area in the 1990s, when I became a politician.

Those two days, 9 and 10 August 1971, were a crazy period, and things escalated very quickly. Nobody in my community had any sympathy with those who were interned; in the then and there, we thought that they must all be active republican paramilitaries. If the 'burning of Bombay Street' in August 1969 was part of republican folklore, then the intimidation of Protestants from areas such as New Barnsley, Moyard and Ardoyne in 1971 became a similar milestone in the loyalist narrative of the emerging conflict. Protestants became afraid, and vigilante groups proliferated and began to be formed in areas where there had been none previously. Since the violence that had erupted in the summer of 1969, there had been a sporadic emergence of vigilante groups in Protestant working-class areas. These groups were formed with the intention of deterring republicans from staging armed incursions into streets off the Shankill and other loyalist districts. The vigilantes had appointed themselves as defenders of the last resort in their communities. They were brave men, who deserve credit: often older men whose primary concern was the safety of their families. They spent their evenings standing around, warming their hands at braziers behind wooden barricades that were wrapped in razor wire. They carried big sticks and took turns at patrolling streets off the Shankill, keeping an eye out for any suspicious behaviour or unfamiliar cars. Like other youths, I joined in and did my bit at the barricades at the top of my street and in the nearby Tennent Street and Ambleside Street. It was symbolic more than anything and designed to give some reassurance to people living in the Shankill and other loyalist areas that the men in these districts were finally doing something. I felt frustrated that we were walking around like we were still in the Boys' Brigade or the Scouts when, at the same time, we were watching footage on the news of heavily armed Provos openly patrolling and stopping cars in 'Free Derry'. In comparison, loyalists seemed woefully unarmed and underprepared for the worst case scenario. If a carful of IRA bombers decided to drive through the barricades on the Shankill at this time, they would have found little resistance in the flimsy structures manned by the fathers and grandfathers standing around with only cudgels to protect themselves. Fear of the IRA was intense, and in the truest sense they were successfully terrorising people in the loyalist community. Men, women and children lived under a constant cloud of fear and anxiety, not knowing where and when the bombers and gunmen would strike next. If the IRA wasn't bombing pubs on the Shankill, they were blowing up premises in Belfast city centre and shooting soldiers dead. We didn't feel safe anywhere.

As anger and uncertainty intensified after the violence that surrounded internment in August, the vigilantes, known as 'defence associations', formed into a larger umbrella organisation called the Ulster Defence Association. A lot of lads who were around my age were eager to join the UDA, but the organisation didn't appeal to me. At the time it seemed more like a sort of home guard. It didn't help that the UDA appeared to be intent on putting out black propaganda about the UVF. The UVF was obviously keen to create a coherent strategy and identity for loyalists who were interested in taking direct action against the IRA. This involved encouraging the vigilantes and the better-quality UDA members into joining the UVF, then still to emerge fully from Tara. Tara was a loyalist 'doomsday' organisation led by the maverick William McGrath, a nefarious individual who was later sentenced to jail for abusing boys in his care at the Kincora home in East Belfast, where he was employed as a housemaster. The UVF, all but dormant in the wake of Gusty Spence's arrest, had infiltrated Tara in the late 1960s in order to gather intelligence and weapons. Men were ordered to join up and report back on what was being planned by this strange organisation. When the UVF had plundered Tara for its guns and information, it withdrew its men and began to resurface in the spring of 1972. One of the early UDA bulletins took a dig at the UVF in what was an extremely disorientated tirade:

> Extremist groups have been surprised by the growth of the UDA. They know it poses a threat to their existence.

> These extremist groups put themselves first and the UDA second and Ulster a very poor third. At the moment these extremists are trying to take over the local defence groups. Don't let them. Already they have tried to involve the UDA in unjustified discrimination. We know who they will discriminate against, and this includes protestants whose only interest is their own interests.

Despite the UDA's apparent resentment of the emerging UVF, I could relate to some of the slightly older men in the organisation, like Andy Tyrie. These were ordinary working-class guys who suddenly found themselves thrust into the role of community defenders. A lot of good people joined at the beginning, including many of my neighbours, but while standing around in matching khaki and bush hats probably reassured people that loyalists were finally doing something to defend their areas, things had moved beyond that stage in my opinion, and the UDA was still to catch up with the UVF as defence gradually turned to attack. My gut feeling was that we needed to fight fire with fire and proactively go after republicans. The British government, the army, the police – none of them were able to provide us with protection. We had to take the situation into our own hands and defend loyalist communities. When I read statements like the one published by the UDA in its bulletin, it made me wonder whether those behind it were keen to fight the IRA, or did they just want to set Protestants against each other? It often seemed like the latter.

As the summer nights grew shorter and turned to autumn, there was still a tangible sense of fear in loyalist areas of Belfast. News-sheets produced by some of the defence associations warned people to guard their streets; vigilantism became a regular nightshift for guys who had already toiled hard during the days in the shipyards or factories.

At the beginning of the 1971/72 football season, I was walking down the Shankill when I was approached by two local men who I knew to see. I didn't know their names, but I got the impression that they must have been involved in something. They just had that way about them; they conveyed a sense of authority. They asked me to come and speak to them in private, where they told me that they had noticed how I was able to lead the Linfield supporters coming back to the Shankill past Unity Flats. There was a match coming up on Saturday, but the men told me that they wanted us to bypass Unity Flats and that under no circumstances should we stop and sing 'God Save the Queen'. One of them asked me would I be able to ensure that my mates didn't get involved in anything on matchday. 'Can you do that, young fella?' I was confident that I could and promised them as much, though I wasn't sure why they were asking me. Despite this, I knew not to question them. In the back of my mind, I thought they must have been planning something, and that they wanted us out of the way.

As Saturday approached, I constructed a plan. I had identified a guy from the West Circular who went to the matches, and I knew that he was unable to keep a secret to himself. Early on the day of the match, I got a hold of this guy: 'We can't stop at Unity Flats today on the way back from the match. I've been told that the lads are going to do something.' 'What do you mean, the lads?' he asked. 'The lads – the UVF. They're going to fire a few shots at Unity Flats, and they want us offside,' I replied. I left it at that and told only a few other people what was happening, minus the specifics about the potential shooting, which I had obviously made up. Later, when we got close to Unity Flats, rather than doing the 'hula' and singing 'God Save the Queen', we moved on to Brown Square. I told the guys around me to start making their way on up the Shankill toward Dover Street on the left-hand side. After a few moments standing there, people started to ask what the hell was going on. Suddenly there was a frisson in the crowd. 'I saw yer man with a rifle! Let's get away, there's going to be shooting,' said one young lad. Of course, there was no gun and subsequently no trouble.

Later that evening, I was again approached by the two men who had asked me to stop the crowds from assembling at Unity Flats: 'Okay, young fella. Good job. How'd you do it?' Arrogantly, I replied, 'Does it matter how I did it? You asked me to do it, and I've done it.' I subsequently discovered that this was the first test that the UVF had set me. Over the next few months, I would periodically meet with these men to discuss the ongoing situation, and what myself and my friends could do. I'd stand outside the Standard, a bar favoured by UVF men, and a car would pick me up. We'd go off and have discussions in private, away from prying eyes, and with their approval I would feed the information back to those of my mates who were of a similar mind to me. I was meeting senior UVF men like Bo McClelland, who was a war hero; I was hearing stories about how the UVF had raided an Official IRA arms dump in Leeson Street and how a UVF man who worked for the Belfast Corporation had retrieved guns from a place on the Antrim Road having discovered them while carrying out routine services. To me and my mates, this was exactly the kind of thing that we needed to be doing, and we finally felt like we were getting somewhere. Events on the Shankill over the next few months would only exacerbate our desire to take up arms and fight for the UVF.

On 29 September my friends and I made our way to Windsor Park for the second leg of Linfield's first-round European Cup tie against Standard Liège. The Blues were 2–0 down from the first leg in Belgium, but there was cause for optimism as we always seemed to be up for it in European games. In the event, Linfield lost 3–2 on the night, but goals from Eric Magee and Albert Larmour gave us reasons to cheer. Isaac Andrews, our local hero, made a brief appearance from the bench. The tie wasn't as eventful, on or off the pitch, as the Cup Winners' Cup matches against Manchester City a year previously, but the date will forever be etched in my mind due to what happened after the match.

As was the tradition, hundreds of Bluemen made their way back to the numerous public houses on the Shankill to have a post-match drink and analyse what they'd seen. At times like these, everyone was an armchair manager and it was always good banter. One pub, the Four Step Inn, was a Rangers bar owned by a Mr Moffett. It was immensely popular with Bluemen and was thronged after the Standard Liège fixture. At 10.20 p.m. a bomb, which had been placed at the door of the pub by Provos from Ardoyne, exploded, tearing most of the building down. As with many of the no-warning bombings, there followed an eerie silence for about a minute until people realised what had happened and screams and shouts rung through the night air. Men ran up the Shankill, down from Woodvale and out of the side streets near the Four Step to offer assistance.

There was mass hysteria. Basher Bates, who went to the Linfield matches, was one of those on the scene. He knew that his uncle and father had been drinking in the pub and he was desperate to rescue them. He later recalled how he had clambered through the debris with blood from the dead and injured seeping through his socks and trouser legs. His uncle, Ernie Bates, who lived in Battenberg Street, beside the Four Step, was dead. Basher's father was rescued, but one of my near neighbours was also killed. Alexander 'Joker' Andrews lived around the corner from me in Derry Street and was a relative of the Linfield player Isaac Andrews. Joker was one of the last true characters on the Shankill, and everyone knew him and enjoyed the way he liked to skip up and down the road singing 'I'm the champ.' His son, Bear Andrews, was also someone I knew.

The Troubles were now on my doorstep. Ernie and Joker were two people that were known and loved on the Shankill. They weren't just strangers or faces in a newspaper, they were neighbours and family of friends. My friends and I were one of several groups of people standing around, shocked, talking about what had happened as ambulances sped up the road. Even in those days, when there was no social media, Chinese whispers were a problem and inevitably stories became laced with people's personal feelings and fears by the time they reached a dozen others. There was a real fear that the IRA were going to come back onto the Shankill and shoot dead as many people as they could. I heard women saying that they were terrified that they and their families would be murdered in their beds as they slept. From Springmartin right the way down to Peter's Hill, people were on edge. Fear stalked the Shankill, as the spectre of the IRA was ever-present. No one knew where the next shooting or bombing was going to happen.

In what would become a recurring theme throughout the conflict, Ian Paisley seized on people's grief and anger to boost his own profile. He arrived on the Shankill to tell the assembled crowds that everything would be ok because he had formed a new political party called the Democratic Unionist Party (DUP). Paisley was always there, manipulating the Protestant working class for his own agenda. There were calming voices in the middle of the madness. Billy Boyd, who had formerly been an NILP MP for Woodvale, called for people not to react in the heat of the moment. He was recorded in the *Belfast Telegraph* as saying, 'I appeal to people in the area not to fall into the trap of the Provisionals by retaliation, but leave the pursuit of these murderers to the security forces.' Although men like Boyd had the best of intentions, any hope I or many other guys on the Shankill like me had that the police or army would deal with the Provos was rapidly diminishing. The bombing of the Four Step was a deliberate provocation, with the IRA obviously hoping that they could draw their Protestant working-class neighbours into a bloody civil war. The twisted logic of this was that all-out war would make Northern Ireland ungovernable, thus quickening the republican aspiration of a reunified Ireland. This rhetoric had been articulated by Ruairí Ó Brádaigh, president of Sinn Féin, at a rally in Londonderry in July, where he had said the following to a rabid crowd of republicans: 'We're on a high road to freedom, and what we need to do now is to rock Stormont and to keep it rocking until Stormont comes down.'* It is certain that Ó Brádaigh and his fellow travellers in the Provos weren't advocating peaceful protest or democratic means to bring Stormont down. They wanted a backlash from loyalists in order to create a situation where the British government would have no alternative but to prorogue Stormont. It was fascism, pure and simple. The ordinary Protestant working-class people of the sort who frequented the Four Step Inn were just collateral to the Provisional movement. Rubbish to be discarded in their quest for power.

The funerals for Joker and Ernie were held on Saturday, 2 October and saw 50,000 people converge on the Shankill. Joker's remains had lain in West Belfast Orange Hall on the Friday night and into Saturday morning. I and my friends went to pay our respects and the queue outside the hall was four deep. On the day of the funeral, the hearse was followed by a flat-bed lorry containing over a hundred wreaths. People were crying openly as the procession moved down the Shankill toward the city centre.

Although people were naturally despondent in the wake of the Four Step atrocity, there was a sense of solidarity and a resolve to ensure that we remained part of the UK.

***

---

* Ed Moloney, *A Secret History of the IRA* (London: Allen Lane, 2002), p. 112.

In early November a 19-year-old man named Tom Kells, who had recently served a sentence in Crumlin Road Gaol for car theft, was found dead near the Dundrod racetrack at Nutts Corner on the outskirts of Belfast. I wasn't friends with Kellsy but knew of him, as he was into cars and he would have associated with other young loyalists that I knew well. After his body was found, there was a lot of macabre talk on the Shankill about how he had met his end. People said that he had been tortured in the most horrible ways imaginable. It wasn't just on the Shankill that people were talking about Kellsy; during a discussion in the Stormont chamber, Ian Paisley and Johnny McQuade were prominent in seeking clarification from Brian Faulkner, the Prime Minister of Northern Ireland, as to whether Kells had been tortured before he had been killed. McQuade asked of Faulkner, 'Could he tell us if there were any marks of torture upon his body? Is it a fact that his fingertips were burned when his body was recovered? Is it a fact that other marks were found upon him indicating that he had been subjected to ignominious savagery of the worst and most terrible character?' Despite assurances to the contrary by John Taylor, the Minister of Home Affairs, who was said to be acting on information received from the police, Johnny McQuade, whose Woodvale constituency neighboured the streets Kells and his family were from, stated that he was adamant that a torture-style killing had taken place. It was McQuade's theory that Kells, a petty criminal who stole cars, was attempting to evade the clutches of the RUC when he was apprehended by republicans:

> Let me tell the Minister of State for Home Affairs how his murderers got him into Ardoyne. In his anxiety to get away from the police he knew that there was one place where the R.U.C. could not get him. He went to Flax Street, and in Flax Street-Jamaica Street he was taken by the I.R.A. That

> is on good authority. May I add something about his being tortured? Nobody in the Shankill or Woodvale area will believe anything other than that young Kells had a tattoo on his arm cut off before the bullets were used on him. This was not the first time that he had suffered torture by the I.R.A.; it was the second or third time.

Johnny wasn't a bullshitter, and he wouldn't have spun a yarn that would have potentially caused huge distress to Kellsy's family for no reason. We soon came to know for sure that Kellsy had been tortured; macabre photos were being passed around the Shankill that showed his body. Was this the police looking for a reaction from the UVF? Probably. Did young loyalists need spurring on? Absolutely not. We now knew that Protestants weren't safe drinking in their local pubs, or as had happened to Kellsy, walking along a footpath.

***

There was very little in the way of formal paramilitary organisation at this time. Aside from the UDA, the UVF was still intelligence-gathering in Tara. It was putting together the pieces of a complex jigsaw, and the last, crucial piece was getting access to the Tara arms dumps. In the main, however, the loyalist paramilitaries in the autumn of 1971 were just a number of small groups of self-starters popping up here and there, experimenting with whatever weapons they could get their hands on. One of the most impressive of these groups consisted of a number of young men around my age who met in the upstairs lounge of the Bricklayers Arms at the top of Wilton Street on the mid-Shankill. They were known as the Red Hand group (later to become the Red Hand Commando) and were commanded by the former Paisleyite and Shankill Defence Association leader John

McKeague. My friend John McAllister encouraged me to go to one of these meetings with him, where I discovered that Frankie Curry, Gusty Spence's nephew, was one of the Red Hand's cohort and that there were other familiar faces from around the Shankill in attendance such as Ronnie 'Flint' McCullough, Jimbo Tipping, William 'Plum' Smith, John McFarland and Dick Henderson. All of them were teenagers we had grown up with, and, like us, they were committed and proactive loyalists who were looking for a way to hit back at the IRA. I and a few others attended some of the meetings of the Red Hand, where McKeague and his associates discussed the political issues of the day and we were trained in unarmed combat techniques. In these early days of the loyalist organisations, there was a lot of crossover between groupings; there wasn't the ingrained regimental loyalty that would come a bit later. The Red Hand would often co-operate with the UDA on the Shankill, staging snatch squads and unarmed combat routines for the television crews and newspaper photographers.

My friends and I appreciated what our peers were doing, but we were that bit younger and were attracted to the mystique of the UVF. We often complained that the organisation was only writing on the wall. Although we knew that there had been a UVF in the 1960s, the only remnants of it were large white painted letters in the streets off the Shankill and outside Joe Watson's pub in Malvern Street, where young Peter Ward had been shot dead. We soon decided that we would form our own unit. Coming up with a name wasn't difficult – Young Ulster Volunteers was an obvious choice that we hoped would get us noticed by the UVF. We didn't have a uniform and we didn't seek any publicity, but reputations grew and spread fast on the Shankill in the early 1970s. I had made my name during the Milanda riot of September 1970 and the army's harassment of me continued as I surreptitiously began to form my own paramilitary organisation. The army was always keen to exert pressure on groups of individuals they identified as organising at the time. Obviously, they thought that if they put the frighteners on young lads at an early stage by bashing in their doors and pulling up their floorboards, then there'd be a lack of appetite for anymore. The one thing the army and the police didn't count on was the burning passion of young loyalists like me. No amount of hassle from them would deter us from defending our community.

By this stage my mother and father had separated, and I was living with my mother in a house on Jersey Street, not far from Matchett Street. By now it was often difficult for me to return home for any length of time before the army would arrive at the front door and make a mess of the place. Sometimes I sent a friend around – a young guy with long hair like myself. Not long after, the army would be there, thinking they had me. My mother's love for me was unconditional. She obviously knew I was up to something, but I don't think she knew exactly how far I had gotten into things. In the years to come, if something had happened at the house she would have told UVF people to pass a message on to me to stay offside for a while. She always had to clear the house up after it had been wrecked during a raid. There were neighbours or a neighbour in Jersey Street who didn't approve of what I was doing, and from behind their twitching curtains they must've tipped off the army anytime they thought they had seen me arrive at my mother's. One of the criticisms that many loyalist paramilitary volunteers have faced from within their own communities is that we could have taken a different, legal route by joining the RUC or the army. The RUC had been disarmed in 1969, and the British Army appeared to be taking a soft approach to republicans during the first couple of years of the conflict. So, many thousands of men across Ulster decided to take the law into their own hands; my friends and I were no different. We didn't see an alternative.

A mixture of fear, anger and hopelessness pervaded the Shankill as autumn turned to winter. Things were about to get worse.

***

For young men, myself included, who joined the loyalist paramilitaries in the early 1970s, there were several forks in the road where we decided to take a certain course of action. Some events, however, angered people from across the board and were felt in the Shankill and other loyalist heartlands. One such event occurred on Saturday, 11 December when another IRA bomb went off on the Shankill Road. A week previously the UVF had targeted McGurk's public house near the New Lodge on the north side of Belfast city centre. Fifteen people had died in an explosion that was initially attributed to the IRA as an 'own-goal'. The Shankill had always been a busy shopping thoroughfare, and although society was becoming more polarised, the shops on the road still attracted people from across the city at the time. Shortly before 12.30 p.m., when large numbers of people were doing their pre-Christmas lunchtime shopping, a Provo bomb squad left a device at the steps of the Balmoral Furniture Showrooms in the Lower Shankill. Moments later there was a massive boom and the furniture shop collapsed. As it was a Saturday, there were many young people on the road, most of whom were heading off to the football or into the city centre to buy records. I was one of them and can remember the chaos that followed the bomb. As I rushed to where the Balmoral had been, I was met by an absolutely appalling scene, with dust and rubble everywhere. Just like they had nine or ten weeks before at the Four Step Inn, people were clawing with bloodied hands through the rubble to dig out any survivors. Women were screaming and men were shouting. I did my best to help, but none of us were equipped for this type of rescue effort. Even the ambulance services found it difficult to deal with such a bloody massacre. Tracey Munn, 2 years old, and Colin Nicholl, 17 months old, were killed instantly when part of a wall fell onto the pram that they were both in. The image of a dead baby being carried away from the scene in a bloody blanket by a fireman would become one of the most enduring and horrifying images of the Troubles. Once again the IRA had hit families that I knew well, leaving devastated and shattered parents to deal with the death of innocent infants. I was a methodical person, but on that day even I felt a surge of hatred course through my body.

The Balmoral bombing led to an upsurge in recruitment to the fledgling UDA, with an entire unit of what became the Ulster Young Militants being sworn into the organisation in the Highfield estate the very next day. The atrocity confirmed my belief that the Young Ulster Volunteers needed to be able to hit back hard, by whatever means necessary, at republicans and those who supported them. The IRA and republicans needed a dose of their own medicine. That obviously meant getting guns. Although we had all messed about with the DIY zip guns that had become a cottage industry in Mackies, we needed a proper armoury if we were to convince the IRA that we were serious about defending the loyalist community from attack. What weapons we had in those early days and weeks were sourced from within the community. We had in our possession a couple of .35 and .45 small arms. A friend of one of the members of our group was also careless enough to show off his dad's privately-owned Sten gun. Needless to say, it was soon added to our small but steadily growing arsenal. Around this time, I was approached by an older man from the Greater Shankill area who told me that he was impressed by our organisational skills and ability to respond to ongoing events. I'll call him Mr A. He said we should call ourselves the Red Branch Knights, and he regaled us with tales of ancient Ulster. I thought that the name sounded a bit silly and wanted to stick with something closer to our recent history of conflict and retain that link with the UVF, so the Young Ulster Volunteers stuck for the time being. More importantly, Mr A. knew of an arms dealer (Mr B.) who would be willing to do business with us. Mr A. arranged a meeting, during which we explained our needs to Mr B. He was clear that no matter what organisation we ended up joining, his name could never be revealed to any third parties. I made a firm commitment to him there and then that whatever might happen in the future, no matter how much pressure was applied in interrogation situations, his name would always be kept secret. That remains the case to this day.

Other young loyalists from across Belfast began to hear about us, and we agreed to work with any who we felt had the same vision. We met regularly in a pigeon club on Ambleside Street and it was there that we sold ammunition and arms to other emerging groups. The floor was covered in sawdust and the gear we had was well hidden in the straw that was used for bedding the bird cages and pigeon lofts. We certainly weren't pros, but we all thought we were very sophisticated, and sometimes there was evidence of the naïve but ingenious thinking typical of 16-year-old boys who saw themselves as soldiers. One Saturday two lads from East Belfast came to the pigeon club and bought a handgun and bullets from us. Before they left, one of them took the gun and concealed it in his pilot jacket while the other put the bullets in the turn-ups of his Wrangler jeans. When the transaction was complete, they walked off down the street and onto the Shankill Road, where they went their separate ways back across the Lagan.

***

The tail-end of 1971 had been a dreadful and bloody period of tit-for-tat bombings and innocent lives lost. The Shankill bubbled with anger as the New Year bells hailed the arrival of 1972. There was a growing sense of tension and uncertainty, and I knew deep within my gut that the year ahead was going to be a violent one. With the army and police seemingly impotent, loyalists would be forced to take the law into their own hands to try and defeat the IRA. I wanted the Young Ulster Volunteers to be at the forefront of the campaign against the Provos.

At the end of January, the eyes of the world returned to Ulster when the Parachute Regiment shot dead thirteen people in Londonderry during a march protesting against internment. There was widespread shock and revulsion at what had happened, but in the immediate aftermath of Bloody Sunday, the feeling among hard-line loyalists was that the people who were killed were nothing but IRA members or supporters. The atmosphere was so volatile in the days and weeks following events in Londonderry that all rumour and conjecture was taken as the truth.

'NICRA is a front for the IRA.'

'The IRA opened fire on the soldiers.'

The Provos had shot a couple of policemen in the city a few days before, so it wasn't a stretch to think that they were responsible for starting the shooting that Sunday. The context leading up to Bloody Sunday, from a loyalist perspective, was that the IRA was heavily involved in trouble and the marchers were just an extension of their violent aims. Talk of the casualties being anything other than IRA personnel was regarded by unionists as a pernicious plot designed to discredit the British Army. If the people were innocent, then it appeared that the IRA was content for people within the nationalist community to become collateral just so the 'Brits are bad' line could keep being pushed. In the midst of this toxic atmosphere, no one was willing to take the time to step back and try to analyse what exactly was going on. It was impossible. Naysayers and critical voices were shouted down and marginalised. We were heading toward oblivion.

All the talk of doomsday, sell-out and surrender seemed to be coming to a head. The newspapers were constantly talking about a potential 'Protestant backlash'. In the midst of this crisis, Bill Craig, a former Minister of Home Affairs, formed the Vanguard movement in February. Vanguard was a vehicle for unionists and loyalists to coalesce around an anti-Faulkner agenda. During an early meeting of the organisation in Lisburn, Bill Craig told those assembled, 'God help those who get in our way for we mean business.' Subsequently, Vanguard staged a series of massive rallies across Northern Ireland in the late winter and early spring of 1972, the most famous of which was the one held in Ormeau Park on Saturday, 18 March.

As I and thousands of other loyalists from across Northern Ireland made our way to Ormeau Park, the atmosphere felt militaristic, but it also reminded me of the normal Saturday match routine. I was in the middle of a large group of guys from the Shankill, and as we made our way across town and through the city centre, we marched behind a big flag that read 'Shankill Young Tartan'. People were at fever pitch as they descended on the park from the Ormeau and Ravenhill roads. Some lads were banging big Lambeg drums, while others were playing flutes and accordions. The following morning the *Sunday News* described the intoxicating atmosphere at the rally as being like 'the Twelfth, a family reunion and the football match of the year, all rolled into one'. There was a strong sense of solidarity, and it was exactly what loyalists needed in this time of crisis.

Bill Craig arrived at the speaker's podium in an open-top touring car, flanked by motorcycle outriders from the Vanguard Service Corps. As he surveyed the masses of loyalists in attendance,

Craig declared that 'We must build up the dossiers on the men and women who are a menace to this country, because one day, ladies and gentlemen, if the politicians fail, it may be our job to liquidate the enemy.' Most people didn't really catch what Craig had said at the time, as the public address system was terrible, and the wind made it impossible to understand. That evening, during television news bulletins, the message was transmitted without interference. It created a frisson of excitement and nervous energy among many young loyalists, some of whom described the speech as being the 'green light' to go ahead and take action against republicans.

Despite this, I couldn't help but feel cynical about Craig and his colleagues in Vanguard. Although a paramilitary grouping did emerge from the movement, the Vanguard Service Corps was absorbed into more established organisations such as the Red Hand Commando. Like many other individuals at the time, Craig used Ulster's political crisis to feed his own ego. His orations were made from a relatively safe distance, and although flirtations were made with the loyalist paramilitaries, it certainly wasn't going to be the grammar school-educated Craig or any of his ilk on the political scene who actually lifted the gun during this period. Of course, that didn't deter him from making outrageous speeches to those who were titillated by such rhetoric. Later in the year, Craig told the Monday Club at Westminster that he could mobilise up to 80,000 men who would be prepared to 'shoot and kill'. Undoubtedly under the influence of alcohol, he continued: 'Let us put bluff aside. I am prepared to kill and those behind me have my full support.' It was tough talk and it was embarrassing. While Craig slept soundly in his bed at night, it was young loyalists like me who were getting our hands dirty to ensure that the enemy was 'liquidated'.

***

As the UVF began to emerge from the shadows of Tara in the late winter and early spring of 1972, I was approached again by the two local men who had asked me to orchestrate things after the Linfield game. Having had a few meetings with them over the winter, I now realised they were senior UVF figures. They told me that they had been impressed by my organisational qualities after the Linfield match earlier in the season but had heard me giving off about the UVF being 'writing on the wall'. They questioned me, asking me my opinion on the organisation. I told them the honest truth about how I felt: that I liked the idea of the UVF but felt that it was what I had previously stated – just writing on the wall and of no use to loyalists if it was dormant. I had heard plenty about it from these men but saw nothing to back it up apart from a few good stories. I was upfront in my opinion that loyalists were proving slow to react to the ongoing crisis and that the British government had tied the hands of the police and done away with the B-Specials.

Although I subsequently learned about the complex sequence of events that shaped the UVF during this period, I had had no idea at the time that they had been carefully infiltrating Tara. They began to tell me of the shadowy reconnaissance work they had been doing in Tara. 'Sure from what I hear they're just a bunch of MI5 agents!' I said. I'm sure I came across as an arrogant young man, but the two UVF men knew more about me than I had imagined. 'Yes, you're right, and that's why we're in there – to identify the guys we want off the scene, and more importantly to make sure we take their weapons before they're rendered useless as intelligence assets. We've been watching you and your mates. We're very impressed. Youse are young and enthusiastic and most importantly youse have weapons.' The Young Ulster Volunteers hadn't set out to impress anyone. We were independent and dedicated to what we were planning, but to finally get an approach from the UVF gave us a lot of confidence in what we had done so far in terms of organising. These men, one of whom was Ken Hagan, were obviously keen to get me and my mates involved in the UVF during this period of regeneration.

In the months leading up to the summer of 1972, the Young Ulster Volunteers became part of the UVF, with most of the eighteen or so members joining in stages. We became a unit within the 1st Battalion and were initially known as 'S' (support) Company. Gusty Spence's family lived in the Springmartin estate, just across the Springfield Road from the republican stronghold of Ballymurphy. By May, Springmartin and Highfield estate, which ran parallel, were under almost daily sniper attack from the IRA in Ballymurphy. Protestants had already been intimidated out of the nearby New Barnsley estate, and it seemed obvious that the IRA was trying to push Protestants out of Springmartin and back down the Shankill Road. The intimidation was so severe that many parents eventually sent their children to Liverpool or Glasgow for their own safety. In the event, S Company (later to become C Company) was deployed in Springmartin by the UVF Brigade Staff to protect residents, with specific attention being given to Gusty's wife and children.

From April 1972 the Springfield Road became a no man's land. There were constant gun battles, which grew in intensity after dark when the unlit streets were punctuated by the muzzle blaze of sniper fire. Vigilantes on both sides threw up makeshift barricades such as hijacked cars and buses, which were often set on fire to deter any potential forays into each community. It was an extremely tense time in Belfast and it often felt like things were threatening to spill over into a bloody civil war.

The febrile atmosphere mixed with the ongoing intimidation of Protestants in the area gave the UVF an impetus to launch an attack that it hoped would provide a warning to republicans and those responsible for the constant attacks on the people of Springmartin. The UVF, by this stage, had taken up positions all around the estate. Many of the volunteers were strategically posted in maisonettes at the edge of Springmartin. The maisonettes had been abandoned by residents due to the number of pot-shots the IRA had been taking at them; life had become unbearable for those living there.

On the evening of Friday, 12 May, UVF personnel from across West Belfast took up positions on the top floors of the maisonettes facing across to Ballymurphy. Rifles, many of which were like artefacts from a Second World War museum, were brought into the estate from an arms dump. The following day, the UVF launched its attack. I always remember that England were playing West Germany in the European Championship quarter-final play-off. Like many other bars across Belfast, Kelly's at the top of the Whiterock Road, at the junction with the Springfield Road, was packed with people watching the match. Shortly after 5 p.m. a car bomb exploded outside Kelly's, the UVF men in the maisonettes opened fire on the bar and on the people scrambling from the explosion. It was brutal but effective. Later that evening, my good friend Trevor King was arrested at a house in Black Mountain Pass. He was caught red-handed in the backyard trying to fix a rifle that had jammed. In addition, the police discovered Steyr rifles and ammunition. Trevor had been heavily involved in the sniping from Springmartin and he was unlucky to be caught.

On Sunday we had to drive back into Springmartin and up to Black Mountain Parade to meet with Ken Hagan and discuss the ongoing situation. The UVF and the Provos were still engaged in a shooting match while we convened in Ken's kitchen. Out of the corner of my eye I noticed a figure moving around at Corry's timber yard. Instinctively I warned the fellows with me to watch out – I knew that it was possibly an IRA sniper up there. Before we could hit the floor, the kitchen window came in around us. There were shards of glass and debris everywhere. We were half crouching and kneeling behind the sink. As I rose to dust myself off, I noticed that there was blood coming from a cut on my face. My friend Bill Foster also clambered off the floor and surveyed the mess in the kitchen. A bullet had gone through a door, a wall and a water boiler. After a few minutes someone noticed a dark stain on Bill's Wrangler jacket. It was only when we pulled his jacket off him that we realised that the same bullet that had made its way into the boiler had gone straight through Bill's shoulder. To say that Bill was lucky would be an understatement. If he had thrown himself down a few inches the other way, the bullet would have gone straight through his head. During the shooting that Sunday, a young Protestant named John Pedlow wasn't so lucky. An IRA sniper's shot took a ricochet and killed the young man before injuring his friend. In a strange twist of fate, Bill Foster later met Pedlow's sister during our time in Springmartin and ended up marrying her.

***

Even though we had joined the UVF, there were still attempts made by the UDA to coerce all young men in the Shankill into joining the new, larger organisation. In the early summer of 1972, a huge meeting was organised in a big derelict building in a side street off the Shankill. There must have been a couple of hundred young loyalists in attendance, and some older men too. A man who spoke to the crowd from a platform told us that we were all to join the UDA. There was a lot of pressure on young lads at this time. The UDA weren't afraid to be physical when they wanted to get people under their control, and I heard of fellas getting their arms broken for not towing the line. Often, if the commanders saw you at Vanguard parades or any of the big protest rallies, they assumed you were now part of the UDA. This happened to me later on, in 1972, when I was on UVF business at a house in

Heathfield, a particularly volatile part of North Belfast, which, like Springmartin, was always under attack from republicans. I was there to get a message from the local UVF commander, Sam McCorkindale. The local UDA brigadier, Sammy Doyle, who was also there, turned to me and said, 'Hey, I thought you were one of my men.' I quickly enlightened him to the fact that I was not – that I was actually in charge of my own organisation. Sammy was an amateur actor who had starred in a few television commercials on UTV, but even he couldn't hide his disappointment on this occasion.

While some lads were getting their arms broken or were given the wet towel treatment by the UDA in East Belfast, aggravation didn't always come from the organisation directly. There were also demands from some of the older men and women in the community for everyone to coalesce under the UDA banner as one big force. The community obviously saw safety in numbers, and I'm sure the sight of the UDA on parade did reassure many loyalists that something was being done in response to the IRA. Those promoting the UDA weren't seeing the full picture, however, just as I hadn't when I had been dismissive enough to describe the UVF as mere writing on the wall. One day my friends and I were on the Shankill watching the UDA marching in their hundreds down toward the city centre and there were a few local women giving me and my mates dirty looks and saying, 'Youse should be ashamed; youse should be in there with them! Thon men are fightin' for our country!' If only they knew who we were and what we were planning. We didn't need to parade around in army surplus fatigues. Actions would speak louder than words. While the UDA were parading around Northern Ireland in their uniforms, we were travelling around the country as well. We were getting trained in handling weapons, methods of warfare and anti-interrogation techniques. The Young Ulster Volunteers wouldn't just be another group that stood around at night waiting for the IRA to come into the Shankill. We were focused on taking the war to the IRA's door and were determined to be part of the 'Protestant backlash' that the newspapers seemed to mention on an almost daily basis in late 1971 and early 1972.

CHAPTER 4

Youth Battalion

Although I knew of Gusty Spence through his reputation as a loyalist legend, I had never met the man himself. When he was arrested and incarcerated in 1966, I was just a 10-year-old boy. By the early 1970s I had become friendly with his family, and as a young volunteer I moved in the same circles as his brother Bobby and our unit looked out for his wife and children in the volatile Springmartin interface. His daughter Liz was due to marry Winston Rea on 1 July and Gusty was granted parole to attend the wedding. Everything went according to plan, and when the wedding and celebrations were over, Gusty, as agreed, prepared to return to Crumlin Road Gaol. His nephew, Jim 'Butch' Curry, was driving him out of Springmartin when the car was brought to a juddering halt. Two other motors penned him in, and he was pulled from the car by unknown assailants and driven off. News spread quickly about Gusty's capture, and like most other people I immediately assumed that the Provos had claimed a major scalp. It was devastating to think that this great man who had been happily celebrating his daughter's marriage only a few hours previously could now be at the mercy of republicans. Was he being tortured? Or worse?

It was soon made clear to us that Gusty was in fact being held by the UVF and everything had been planned on a need-to-know basis. Before this news became public, some volunteers were preparing to exact deadly revenge. Word came through that he was safe, and we all breathed a collective sigh of relief. I should have trusted that the UVF would have had a plan for Gusty, but in the immediacy of July 1972 you always feared the worst when someone went missing.

The UVF claimed that they had taken Gusty due to his intimate knowledge of the old UVF and its military structure, which was modelled on the British Army. The UVF had reformed in 1965, but the organisation that emerged from the shadows in April 1972 may as well have been a totally new grouping again. It had structure, but it was crying out for an identity. The UDA was hoovering up recruits in loyalist areas of Northern Ireland, and its membership was almost 60,000. Many of these recruits would have been ordinary guys with little or no military experience, but the sheer numbers that the organisation had attracted gave the leadership of the UVF much to ponder. Gusty liaised with the UVF leadership and created a fresh structure for the organisation based on platoons, companies and battalions across the province.

One of the young guys from the Bricklayers Arms group was very close to Gusty and his older brother Billy Spence. Ronnie 'Flint' McCullough, a 20-year-old from the Old Lodge Road area, had been instrumental in organising other young men into the Red Hand organisation back in 1970, and Gusty and Billy obviously recognised that his personality, ability and intelligence were invaluable to the loyalist cause. He was a member of the Prince Albert Temperance L.O.L. No. 1892, the same Orange Lodge Gusty and Billy had belonged to. It didn't come as a surprise that Gusty and Billy were keen that Flint and his comrades in the Red Hand would be a part of what the UVF was trying to do. Shortly after Gusty went 'on the run', the UVF and Red Hand produced a document which stated:

Senior Officers of Red Hand Commando and Officers of the Ulster Volunteer Force Brigade Staff sat in discussion of various points relating to the UVF and RHC in July 1972, in which the following points were agreed.

1. Red Hand Commando, shall be aligned to the Ulster Volunteer Force and shall work hand in hand in a joint effort to aggregate all resources of both groups and devote all their energies to the war against the IRA.
   (a) This alignment is taken because;
      (i) Red Hand were in complete agreement with UVF policy on all matters.
      (ii) The UVF recognises the right of Red Hand units to retain their own separate identity, as a regiment with its own prides and particular style of internal organisation.
      (iii) It is deemed desirable that both groups become aligned in order to provide assistance and support to each other, politically, physically, financial or materially.

2. Consistent with this agreement, Red Hand shall retain its own command structure of Red Hand personnel, appointed from within Red Hand, to legislate and administer to the internal affairs of Red Hand.
   (i) Only a Red Hand Officer can give an order to Red Hand personnel.
   (ii) No Red Hand officer can be appointed or 'stood down' except from a more senior Red Hand Officer.
   (iii) Wherever UVF policy requires specific action to be taken, the UVF senior officers shall liaise with senior RHC officers in order to have both UVF and

RHC working in conjunction in accordance with UVF policy.

(iv) Wherever it is decided that disciplinary action is to be taken against Red Hand personnel, this must be done by Red Hand Officers. However, if UVF officers request that an observer is present during disciplinary action, then so be it. The opposite can also be agreed to, allowing an observer from Red Hand to witness the carrying out of disciplinary action, in specific cases, where an observer would be required.

3. Red Hand prisoners shall be housed along with UVF prisoners, under a joint structure of command from senior UVF and RHC officers. Both sets of prisoners shall be regarded as one body of men and will be under the umbrella grouping of the Ulster Volunteer Force. No disagreement between UVF and RHC outside shall be allowed to affect the good-relations and oneness of UVF and RHC prisoners.
4. All members of Red Hand Commando shall be administered the oath of allegiance from the senior Red Hand Officer. This oath of allegiance shall be an exact oath, as that taken by UVF personnel, with the exception of three words thus; "Red Hand Commando" as opposed to "Ulster Volunteer Force". No other oath shall be recognised by Red Hand other than that adopted from the UVF oath.

The above agreement was made in July 1972 in Belfast and was established with the will and sanction of representatives of Red Hand Commando and representatives of the Ulster Volunteer Force.

Signed (Gusty Spence)
ULSTER VOLUNTEER FORCE (BRIGADE STAFF)

Signed (John McKeague)
RED HAND COMMANDO

It is my view that Flint would have been the driving force behind cementing the relationship between the UVF and the Red Hand in July 1972. John McKeague, as figurehead of the Red Hand, may have been the one who put his signature to the agreement, but most of the senior UVF men at the time would have had a lot of respect for Flint in particular. Gusty loved his nephew Frankie and Winkie Rea, now his son-in-law, but in terms of operational matters and a coherent vision of what was occurring in 1972, he would have been drawn more to Flint. It was exhilarating for young volunteers seeing Gusty Spence in their midst. Flint and William 'Plum' Smith would have shadowed Gusty wherever he went, carrying out the necessary bodyguard duties for the man the press was describing as the 'Orange pimpernel'.

A week or so before Gusty had been released, the Provos had declared a temporary ceasefire to facilitate secret talks with the British government. They were demanding a complete withdrawal of the British by 1975. On top of this, they wanted their prisoners released. There was no way the British government would accede to this request, and predictably the talks broke down. With the collapse of the talks, the Provos ended their ceasefire on 9 July and the rest of the month became the bloodiest of the conflict.

Every person who joined a paramilitary organisation in Northern Ireland had a reason for why they decided to volunteer. Friday, 21 July 1972 is a date that is often cited by former loyalist combatants as the day they crossed the Rubicon and decided to join either the UVF, the RHC or the UDA. On what became known as 'Bloody Friday', the Provos exploded several bombs across Belfast as people went about their daily tasks. In the space of seventy-five minutes, twenty bombs were detonated throughout the city. Nine people were killed and 130 more were injured and mutilated. People were terrified. In the confusion, they ran in all directions around the city centre, unsure of where the next bomb would explode.

That evening I was glued to the news like everyone else and was horrified when I saw the footage of burnt human flesh being shovelled into plastic bags. On the Shankill, the blood was up. It was a primeval atmosphere, which was only exacerbated by the warm weather. Loyalists were expecting another attack on the area, and armed paramilitaries patrolled the main Shankill and arterial routes on the back of flatbed trucks and Land Rovers. Later that night the UDA threw up roadblocks on the Crumlin Road and other areas. They took it upon themselves to stop traffic and check people's identification. The temptation after an event as horrific as Bloody Friday was to go out and shoot a few Catholics in pure and simple revenge. This did happen, and innocent people were killed in the most horrific of circumstances as loyalists sought to settle the score.

I was trying to think more tactically about how we could get at the perpetrators of Bloody Friday and make them pay directly rather than just killing a few random Catholics to settle the score. On a personal level, I was influenced by the political leadership imparted by Billy Spence, who was a strong unionist and staunchly defended loyalist culture; older UVF men like Jim McDonald, who was a trade unionist in Michelin, also mentored me. They were two very different sides of the coin, but importantly, would have counselled against acting in a kneejerk fashion. It was the quiet influence of such men that ensured that the bloodshed wasn't greater at that time. Indeed, the day after Gusty had gone missing, the UVF had issued a statement promoting this line of thinking:

> To the majority of the Catholic population we would say, Unite and join us in defeating the IRA as a means of keeping sectarian warfare from becoming a reality. Sectarianism plays no part in our policy and we contend that the working class people of whatever creed are the real inheritors of peace and prosperity.*

I know that a lot of people will be reading that statement with a feeling of incredulity, but it is important to remember that at this stage in the organisation's history there were a few former NILP members in senior positions within the UVF, and very few rank-and-file members who were under their influence wanted to see innocent Catholics being killed. Individuals who enjoyed killing did engage in romper-room style murders as a response to Bloody Friday, but the people I associated with wanted to take co-ordinated action against those specifically responsible for the events on 21 July. We analysed the situation and soon discovered that it was D Company of the Provos that had carried out the Bloody Friday bombings. That meant that the perpetrators were most likely a unit based in or around Albert Street in the Lower Falls. This was an area that you couldn't just drive into without raising suspicion in July 1972. Barricades had been erected across streets, and armed IRA men stood around watching for any suspicious cars.

Sending UVF men into the Lower Falls to exact revenge would have been tantamount to a suicide mission. It was a frustrating situation, which was made worse by the loyalists who had decided that stopping Catholics at UDA checkpoints and rompering them was the best way of hitting back. This was counterproductive on two levels. It meant that yet more innocent people were being

* David Boulton, *The UVF: An Anatomy of Loyalist Rebellion, 1966–1973* (Dublin: Torc, 1973), pp. 170–1.

killed, which was no better than what the Provos had proved themselves capable of with Bloody Friday, the Abercorn bombing, and numerous other shootings and bombings throughout the first half of 1972. In turn, it meant that we were unable to get to the people who we knew were responsible for carrying out these atrocities. Once the Provos realised that Catholics were being killed at random in retaliation for their bombings, the operators in areas such as Albert Street melted into the background like cowards; these republican enclaves changed, and the key figures began to move to safe houses. I felt that we were sailing in the right direction but that the wind generated by the sectarian killings blew us off course.

Unfortunately, it was almost impossible to try and stop that gut reaction, which was prevalent among so many loyalists. The blood was up because the city was being destroyed by bombs. Random killings were a counterproductive tactic that characterised the rest of the early to mid-1970s, but it was justified within loyalist organisations as 'terrorising the terrorists'. Due to a dearth of quality intelligence on the IRA, the strategy that influenced much of the loyalist paramilitary thinking during these years was that if they killed enough Catholics then the Catholic community would in turn put pressure on the IRA to disband: 'If you weren't here killing Protestants and soldiers, then we wouldn't be getting attacked at random by the loyalists.' This was pure sectarianism, and it didn't work. It had the opposite effect and dramatically strengthened support for the IRA in working-class Catholic areas. At the time, however, I truly believed that if we pushed the Catholic community to the edge, they would go begging to the IRA to stop their terrorist campaign.

A week after Bloody Friday, Flint and Plum were arrested after shooting and seriously injuring a Catholic man they had spotted walking past Unity Flats late at night. This was obviously a huge blow to morale, and although we were reeling at the capture of two active operators, things moved very quickly, and the organisation knew that Gusty would continue to require close protection around the clock. The Young Ulster Volunteers were given this task, and I believe that this was due to the respect that had grown between myself and Billy Spence. Billy had been encouraged by the organisation of the young lads in the Red Hand, and when he saw myself and my friends emerge onto the scene, he spoke highly of us to Gusty. He knew that it wouldn't be older men like himself who would be involved in the war; he understood that we were the future. With his foresight and vision, Billy Spence encouraged us to change our name to the Young Citizen Volunteers (YCV) in order to fit in with the restructuring of the UVF that Gusty was involved in spearheading. Like Gusty, Billy understood the importance of an identity, a vision and, above all, a historical lineage to Ulster's past crises. It made sense. We saw ourselves as the inheritors of the original UVF and YCV, which had fought against Home Rule and paid the ultimate sacrifice at the Somme.

Billy may not have been a fighter like Gusty, but he had an important political influence on the UVF and the loyalist cause. He didn't act on impulse, and I suppose if he had been around nowadays, he would have been a well-paid special advisor in politics. He had an ear to the ground and knew all the people who mattered. Billy had been a member of Ulster Protestant Action and he kept the cogs turning behind the scenes in the Unionist Party's Court ward branch, where many years later I would be elected as a councillor for the PUP. Along with his son, Edward, in 1971, he formed the Orange Cross. This was the first loyalist prisoners' welfare organisation, and Billy and Edward organised it for many years in the 1970s. I know that they both worked tirelessly and acted selflessly to ensure that those young men who found themselves inside Northern Ireland's jails in the early to mid-1970s were not left wanting for anything.

This was an exciting time to be a young volunteer, and it was an honour to be assigned the task of acting as Gusty's bodyguard. It also brought with it a huge amount of personal responsibility. Up until this point, I had been expected to analyse and plan how best to respond to the ongoing security situation. Now I had to factor in the constant protection of a man with an almost mythical status. Gusty was a loyalist icon. The first time I met him was in the Liverpool Club in Woodvale, and he said to me, 'I hear you're out organising the younger ones? I take it that it's the YCV?' I just played it cool, looked him straight in the eye and said, 'Yeah'. I didn't want to give too much away to anyone, not even someone with the legendary status that Gusty had. His response reassured me that I and the twenty or so young lads under my command were being given our place within the fresh UVF structure: 'I'm glad you're onboard Hutchie, and that you're going to be working with me, because I heard all about you when I was in jail.' A young man likes validation, and despite my independent mind, I was excited to receive such a commendation from a living loyalist icon.

The UVF was galvanised by Gusty's presence on the streets of the Shankill and other loyalist redoubts, and he conducted a number of large swearing-in ceremonies in venues across Northern Ireland throughout the summer. Volunteers were expected to take an oath of allegiance to the organisation – a solemn vow that they were dedicated to fight for Ulster's freedom and its people against IRA violence.

With the emergence and rapid growth of the YCV, my friends and I consequently had a lot more responsibility. Things had escalated and developed extremely quickly, and I had gone from being a Tartan gang member to becoming a founding member of a paramilitary organisation. We weren't just a group of young loyalists trying to find our feet anymore; we were now an integral part of the newly restructured UVF, with officers in place. I didn't regard the YCV as a mini-UVF, and it certainly wasn't just a feeder for the organisation. Anyone who thought that was quickly disabused of the notion. The YCV would have input at the highest level of the UVF. As a leader of the YCV, it was my duty to attend meetings with other company commanders and debate tactics and other house-keeping matters within the entire organisation. My seventeenth birthday wasn't until December 1972, and yet here I was with several enormous responsibilities amid what was the most violent period of the Troubles. I had to ensure that Gusty Spence wasn't targeted by the IRA or rearrested by the police or army; I had to walk into venues around the country and exert authority over men who were often three or four years older than me.

Many other 16-year-olds were worrying about standing in front of their class in school to give a talk about science or history, but I was a leader of a paramilitary organisation giving lectures on weapons and the tactics of urban warfare. I called in favours wherever I could to ensure that my men were equipped with both a knowledge and practical understanding of what they had committed themselves to. Weapons training was provided by the Orange Volunteers on the Shankill. Bobby Ramage, a local engineer and former soldier, provided classes on the design of explosives in a derelict house in an area that had been bought up for slum clearances. Many other nameless figures assisted in making the YCV a cohesive and forceful organisation, whether they were raising funds for prisoners and weapons, or bandaging wounds received during active service. People all had their roles to play.

As a group of young men, we talked continuously amongst ourselves about the political situation and the conflict that had been created by the PIRA. We were frustrated by the collapse of Stormont, which had been prorogued in March 1972 – it seemed to be a culmination of everything that had gone wrong locally in terms of dealing with the ongoing situation. In addition, we were angry at the inability of the local forces of law and order to do anything about violent republicanism. If the British government wouldn't step up to the mark and defend the Protestants of Ulster, then young men like me would.

Although the era we were living through was different to that which the original YCV had initially encountered in 1912, some of the core tenets of that organisation resounded in the grouping I established:

> To cultivate, by means of a modified military and police drill, a manly physique, with habits of self-control, self-respect and chivalry.
>
> To assist as an organisation, when called upon, the civil power in the maintenance of the peace.

From the outset I promoted the YCV as a tight, disciplined group of volunteers who would take the war to republicans and 'return the serve' for IRA atrocities perpetrated against Protestants. Initially I recruited within the neighbourhoods closest to where everything was happening in Belfast in 1972: the west and the north of the city, as well as the south and east. Thereafter I contacted the various UVF battalion commanders across Northern Ireland and commenced the process of working together with them for the overall benefit of the organisation. The YCV had started small as the Young Ulster Volunteers. I had to approach the best young men across the country to get them involved in what the UVF was doing.

Travelling to all these different locations outside Belfast and liaising with other volunteers was all well and good, but the secretive nature of the YCV was such that we could hardly arrive in town and openly advertise a recruitment night in a local hall. Instead, we booked such venues under the auspices of karate lessons and other similar physical pursuits. I was going to places like Mid-Ulster and East Antrim, where people's desire to defend Ulster might have been the same as us in Belfast but where the local challenges from republicans might have been slightly different. This had to be considered when approaching new recruits, and lectures on tactics were tailored to suit the specific needs of the local unit. The segregated geography of Belfast, particularly after August 1971, made it easy to identify the enemy based on where they lived or socialised. For those loyalists in rural areas where communities were mixed and farmers relied on their neighbours, it could often be more difficult to predict where an attack might come from.

There were very few people who knew that I was only 16 years old. The UVF wouldn't even realise my young age until I was later arrested. No matter where I went, I was treated like a man. I could tell that people had been talking about me, and that a bit of a reputation had been constructed around 'Billy Hutchinson'. It was a bit like the army and the police in 1970 and 1971. They obviously had an image of who I was and how I thought, but they didn't know the real me. To the local loyalists who had only heard about me, I was not only a man, I was *the* man. Doors were opening for the YCV. I was getting slapped on the back and told about how I was doing great things for Ulster in its time of need. This could've gone to a lot of people's heads, and they could have taken advantage and gone on a power trip, but I was consumed by an intense focus on what needed to be done for the greater good.

Since Gusty's arrest in 1966, his family had worked hard to ensure that he and other loyalist prisoners and their families were looked after. The Orange Cross, formed by Billy Spence and Ed Spence, was the logical outcome for this cause, but as time went on the welfare side of things broadened out and the Loyalist Prisoners Welfare Association, headed by Jackie Hewitt (a member of Headquarters Staff involved in the welfare side of the UVF) and Jim McDonald, became an important component of the organisation. In these early days, the YCV often had to carry out bank robberies to ensure that money was available for the families of prisoners.

Some of our lads were still schoolboys – some were going on operations with boiler suits over their school uniforms before arriving at the classroom to take lessons. The only rationale for paying someone was expenses if they were forced to take a day off work to carry out duties for the organisation. This was usually only the case if someone had a specialised role, such as a driver or an Ammunition Technical Officer (ATO).

I was also very firm with regards to my stance on alcohol. I didn't drink and I didn't like the effect that alcohol had on a lot of people. I expected the men under my command to abstain from drinking when they were on duty or on a 'stand-by' situation. Alcohol lowered people's inhibitions and made them careless; my volunteers needed to be disciplined and flexed, ready for action when the time came. The YCV was an army in defensive mode, so volunteers were expected to keep a clear head in case they were called on. This was part of the psychological preparation for war that I hoped would ensure discipline; if a guy knew that the one time he was called upon happened to be the time he was drinking, it would have made him less likely to indulge while on duty. Young men are young men, however, and often I would walk into a room in one of the pubs where we met and would suddenly see all these big pint glasses of Coca-Cola being shuffled to the front of the tables. I wasn't stupid, and I certainly wasn't a puritan, but I needed volunteers to keep a clear head and take their YCV duties seriously. If I caught anyone disobeying these rules when they were active, they had to do the door at one of the bars on the Shankill without any breaks. There were one or two persistent offenders who only got away with it because they were longstanding personal friends of mine.

Commanding my own UVF battalion was becoming a full-time occupation, but I also kept up my apprenticeship at Mackies throughout the spring and summer of 1972. Nevertheless, it wasn't long until the rumour mill began to spread. Belfast is a very small city – more like a village, in fact. Republicans detested me during the Tartan and Linfield period, but word must have somehow begun to spread about my involvement with the UVF and those republicans who had previously wanted to kick the lights out of me were now intent on killing me. There were three or four of us from Mackies who went to Millfield technical college (or 'tech', as it's called in Belfast) together. Millfield is an area close to the city centre that lies at the bottom of Divis Street and the Falls Road, but which is also close to the foot of the Shankill. One afternoon my pals from Mackies and I were leaving the tech when we heard the unmistakable crack of gunfire followed by the screech of car tyres. I looked around and was relieved to find that no one was hurt. We hurried off to Brown Square and onto the Shankill, where we would be safe. I thought nothing more of it until a few weeks later, on a Saturday morning.

As I walked to Mackies for my shift, I heard gunfire coming from Lucknow Street. By this point in the Troubles, the sound of shots being fired was just part of the regular soundtrack to daily life in Belfast. I put it down to republicans firing at the army or whatever and walked down to work, clocked in and took my place at my lathe. After a couple of hours, a mate's dad, who was in charge of my section, 'S1', came to seek me out at my lathe, which faced the wall. I felt the tap on the shoulder and turned the machine off. 'Look, Hutchie, I don't know what's going on, but one of the Mackies has phoned me asking do I have a "Hutchie" that works here, with long hair. I said, "Yeah – he lives in Matchett Street", and they said "Yeah, that's him."' Apparently, they needed to speak to me urgently; it was a matter of life and death, I was told. My mate's dad was concerned and accompanied me through the foundry and into the big offices at the front of Mackies on the Springfield Road. We had no idea what was going to happen. As we stepped into the office, we saw one of the Mackies, a couple of policemen and a few soldiers. My heart sank; I thought I was going to be arrested. The manager said, 'These gentlemen want to talk to you. You can use that room.' I wasn't sure about going into a room by myself with the police, so I fell back on my age. 'I shouldn't be in a room by myself with these ones, I'm only 16.' They assured me it was in my best interests, so I asked my mate's dad to accompany me, which he was only too happy to do.

First of all, the police asked me had I been shot at earlier in the morning on my way into Mackies. I said no, because I hadn't even entertained the idea that anyone was shooting specifically at me. They then asked had I been shot at a few weeks ago, on a Thursday. I told them no. They then asked me had I been at Millfield tech when shots were fired. I confirmed that this had happened. I was then asked did I know one of the guys I'd been with, who worked in the foundry over at Woodvale (which was a part of Mackies). 'Yes,' I told them, 'what about him?' The police told me that on the Friday evening after shots had been fired near us at Millfield, a few of the guys had gone out on the town for a couple of beers after work at Mackies. On the way home to the Mountainview area between the Woodvale and Crumlin roads, one of the guys who I was very friendly with (the one who worked at the foundry at Woodvale) stopped off at a chippy in Ardoyne. As soon as he walked back out onto the Crumlin Road with his bag of chips, he was bundled into a car and taken to a house in the republican part of Ardoyne, where he was tortured for several hours. During a break in his interrogation, he managed to throw himself out of a window and make a bid for freedom. Luckily, some sympathetic locals discovered him, and he was rushed off to hospital, where he was eventually able to make a full recovery and speak to the police after a period of three weeks. The police asked him what he had been questioned about. 'Hutchie. From Mackies. They wanted to know everything about him.' After they had finished telling me this, the police advised me to leave Mackies immediately and to never come back. My mate's dad offered to drive me back to Matchett Street, but the army said he needn't bother, that they would leave me home. Always keen to make me feel uneasy, the soldiers drove me down Cupar Street, where they left me off on the Falls Road end.

'You're on your own.'

As I walked into Lawnbrook Avenue and back onto the Shankill, I thought of my mate. He was completely innocent of any involvement in paramilitaries. We both loved rock music, and that was the main basis for our friendship. The other guys I had been with outside Millfield were also civilians who weren't political in any way. People who I was friendly with were now beginning to get caught up in trouble because of my reputation. It wasn't fair on them, and I made a conscious decision there and then not to get too close to anyone in the future. I had to keep my eye on the ball and make things as simple as possible. I also thought back to my interactions with some of the Catholics who I had worked with in Mackies. There was always political debate going on, very little of it highbrow; this was natural due to the ongoing situation. Then I recalled one guy from West Belfast who used to throw the contents of his wage packet on the ground every Friday and stamp on the Queen's head. 'Fuck the Brits and fuck you,' he would say to me. He had a mate from the Ardoyne, and I think they were both members of the Fianna Éireann. The guy from West Belfast would shit himself if I ever challenged him over his antics with the money, but his mate from Ardoyne was always deadly serious. He had said to me regularly, 'I have one with your name on it, and its going into your head.' I was fearless and always said back to him, 'Well, come on then. Go and get it.' One of the Protestants had pulled a zip gun on a mate of these guys, and obviously their attitudes had hardened even more after that. With my reputation stretching back a couple of years, I was always a lightning rod for this sort of hassle from republicans. There was no point complaining about it. We were now in a war situation, and people had taken their sides. I was no different. My dedication to the UVF was the most important part of my life.

Although the UVF was firmly on the scene by the end of the summer of 1972, there was still a mystique surrounding them in the loyalist community. Among the ranks of the UDA men parading through Belfast and elsewhere, there were many guys wearing UVF enamel badges on their peaked caps, and Flint had always been very prominent at the no-go areas with the Red Hand, wearing his Ulster Special Service Force cap badge on his beret. Apart from this and the press conference Gusty had held back in July, there was no sign of the UVF. We were active, but people would still ask each other, 'Who are the UVF?' That's the way we wanted it, and the YCV was no different. Volunteers were never encouraged to speak publicly about what they were involved in, even with their friends, families or wives or girlfriends.

The UVF had been busy creating an image for when we needed to go public, and the uniform was very much modelled on what Gusty was wearing when he spoke to David Boulton on television, on a special episode of *World in Action*, shortly after he had been 'kidnapped' by the UVF. Cap comforters, black polo-neck jumpers, dark leather jackets, dark trousers and black boots. This uniform would become synonymous with the UVF throughout the 1970s. The first opportunity for the UVF to appear en masse and in uniform in public came in tragic circumstances for the organisation.

In the middle of September, some loyalists in the predominantly Protestant County Antrim coastal town of Larne descended on a Catholic enclave. There were rumours that locals had been involved in the IRA, and the Protestant defence association had decided to take matters into their own hands. Rioting broke out, and in the melee that ensued Sinclair Johnston, a 27-year-old volunteer in the UVF, was shot dead by the RUC. Sinclair had been a sergeant and intelligence officer and was a huge loss to the organisation. The UVF wanted to ensure that he received a military send-off, and volunteers were asked to attend the funeral and to be prepared to change into UVF uniform. A few of us from the Shankill hired a minibus to travel the twenty-five or so miles up to Sinclair's funeral. When we arrived in Larne, we changed into black trousers, black polo-neck jumpers, leather jackets and cap comforters and formed a colour party with flags among the 3,000 or so mourners. Sinclair Johnston's funeral was a solemn occasion and the UVF had proved that it was a disciplined military outfit.

Before we left Larne, we all got changed back into our civvies: Wranglers, shirts, denim jackets. Someone took all the UVF uniforms and paraphernalia and put it in a black bag, which was ferried away in a clean car. As the minibus reached Clifton Street in Belfast, we were flagged down by a police patrol from Glenravel Barracks. 'Ok, you lot – out of the bus and across the road.' Once the fifteen of us, of various ages, had all been marched across the road and into the police station, we were each questioned about what we had been doing. 'How well did you know Sinclair Johnston?' 'Are you a member of the Ulster Volunteer Force?' The police must have questioned us about nearly every unsolved murder in the district.

By the latter months of 1972, I was firmly ensconced in the UVF. I lived every day, as much as possible, like a normal teenager, going to my job and chumming around with my friends, but I was beginning to have a lot less time for the latter and I was spending most of my time with the guys who had moved into the YCV. There was a core group of about twenty-six of us who were deeply involved in the YCV. Tom Winstone and I were engaged in recruiting new members. Tom was one of my closest friends, but some of my other good friends, who weren't that way inclined, were the kind of guys we tried to keep our paramilitary lives separate from. I'm sure they may have guessed what we were doing, but my feeling was that if they were privy to the details then they could be harassed by the police, army or, even worse, republicans – like my old friend from tech had been.

Any paramilitary organisation will attract a broad church of individuals who come together in common cause. The UVF was no different. Some guys could lift a gun and carry out assassinations like the soldiers they were, while others were better at the welfare side of things, ensuring that prisoners and their families had everything they needed. We had the guys who were supremely talented at creating and experimenting with explosive devices, and others who were 'wheelmen': good drivers. These were the various roles played by people who joined the UVF, and they were all equally crucial to the organisation. I have met guys in the UVF who were quiet, some who were ostentatious, others who were deeply conservative and a number who were like 'hired guns' – professionals who were purely focused on what their specific role in the organisation was.

Around this time a young guy called Lenny Murphy became interested in what the YCV was doing. I'd known Lenny since I was a young boy, and although he was a few years older than me, he was keen to meet up and have discussions about the ongoing situation in Ulster. Lenny was always dressed in the best clothes, drove a car, and had girlfriends; he was somebody who younger guys looked up to. I also knew that he had a reputation for being able to handle himself. At this stage, in 1972, he was constantly busy, trying to make friends with people in the various loyalist organisations; during this period, he started to try and make inroads into the YCV. I was on friendly terms with him, but he already belonged to A Company of the UVF, so I was hesitant about him being privy to anything we were doing.

Despite Lenny's dedication to the cause, it was noticeable by late 1972 that he was becoming a larger-than-life version of the average UVF volunteer. We were a secretive organisation and by necessity volunteers were expected to shun the limelight; however, Lenny seemed consumed by the need to be recognised. He appeared to have a steely determination to make a name for himself, and the kudos he began to receive within loyalist circles apparently wasn't enough to satisfy his burning desire to become infamous.

I felt that Lenny was getting way ahead of himself, and I didn't think his approach – instilling fear in those around him – could work in the long run. You can't motivate or rule by fear. I told him as much, and after a few discussions he seemed to have taken my advice; I thought I had got through to him.

One Saturday morning around the end of the summer, I bumped into Lenny on the Shankill Road and we began walking up past Crimea Street and talking about all and sundry. Out of nowhere, he asked me had I seen an article in one of the newspapers. According to the story, Lenny said that there had been a coup within the UVF and Captain William Johnston had been overthrown by Captain Henry Wilson. I found this all strange. First, these were two historical figures, and the Johnston moniker in particular was used by the UVF to sign off on communiques and press statements. It wasn't a specific person. I asked Lenny what he had heard; he told me that someone on the UVF Brigade Staff had mentioned this wrangle between Johnston and Wilson to him, and it was now all over a newspaper. After a few minutes of walking and talking about this, we reached Moscow Street, where we were suddenly surrounded by a large squad of soldiers and police. I was shoved up against the wall and given hassle about Gusty and his whereabouts before being unceremoniously thrown into the back of a Land Rover, something that was becoming par for the course for me. Lenny was left standing on the street with his mouth wide open. When I was brought to the police station at Springfield Road, the soldiers started questioning me about Johnston and Wilson. They were accusing me of being Wilson. I denied being Wilson and told them that I didn't have a clue what they were talking about. They then accused me of being sympathetic to Wilson's plans to overthrow Johnston. It was bizarre, and I honestly didn't know what they were talking about. They began asking me about the leadership of the UVF and the whereabouts of Gusty. I told them I was just a kid, that I didn't know anything about that sort of stuff.

After a few hours of this the soldiers dumped me back out onto the Shankill, frustrated in their efforts to get any clarity about the situation. Later that evening I saw Lenny and he was in one of his regular dark moods. I asked him what the matter was. He was annoyed that the soldiers and police hadn't arrested him. While the rest of us were trying to keep our heads down, he was trying to earn notoriety no matter what effect it had on the security and secrecy of the organisation. I took him aside and told him that I thought it was a bit strange that he had brought up the subject of this supposed coup within the UVF, the figures of Captain William Johnston and Captain Henry Wilson, and a minute or two later I was being arrested and taken in for questioning about that very issue. I reassured him that I wasn't accusing him of anything, but from then on I often wondered what Lenny's motivations were.

It slowly became obvious that if he couldn't control the YCV, Lenny was going to try and poach some of its members. It soon came to light that, for some time, Lenny had been trying to recruit guys who I had utilised for specific roles in operations. When I found out what Lenny had been up to, I decided to call a meeting with some of the YCV. One of my guys had come to me a few weeks before and told me that Lenny had approached him, asking whether he would leave the YCV and join up with him. 'And what did you say?' I asked him. 'Well, I'm here now, telling you – so obviously I said no.' When a second fella came to me with the same information, I decided that I would have to find out what was going on. At the meeting I had convened, I asked those who had been approached by Lenny to make themselves known. Four lads raised their hands. I told them that they could leave and go with Lenny but that they wouldn't be privy to any further details about what our team was doing. If any information about us came to light, I would know who had spoken out of turn. It would have been easy to fly off the handle with the guys who wanted to leave, or make threats, but what was the point? If they thought they would be happier under Lenny's leadership, then that was their choice. There was no point in trying to carry deadweight. The four lads were adults and I graciously allowed them to go with Lenny.

One weekend in September 1972, myself and one of the guys who had gone to Lenny's team were socialising with three girls at a dance in the West Belfast Orange Hall. Although this fella had gone with Lenny, I didn't hold any ill-will against him and still liked him on a social level. At some point in the night, a couple of the girls decided that they wanted to go to a shebeen up in Springmartin. The guy said he would drive us up. I was a bit reluctant as I didn't drink, but we all got in the car and headed up the Shankill. The other guy had had a few drinks, and when the car stopped at the traffic lights at the junction at Cambrai Street, he decided he would try and race the car beside us; he suddenly stuck his foot on the accelerator and bombed up toward Woodvale Park, where the car ended up colliding with a lamppost. As it did so, the lamppost fell, and I instinctively threw myself over the two girls in the back to protect them. Miraculously, no one was killed. It was a good job as well, because one of Gusty Spence's daughters was with us. The driver made a run for it, leaving me and the three girls in the car. The fire brigade arrived and were able to cut me out, and an ambulance ferried me to the Royal

Victoria Hospital off the Falls Road. I had a fractured back and was put in traction.

While I was convalescing in the Royal, Lenny came up to visit. Again, he was in a black mood and started telling me that he was going to kill the car driver for this. I told him to leave it, that it was a drunken accident and was nothing to do with him, the YCV or the UVF. It wouldn't look good if he killed one of his own guys over such an innocuous thing.

On 28 September I was watching the news in the television room off the ward I was in. There was a report about a shooting that had taken place at Glenvarlock Street in East Belfast. I was subsequently told about what had apparently happened. Allegedly, Lenny and a young man called Mervyn Connor, one of the four lads who had raised their hands at the YCV meeting, had arrived on the doorstep of an East Belfast man called Ted Pavis. The UVF had supposedly heard that Pavis was selling guns to republicans and decided that he should be killed. It was reported that while Mervyn kept a stolen motorcycle in gear outside Ted Pavis's parents' house, Lenny shot Pavis dead at the front door; Lenny and Mervyn then reportedly made a hasty retreat through the back streets of East Belfast and across the river to the safety of the Shankill.

Some time passed after Pavis had been shot before Lenny and Mervyn were arrested for the killing. They were remanded in Crumlin Road Gaol, where a growing number of loyalists were beginning to find themselves incarcerated as the conflict gained momentum. Apparently Mervyn decided to admit his part in the shooting of Pavis, thus implicating Lenny. It looked certain that Lenny's aspirations to be a big name in the UVF would be curtailed at an early stage and that he would be going down for a long time. Yet another willing operator being put behind bars would be a blow to the UVF during what had developed into an extremely violent and volatile year.

In early 1973, as Lenny languished on remand, I was approached by his mother, Joyce. I'd been in and out of the Murphy house over the past number of months, during my brief friendship with Lenny. I knew that she and Lenny had a strong bond, and while Lenny was generally frightened of nothing, he certainly feared the wrath of his mother. She appeared to be the only person who had any influence over him. I respected Mrs Murphy and I knew her to be a loving mother who was devoted to her children and wider family. It was upsetting to see her so animated as she claimed that Lenny was beginning to question himself and had been asking to talk to me. Mrs Murphy wanted me to accompany her on a visit. After some resistance I eventually relented and went up to the Crum with her. Sitting across from Lenny, I was taken aback, but not completely surprised, by the fact that his usual confident demeanour had fallen away. He was on the verge of tears and kept saying that he should have taken my advice and stayed away from the people he had recruited from the YCV into his unit. He was also torn up over the fact that somebody he had regarded as being close to had apparently betrayed him by making a statement against him. I could tell that he felt paranoid and wasn't sure who to trust any longer. I believe that his desire to talk to me was heavily influenced by his mother. He wasn't in tears because of his incarceration but because his mother was frustrated. She knew that Lenny could trust me and that I would tell him things as they were. I was straight down the line with him. I told him that he had made bad choices; that he had taken on people who were used to carrying out specific roles within the YCV and hadn't thought to assess their capabilities for what he wanted before taking them over to his team. He was putting people into situations they were probably unhappy or uncomfortable with. This could only lead to chaos and poor morale.

Lenny's contrition during that visit was indicative of one side of his dual personality. One minute he would be on the level and easy to talk to; the next he would be apoplectic with rage and an intimidating presence for those who happened to be around him. You just didn't know which version of him you were going to get. It was always one extreme or the other.

In April 1973 Mervyn Connor was found dead in the Crum. The word on the street was that he had been poisoned by Lenny after writing a forced confession and suicide note, absolving Lenny of all blame for the Pavis shooting. The whole thing seemed to me to be a complete and unnecessary mess.

After I had been forced to walk from Mackies, I was fortunately not without a job for long. For the next year I worked as a labourer in a firm of electrical engineers located outside Belfast. This was a busy time for me. On top of my day job, I had to ensure that Gusty wasn't rearrested. This was a duty that the YCV was proud to carry out. On a personal level, I learned a lot from him during this period, and it was the genesis of a relationship that would be developed later in Long Kesh and reinforced by the time the UVF called a ceasefire in 1994.

Gusty's experience of soldiering meant that he was a veritable well of information and good advice on how I could develop the YCV and turn it into a ruthless war machine. Importantly, since his incarceration in 1966, he had also learned a lot of psychology. He always had a strategy in his head, and he knew how to influence people into doing things. Gusty taught me to trust my own instinct with people.

On a few occasions while he was on the outside, Gusty got lucky. On other occasions there may have been a subtle agenda at work to keep him on the streets to ensure that the UVF didn't descend into anarchy. A good example of this was on 11 October 1972, when there were a large number of senior UVF men conducting a meeting in Brennan Street Social Club. There had been a crackdown on the UVF that day, with paratroopers discovering arms and ammunition secreted at The

Oval, the home of Glentoran F.C. Elsewhere in East Belfast, a UVF volunteer named Joe Bennett was arrested at his house, where it was discovered that he had four guns, 277 rounds of ammunition, two home-made pen guns and a variety of other gun parts. Rioting broke out on the Shankill, and Tennent Street police station was attacked by Tartans. Paratroopers stormed the meeting at Brennan Street, and all who were caught, including a heavily disguised Gusty, were brought to Castlereagh. Billy Spence was also arrested, as he happened to be there solely at the invitation of the UVF leadership to allow him to see Gusty.

At Ladas Drive, Billy was initially mistaken for his younger brother, and Gusty later told us that as everyone was being brought into Castlereagh, he had seen a policeman who knew him from 1966 but that the guy just walked past him. I'm sure if someone had wanted Gusty back in jail that evening, he would have been in Crumlin Road Gaol within an hour. It suited everyone to have Gusty in the midst of things.

This close shave might have made others go deeper underground, but maybe Gusty started to feel omnipotent. I can't say for certain. On the morning of Saturday, 4 November, we were sleeping in the maisonette, where we were staying with Gusty, when he arose early and deviated from the normal routine we had agreed on, leaving by himself to go out. This was a very risky move, particularly given the close shave he had had at Brennan Street the previous month. Usually, if he had told me that he wanted to go out, I would have ordered a reccy first to get a feel for what was going on and what the streets were like on that particular day. Maybe Gusty had become too complacent about his security, but the Paras, always on the look-out for suspect activity, noticed a suspicious looking car in the West Circular area. When they stopped it, they discovered that Gusty was at the steering wheel. When the news was relayed back to me, I was absolutely devastated. I was also angry. I couldn't figure out why he had decided to take such a big chance; it just didn't make sense. He told me that he had decided to go out and fetch food for the breakfast, but I believe that he either wanted to meet with his wife, Louie, or have a private meeting about UVF business with someone on his own. We had been put in a really bad situation and I felt like I had let the UVF down, but ultimately I realised that there was nothing I could have done. Gusty was a 39-year-old man with a family. We were 16-year-old boys. He had free will, and he decided on that Saturday morning, for whatever reason, that the risk was worth it.

It wouldn't be the last time I would see Gusty Spence, however.

My father, William, and my mother, Elizabeth, with my older siblings, Elinor and George, in Dublin, sometime in the 1950s. My father was better known as 'Big Hutchie' and my mother was called Lily. I think you'll agree there is a clear resemblance with my mother.

The aftermath of the IRA's bomb attack on the Four Step Inn in September 1971. The pub was packed with Bluemen after Linfield had played Standard Liege at Windsor Park. Along with others, I scrambled in the wreckage for survivors. Two local men, Ernie Bates and Joker Andrews, died. Three months later, another bomb exploded in a furniture showroom on the Shankill Road on Saturday, 11 December 1971, killing two babies. Once again, my friends and I were on our hands and knees looking for survivors. The next day scores of young loyalists volunteered for the paramilitary organisations. Image courtesy of Victor Patterson.

On muster parade (me in the centre) in Long Kesh. Image courtesy of www.longkeshinsideout.co.uk.

A recruitment ad for the Young Citizen Volunteers in *Combat* magazine, *c.*1974.

With Gusty Spence and Eddie Kinner in Long Kesh. Image courtesy of Eddie Kinner.

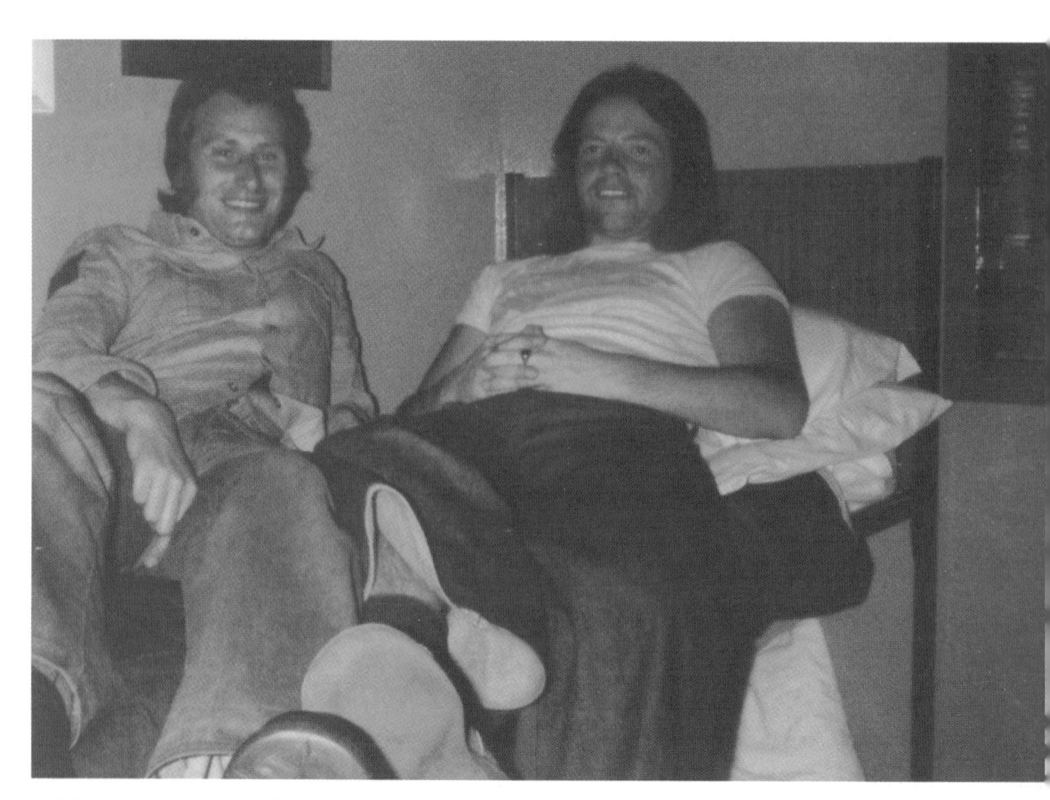

Eddie Kinner and I having a chat in Long Kesh. Image courtesy of Eddie Kinner.

When I was incarcerated in Long Kesh, I was reunited with some familiar faces who I had a massive amount of respect for. Left to right in this picture are senior officers Bobby Spence, Ronnie 'Flint' McCullough (who formed the Red Hand Commando) and Gusty Spence. Bobby was another big influence on me, and I was devastated when both he and Billy died in 1980. Image courtesy of Ed Spence.

The summers in the 1970s seemed often to be very warm. Given the location of Long Kesh and the lack of any foliage or tall buildings, we were able to avail of the sunshine. From left to right: me, Flint McCullough, Jakey Kane and Trevor King. Image courtesy of Ronnie McCullough.

Officers, from left to right: Trevor King, me and Billy Mitchell, with the UVF colours and the huts behind us. Image courtesy of Eddie Kinner.

Gusty with Freddie Stevenson. Freddie was a fantastic artist and muralist and this painting of the pawn shop on the Old Lodge Road reminded many of us of our childhoods. Image courtesy of Ed Spence.

One of my original Open University textbooks with my name in the corner. Ironically, the cover looks like a bonfire! The module number is referred to in my letter to the Secretary of State (see Appendices).

Standing outside Parliament Buildings, Stormont in December 1994 before exploratory dialogue with the British government. From left to right: Jackie Mahood, Plum Smith, me, Lindsay Robb and David Ervine. Mahood and Robb would ultimately defect from both the PUP and the UVF. Image courtesy of Pacemaker Press.

There is an enduring myth propagated by republicans that loyalists didn't avail of education in prison. In fact, we took up education before republicans and many UVF/RHC POWs came out with degrees. Here I am on graduation day at Queen's University Belfast with my mother. Not bad for a guy who left school at 15.

CHAPTER 5

Eating, Sleeping and Breathing the UVF

I had become close to Gusty's brother Bobby as well. Like Gusty and Billy, he was a dedicated loyalist. Bobby was another important mentor in my development as a UVF volunteer, and although he seemed like an old man to me – he was about 44 years old at this stage – he was extremely fit and was an active operator. Bobby was a war hero, and while in the Royal Navy he had been awarded two medals: a distinguished service medal during the Korean War and a United Nations medal. Like me and other UVF men, he was always being watched by the security forces. Any time they saw one of us out and about, they arrested us and brought us in for questioning. One day Bobby was arrested near playing fields at Ballysillan. He had been waiting on a lift to the Farm (a social club/UVF HQ) in Monkstown and suddenly spotted the police racing toward him. Bobby had detonators on him, which he fortunately managed to throw over a wall before they were spotted. Although he tried to bolt, he was caught. Completely unaware that all of this had happened, I was sitting in the Loyalist Club in Rumford Street later that afternoon when Bobby's wife suddenly rushed in. She was in quite a state and exclaimed, 'Hutchie, I need to talk to you! They're questioning Bobby about the stuff.' Bobby had stashed ammunition at a specific location that I also had access to, and he had instructed

his wife to tell me not to go near any of it in case the police were observing the situation.

I did as I was told, but the police were obviously itching to get hold of me to see if they could apply pressure on the situation with Bobby. The next afternoon I was standing in Agnes Street, chatting away to a couple of lads. As I left them, I turned the corner onto the Shankill Road, where the bank was. Suddenly a squad of army and police appeared and bounced into me, pinning me against the wall. One of the soldiers started searching me. I panicked because I had a revolver in my waistband for protection. I needed to act, and quickly. A charge of possession could earn me a spell in jail. One of the other soldiers called to the one who was beginning to search me, and I took his distraction as an opportunity to swivel on my heels and barge him out of the way. Before he realised what had happened, I was away back up Agnes Street and down Richmond Street toward the Loyalist Club. I ran past the old fella who was doing the door of the club and shouted, 'The army is coming!'

I dashed into the yard of the club and shoved the .38 under some crates. I ran up the stairs of the Loyalist toward the lounge, which was closed to the public. The man on the door came up after me and locked the lounge door so that no one could get in while I laid low. Downstairs, people were dancing, singing and drinking. Then, above all of this reverie, I heard the soldiers and police arrive with a clatter, bashing the doors in and shouting and yelling at everyone. The music stopped. Suddenly there was screaming and pandemonium as I just crouched there in the darkness, totally breathless, in the silence of the upstairs lounge. Eventually the soldiers and police must have got fed up with hassling everyone and left. When some time had passed, I decided that I should move again. I knew the army would still be on the look-out for me, but I couldn't stay in the lounge all night. I made my way downstairs into the bar and told a few people that I

was going to a friend's house to keep my head down. I made the decision to get a taxi, as it would be too dodgy to move about in a car that could be easily identifiable to the authorities. Another friend kept offering me a lift, but I told him that it would be serious business with hell to pay if we were stopped by the army or police. He kept insisting and after a while I relented.

Wrong choice.

As the car moved out of Downing Street onto the Shankill, the police and army immediately hemmed us in with a cavalcade of military vehicles. I thought that my luck had finally run out. There was no way out of this one, surely. A soldier and policeman came over to the car, asked us to get out and frisked myself and my friend. Thankfully neither of us had anything on us. They stripped the car to bits and just left it. They were obviously engineers, as they took the seats out, took everything out of the boot, opened the bonnet and removed everything they physically could. As they moved off, they were laughing and shouted, 'You can put it back together your fucking selves.' We were standing there in utter disbelief, all these car parts scattered around us like kids with a big Meccano set, staring at what had been a fully functioning car a few minutes previously. Breaking the stunned silence, my friend eventually turned around to me and said, 'I didn't think it would be this fucking serious!' I said to him 'I'll get a couple of people to give you a hand putting it back together again, I'm getting a taxi!'

On 5 February 1973, the first two loyalist activists to be interned were rounded up. The game of cat and mouse between myself and the authorities ratcheted up at this stage. I don't know for certain if I was ever on the list of loyalists to be detained, but given the hassle I had had from the police and army over the previous two and a half years, it wouldn't have been a stretch of the imagination to guess that if they could have caught me, the authorities would happily have detained me in Long Kesh. Luckily,

I had become accustomed to being on the move constantly; and Billy Mitchell tipped me off, claiming that he had heard that I was on the dreaded internment list. For several weeks through the late winter and early spring of 1973, I ghosted around the place, avoiding any of the haunts that would be under surveillance by the army or Special Branch.

When things died down a little, I re-emerged to an alarming political climate where the political elites were beginning to talk seriously about the future status of Northern Ireland and the creation of a Council of Ireland to foster cross-border relations. Despite all of this, I had to keep myself focused on what the UVF was trying to achieve. We had to keep fighting back against the PIRA to show them that the loyalist people would not lie down while they tried to bomb us into a united Ireland. We had to keep fighting fire with fire. Soon, we would gain assistance in this endeavour from an extremely unlikely source.

When a 35-year-old Catholic named Arthur McKenna was shot dead by the local PIRA while repairing a van in Ballymurphy on 16 November 1970, it probably didn't even register with me or many other people outside the immediate area. Like many killings during the early 1970s, it was just another statistic. The very fact that it happened in a republican area meant that it didn't directly impact on the people who lived in my community. That sounds callous, but it was the reality of life in Northern Ireland at that time. Later, the full details emerged when newspapers reported that McKenna and his lifelong friend Alex McVicker, who jointly owned the van they were working with, were shot dead together in front of local women and children. To add to the horror, a 10-year-old boy had been assisting them when they were shot and witnessed everything at close hand.

The Provos were apparently unhappy that McKenna and McVicker were running a pitch and toss game without their permission and were keen to demonstrate that it was now

the PIRA who controlled Ballymurphy, not ordinary men like McKenna and his friend. Arthur McKenna had an older brother called James, who lived in Australia. James 'Jimmy' McKenna came back to Belfast for his brother's funeral but missed it by one day. Having returned to his home city, he vowed that he would avenge his brother's murder. Jimmy was an older man, about 47 years of age when he arrived in Belfast in November 1970. He first came to public attention in April 1971, when he was stopped at the junction of the Springfield Road and the Springmartin estate by a paratrooper. Apparently, Jimmy was completely unflustered by this and told the soldier that he was a member of the 'special investigation branch' of the British Army. When the para found a Webley revolver and ammunition on him, Jimmy just coolly said, 'Watch it, it's loaded.' He claimed at his trial that he had taken the Webley from a Provo arms dump behind Corrigan Park GAA ground. He had been tailing some IRA men from a distance and had managed to uncover their armoury. Ironically, when he was remanded a few days later, Jimmy faced the same court as a 17-year-old mill worker from the Springfield Road named Hugh Torney, who was also charged with possessing a gun and ammunition in a separate incident. Torney would earn his place in the history of the Troubles as a chief of staff of the Irish National Liberation Army (INLA). He would also become a prime target for the UVF after he was involved in the murder of Trevor King on the Shankill Road in 1994. By this stage Trevor was commanding B Company of the organisation on the Shankill and was always one of the main targets for republicans. Torney was later killed by former comrades in one of the many bloody feuds that has dogged the INLA throughout its existence.

On 4 June 1971 Jimmy McKenna was acquitted of serious firearms charges, including possession with intent to endanger life, but was found guilty of possession of the gun without a licence.

He was sentenced to one year in jail and was separated from paramilitary prisoners. Later in the year, on 3 October, Jimmy wrote an open letter to Cardinal Conway that was published in John McKeague's *Loyalist News*. He was critical of the Cardinal's support for republican internees and lambasted the Catholic Church for allowing collections for the IRA outside churches in West Belfast. Toward the end of the letter, Jimmy addressed his brother's murder and an attack on him that had occurred shortly before:

> Should you ever meet freedom fighter Joe Cahill in that place called Southern Ireland, where all the murderers flock to, ask him did he ever work for P.F. McDonnell. Ask him is it true, that, on the day of my brother's murder, he was working at the Corpus Christi Chapel at Ballymurphy. Ask him was he there in company with a John O'Rawe, and if he knew that this O'Rawe, was one of the men responsible, for the beating my brother received, at Milltown Provisional Club. Ask him was it coincidence, that he and O'Rawe were together in the Corpus Christi Chapel grounds, only a few yards from the spot where my brother was shot dead. I am in a position to expand on this aspect, and much more also, but I will refrain from doing so, at this time.

Aside from the letter, there was next to nothing heard about Jimmy until he was released from jail. It was then that he began to put a daring plan of action in place. Jimmy made a bold approach to the UVF Brigade Staff on the Shankill, and in 1973 he started a conversation with Tommy West, the UVF Chief of Staff, who had been a marksman in the British army, offering his services to the UVF. Obviously when a guy like this just turns up on the UVF's doorstep, there is a large degree of suspicion, and there were a few people who ended up dead in the early 1970s

after making such rash approaches. Some of the older UVF men were slightly wary of Jimmy, and he didn't really click with any of that generation. Soon after this, he made contact with me. I listened to what he had to say and was impressed. Perhaps it was youthful naivety, but I immediately had confidence in Jimmy, and Gusty spoke highly of him, having known him from before the Troubles. His military brain, thirst for vengeance against those who had killed his brother and his intimate knowledge of Ballymurphy, and republican West Belfast, all combined to make him a potentially valuable resource for the YCV.

Jimmy taught the YCV practices and techniques that, looking back, now seem obvious. However, at the time we were young and, despite our relative experience, the YCV could often be quite unsophisticated in our approach to operations. Jimmy taught us how to refine our methods. He showed us how to cut the toes off socks, which could then be worn over each arm to protect a volunteer's clothing from lead residue after a gun was fired. This was a simple but effective way of ensuring that there was no forensic evidence to link anyone to a specific operation. We did a good bit of proper soldiering during our time spent with Jimmy; recces, long-term observation for intelligence – all the important things that could sometimes go out the window when the blood was up.

Jimmy didn't take any prisoners, and he took on anyone who thought that, because he was a Catholic, he would be easily intimidated on the Shankill. An example of this occurred when Anthony 'Chuck' Berry, a local guy who mixed with the UVF and had aspirations to be a leader of his own team, tried to give Jimmy some trouble. He liked to think of himself as a big shot even though he was a glorified car thief. One of my close friends who was also in the YCV had reported to me that Chuck had cornered him and tried to rough him up a bit: 'You're just a wee boy, and that wanker who leads youse is a cunt.' The very next

day, Jimmy and I were standing in Downing Street and Chuck walked past, in the middle of the road. As he did, he muttered something at Jimmy about his religion. As quick as lightning, Jimmy threw his hand on top of a parked Mini and sprung right over the motor into Chuck's path. It was unbelievable. Jimmy seemed like an old man to us, but he was fitter than most of the teenagers I knew. He grabbed Chuck by the collar and was about to hit him when I said, 'Leave it Jimmy, he's a coward.' Jimmy threw Chuck down and we went on into the Loyalist Club and walked past the fruit machines, which were being emptied by one of the staff. Chuck dusted himself off and followed us into the club, where he tried to corner me, 'See the next time he does that to me; I'll knock your cunt in.' I told Chuck that he should watch what he was saying, and that he would be foolish to start anything with the YCV. He was absolutely seething, and not realising that Jimmy was standing right behind him, he shouted, 'See that Fenian bastard McKenna? He's fucking dead!' Before he could finish his sentence, Chuck was on the ground. Jimmy had floored him and was standing over him with his foot planted firmly on his chest. He pulled out a gun and put it in Chuck's mouth before lifting him up and throwing him against a wall. Jimmy never had any bother from Chuck Berry after that.

We knew who all the main republicans were because they often appeared on television news bulletins, but due to their high profiles they took a lot of precautions to protect themselves and were extremely hard to target. Jimmy had an intimate knowledge of West Belfast and he knew who all the behind-the-scenes key players were in the Provos – those who had been, up until now, faceless enemies. The problem that the UVF had during this period was that without good intelligence it was almost impossible to get near guys who were involved in the IRA rank and file. They didn't wear uniforms like their foes in the British Army. There were plenty of operators that Jimmy knew about, but

crucially he was also able to provide the UVF with intelligence on guys who were fundraisers and others who stored weapons – essentially, those who were crucial to the PIRA's ongoing terror campaign. He knew the geography of West Belfast like the back of his hand – the streets off Andersonstown and Whiterock, and all the sprawling estates like Ballymurphy and Turf Lodge. He knew the most subtle ways to enter these areas without being detected and the quickest ways to get out. These were places that had previously been difficult for the UVF to penetrate. A drive around republican West Belfast with Jimmy heavily disguised in the back of the car could lead to a bonanza of new information and intelligence.

Despite all of Jimmy's excellent traits and his loyalty to the YCV guys he mentored, he became a bit hot-headed, and I think he didn't have the same cold detachment about things that we had. There's a phrase that is often used by guys who have been involved as combatants in the Troubles: 'Nothing personal'. While that wasn't always the case in every operation, it was obvious that for Jimmy the whole thing *was* personal – extremely personal – and that was his main motivation. There was no overarching political aim or wish to defend a community. After a while, the YCV felt that things were starting to get too hot with him around. I arranged with a local businessman to sort out a private plane that would get Jimmy over to Liverpool and then he could make his way back to Australia. I accompanied him to the airfield. Jimmy knew this was the end of the road for him with the UVF and YCV, and I'm sure when he was told the news the thought crossed his mind at least once that he was being taken out to this remote location to be shot. Given that I was accompanying him, I'm also sure that he was assuaged of this fear. There's no way I would have turned on Jimmy like that. Just as we were about to part, he turned to me and said, 'Hutchie, I've got something to tell you.' I immediately sensed that something

was wrong and tried to swerve it: 'Jimmy, don't say it. Don't tell me what I think you're gonna tell me at this stage!' He said, 'I have to tell you, but don't worry ... I didn't incriminate anybody in the UVF or YCV. I was working for Special Branch against the Provos.' Although I was taken aback, I must admit that in the midst of everything that was going on at the time I perhaps didn't fully absorb what Jimmy had told me. I knew that he had a loyalty to me and the YCV, so I didn't worry too much about any of the implications of his undercover role. Jimmy had scores to settle and his intelligence and knowledge of active republicans served the YCV's purpose.

For all this deep intelligence and military preparation, not everything the YCV did was planned. Sometimes I had to respond to events in an ad hoc way and, in turn, the YCV often had to fall back on the basic tactics of rioting and street disorder that we had learned during our time in the Tartan gangs. On one occasion there was trouble in the jail, and we had to do something on the outside to show our solidarity with the guys inside. I was coming out of Studio 10 (a photography studio that was used as a meeting place by the UVF) when I spotted a YCV called Eddie Kinner walking up the road from Millfield tech with a folder under his arm.

'Eddie, where are you off to?'

'Just up the road home, Hutchie.'

'Well wait, there's stuff going on in the jail – see the next bus that comes up the road. I want you to hijack it.'

Eddie was a dedicated volunteer, one of the best. Without hesitation, or indeed a weapon to hand, he proceeded to step onto the next bus that stopped at Aberdeen Street and ordered the driver to go up to Woodvale Park and park it across the road. I then spotted another friend and UVF member called Noel Shaw and asked him to give us a hand; he was asked to hijack another bus and block Agnes Street. For all the weapons training

and bomb-making classes that guys had undertaken, sometimes throwing a bus across a road could be just as effective in making a political point.

Eddie was the sort of person I came to trust implicitly. He was part of a famous Shankill family that was steeped in UVF tradition. Like me, he had been part of the SYT, and eventually I brought him into the YCV when his uncles intervened after he had received a bad beating from some UDA-affiliated Bootboys from the Highfield estate. Eddie's uncles had wanted to exact revenge, but after a summit meeting with UDA leaders John McClatchey and Andy Tyrie, we were able to put a plug in what was threatening to spill over into a bloody feud. Eddie's uncles asked me to approach him, and a week or two later I did so at a disco we both attended in the Alliance Avenue area. It meant that if anything happened to him again, the UVF could take armed action. More than that, though, Eddie was a good and determined loyalist, and a perfect fit for the YCV.

On one occasion Bo McClelland requested that I come down to Millisle to meet with them. As I often did, I chose Eddie to accompany me. Bo was wondering about these two farmers who had come into a bar in Millisle asking about me. He was a bit alarmed, thinking that it might be some sort of undercover thing, or a sting of some sort, but I knew who they were. The YCV had linked up with two specific farmers in the area who were sympathetic to the cause and had offered to allow their land to be used to hide weapons. After reassuring Bo, Eddie and I drove on down to the two farms, where I discovered that the farmers had panicked when guys from Belfast came down asking them questions. I did a bit of investigating and then reassured them, reminding them to stay quiet and never to mention the weapons to anyone else, and definitely not to be whaling into local pubs again asking for me by name. After this long day spent wasting our time was over, Eddie and I were driving home along the

backroads at around five o'clock in the morning and suddenly the car broke down. We were stuck in the middle of nowhere, and Eddie turned to me and said, 'My ma and da'll kill me!' To which I said, 'Just tell your ma and da you were with me!' I don't know if that would have reassured Mr and Mrs Kinner of their son's safety or made them worry even more!

The network of farms we had at our disposal wasn't just useful for storing weapons. Volunteers looking to keep a low profile could often find sanctuary in them. Joe Bennett was a UVF volunteer from Coronation Park in Dundonald who had been arrested at his home and charged with possession of guns and ammunition on the evening that Gusty and others had been arrested in Brennan Street. After his wife passed away on 24 April 1973, Joe absconded while on compassionate parole. Shortly after this, Frankie Curry approached me with word that Joe was holed up in a farm in Co. Londonderry and was eager to come back to Belfast and get involved in the campaign. He was a superb ATO whose very specific skills could be extremely useful for the UVF at this point in time.

I agreed to accompany Frankie on a visit to the farm to have a conversation with Joe. When we got there, I couldn't believe the size of the place; it was all mountainous, like something from the American frontiers. Whoever the shepherds were before they had access to motorised vehicles must have been very fit or constantly tired – I imagine a bit of both! We met Joe in the farmhouse, and the woman who lived there was baking these homemade soda farls. I vividly remember them being served fresh from the griddle, and me greedily devouring them with the warm butter running down my chin. If there were warm sodas to be eaten, I was always happy to oblige, as Sam the baker at Aberdeen Street off the Shankill could attest to.

Joe was itching to return to action; he wanted me to recommend him to Brigade Staff and engineer a return to the thick of things. I

thought it would be better if he stayed where he was and continued working on the various devices he was experimenting with; that way the UVF could access his creations from this remote location rather than run the risk of him bringing attention to his activities on the Shankill. I also knew he had weaknesses which meant that, in all good conscience, I couldn't recommend him to Brigade Staff: 'Joe, you're a chronic gambler!' This was a dangerous vice that could compromise a volunteer if the authorities wished to use them as a hook to hang someone on.

I returned to Belfast with the promise that we would continue the conversation at a later date, after I had consulted with a few senior people on the Shankill. Subsequently I was sent back down, and once again Frankie accompanied me. The stuff Joe was working on when we arrived was almost beyond belief. He had been experimenting with various devices. Luckily, it was way out in the wilds, and no one was any the wiser when they exploded on the opposite side of the mountains.

The first time we visited we were confined to the farmhouse, so on this visit Joe was extremely eager for us to see the livestock the farmer maintained. He brought us into the sty to see the pigs. These beasts were massive and were barging around and snorting and grunting. Although the place stank to high heaven, Frankie was curious and went over to have a closer look at some of the pigs. I wasn't too sure so stood behind him, peering over his shoulder. The next thing, one of these beasts got up on its trotters, right in Frankie's face – touching his shoulders and squealing loudly. Frankie darted out of the sty and I followed quickly behind him as we clambered over each other to get outside. Joe was standing in the doorway hardly able to contain himself and said, 'What good would you two fuckers be for Ulster if youse are afeared of a pig?!'

Joe was eventually brought back to the Shankill, but it wouldn't be long until he came to the attention of the authorities again.

Joe Bennett wasn't the only ATO making bombs from a rural location like this. Other volunteers who had similar skills were experimenting in discrete locations across the country. Several Provos had blown themselves up while making or transporting bombs in the early 1970s. It was perhaps inevitable that a UVF member would eventually befall a similar fate. In the middle of September 1971, two loyalists were mortally wounded while experimenting with explosives in a house on Bann Street, off the Oldpark Road. Jim Finlay died from his injuries a week later, and John Thompson died the following month. John Bingham, who would go on to lead the North Belfast battalion of the UVF, was approaching the house and had just got off his motorbike as the device prematurely exploded. The skin was stripped from his hands with the heat and force of the blast. He had a lucky escape. Many others weren't so fortunate, and sometimes, when I think of the rudimentary bomb-making classes I was attending around the same time, I consider myself extremely lucky not to have suffered a similar fate as Finlay and Thompson. Such was the nature of experimenting with devices that were designed to kill, maim and cause widespread destruction.

Despite this, loyalists continued to create bombs for use against the IRA and its supporters. By 1973, having witnessed the intensification of the IRA bombing campaign the previous year, the UVF stepped up its own bombing offensive. The IRA had claimed that its targets were economic and commercial, but the reality is that they planted bombs in Protestant towns and in Protestant businesses. The UVF was more upfront in retaliating and targeted pubs and clubs where republicans met. Many of these explosions were the work of the YCV, with the Red Hand responsible for some others.

In November 1973, the UVF suffered a crushing blow with the loss of an excellent ATO called Charlie Logan. Charlie was a comrade, but also a dear friend. On the evening of Saturday,

17 November, I was in the Loyalist Club in Rumford Street with Charlie, Jim Hanna (a member of Brigade Staff) and Tommy West. They asked me if I would go to a farmhouse in Desertmartin, Londonderry with Charlie the next day, but I told them I couldn't because I had to go to meet a UVF liaison in East Belfast. They knew the importance of this meeting to the organisation and agreed I should go to it; Charlie would make his own way to Desertmartin. In the event, the meeting was quite short, and I made my way back across the river. As I drove up North Street toward the Shankill, I saw Charlie standing on the corner with Royal Avenue. We waved at each other as I headed on to another UVF meeting.

Later that night Jackie Hewitt approached me, asking whether I had heard the news. I was in absolute despair as Jackie proceeded to describe how Charlie, who was only 26, had accidentally blown himself up in a massive explosion at the farmhouse. It was totally unbelievable that my friend, who I had seen only hours previously, was now dead. Killed by his own bomb. At the inquest into his death the following June, the full harrowing details of Charlie's violent demise became public, with one newspaper reporting that 'The conditions of the remains, the scorching of some of the pieces of skin and a lump of metal embedded in one piece of skin indicated that the body had been disintegrated by an explosion.' His driving license was eventually retrieved in a field a couple of hundred feet away from the seat of the explosion. It was horrible to think about. The police were only able to identify Charlie's body by matching hair retrieved from the scene with hairs on a jacket hanging in the hallway of his house.

When you join an organisation like the UVF, you do so in the full knowledge that you face the possibility of either incarceration, severe injury or death. Like most people who died during the conflict, Charlie had a family. He had people who cared about him and depended upon him. Working as a steeplejack allowed him

to provide for his family, who saw him as a husband and father rather than as a soldier. In some traumatic cases when men were killed, arrested or died, naturally families didn't even know that their loved ones had been members of organisations. Breaking the news of the death of a volunteer to family members was one of the most difficult tasks you could be assigned. Jackie Hewitt asked me to accompany him as he delivered the terrible news in person to Charlie's wife. We drove to Toronto Street, off the Ravenhill Road, where Charlie had lived. Jackie knocked on the door and it was opened by Henrietta. She was surprised to see us, but it soon dawned on her why we were there. Jackie just started telling her what had happened in a matter of fact way. I was thinking, *How does he do this?* I couldn't do it. I was just standing there, looking down at the ground. I couldn't say a single word because I kept thinking about poor old Charlie and how I should have been there with him. It was excruciating having to come to this woman's door to tell her that her husband and the father of their two children had been killed. As a 17-year-old with no dependents, I wasn't capable of processing the enormity of such a thing and the profound effect that it would have on a young woman and her kids.

When we came away from the house, Jackie broke down. I realised then that he hadn't been callous, he had just held himself together for the sake of Charlie's wife. We all had our roles to play in the UVF, and Jackie's was as difficult as anyone else's, if not more so. He wasn't trained in grief counselling or any of the techniques that people in professional roles are equipped with in order to carry out such traumatic and delicate tasks, but he did it and never once complained.

Befitting his rank of major, Charlie was given a big UVF funeral, and his body lay in state in West Belfast Orange Hall, guarded by uniformed volunteers.

Years later, when I got out of jail, any time I was driving and saw those signs by the road that read 'Tiredness Kills', it kept

bringing Charlie back into my head. I often wonder, was it the tiredness that killed him? I've heard stories of other ATOs who were so dedicated to their craft that they would spend hours on end without even a toilet break, concentrating on these devices they were making. One minor mistake and it could be game over.

***

By the end of 1973 I was eating, sleeping and breathing the UVF. From August onwards, I was working part-time as a barman in pubs around the Shankill and was eventually offered the chance to work in the Long Bar. That suited me perfectly, as the pub was a favourite watering hole for UVF men and you didn't have to be on edge all the time.

While the YCV continued its plans along military lines, the UVF was forming its first political initiative. The Ulster Loyalist Front (ULF) was a short-lived enterprise set up in November 1973. Hughie Smyth was the main face of it, and it was intended as a vehicle to carry the message of working-class bread-and-butter issues to people in the Shankill and other loyalist heartlands. It gave the UVF a political voice when the UVF called a ceasefire, paving the way for the Volunteer Political Party (VPP). In June 1973 Hughie Smyth had stood as an independent in West Belfast for the Northern Ireland Assembly elections. Always a popular man of the people, Hughie won a seat. After the ULF was formed, the UVF declared a forty-three-day ceasefire, which commenced on 18 November. In fact, it was announced the day after Charlie Logan had died. The organisation was tentatively open to some sort of way forward, politically, and released a statement declaring that in calling the ceasefire it would assist the ULF in 'working for a political solution to the problems of Northern Ireland, and will bring pressure to bear upon the politicians'. There was still a fear among loyalists that any new power-sharing arrangement would

include an Irish dimension. The UVF spoke to this by adding, 'Any moves leading to the establishment of a Council of Ireland will automatically lead to the cease-fire being terminated.'

I found it strange that we were waiting for the inevitable rapprochement with the Irish government. It seemed like a huge waste of time. In January 1974, the UVF came out in support of Desmond Boal's plan for a united independent Ireland. This would entail an amalgamated Ireland with autonomy for the six counties in the north. A spokesman stated that 'We believe that any policy which may result in the preservation of our Protestant heritage and traditional British way of life and at the same time brings about a real and lasting peace to our beloved Province, deserves to be given consideration.' Some YCV members came to me, complaining that they thought this was all very strange. I understood where they were coming from. The IRA was still in existence and people were being killed, so how could a political agreement that provided concessions of any kind to republicans be considered by the UVF?

In March the UVF released a policy document at a press conference that was chaired by a masked Billy Mitchell (then a senior member of Brigade Staff). The organisation admitted publicly for the first time that the Troubles had been a crisis of reaction; the Provos were forced to react against the political impotence of the Catholic community, and the UVF were forced to react in turn against the Provos. It appeared that the organisation was laying the foundations for a political roadmap. Whether it could work in the climate in which it emerged was another thing.

For the YCV, this was an unnerving time. The UVF had been extremely active in 1973 and had shown its ability to work very efficiently with explosive devices. The organisation was responsible for hundreds of bombings throughout the year, and despite the Provos' ceasefire announcement, the IRA continued to shoot and bomb, so some in the YCV were wondering what the point of

this political initiative was. In simple terms, the organisation had doves – those who wanted a solution through political negotiation – and hawks – those who felt that the answer lay down the barrel of a gun. I was on the cusp of my 18th birthday, and most of the volunteers under my command were of a similar age. There was a lot of hawkish feeling in the YCV at the time, but I personally felt that Hughie Smyth, as a UVF volunteer, should be supported and the UVF given backing for their political initiatives. We had to give the political route an opportunity to flourish and see where it could take the loyalist people. I communicated this to all volunteers under my command.

Interestingly, *The Guardian* published an article by Derek Brown on 30 March, around the time of the UVF's announcement of the policy document, which stated that 'The security forces have long recognised the UVF as a potentially dangerous force, with a small, skilled core of bomb experts and marksmen. Protestant extremists have always shown a greater military flair for military organisation than the IRA, and UVF volunteers have been very difficult to detect.' This fine-tuned machine wasn't going to be turned off overnight. Little did I know it then, but 1974 would be the end of this chapter of my life with the UVF.

CHAPTER 6

The End of the Beginning

In the early hours of Monday, 1 April 1974, I was sitting in Jim Hanna's car in Mansfield Street. He and his girlfriend had just left the Loyalist Club, where he worked on and off as a barman and she as the club secretary. Jim was always in the Loyalist Club, and that evening was no different to any other. We'd been talking about everything and nothing and passing the time. Jim and his girl had gone out the back of the club to get to his car, and a few minutes later I followed them. I needed to talk to Jim about something. His girlfriend offered to get out of the car and leave us to discuss business, but I had a change of heart and didn't want to ruin the end of their night with talk about the UVF. I told Jim I'd see him the next day and ran back into the Loyalist Club. I had only just closed the door of the back entrance when I heard the unmistakable crack of gunfire. Jim had been shot a number of times in the chest, and he died in hospital soon after. He didn't stand a chance, as the cowards who killed him had emerged from the shadows behind his car and positioned themselves behind him and to his right. When I realised what had happened, I was absolutely devastated.

Jim was tough, but he was outgoing and friendly with those he was close to. He was tall and had a big mop of red hair, which earned him the nickname 'Red Setter'. He loved me to bits and was generally well liked, but he had made a few enemies within the UVF. There appeared to have been persistent rumours that he

was passing information to the spooks at Lisburn. Photographs emerged of two soldiers in his house handling weapons. For those who felt that he was a tout, this was perhaps concrete evidence. I personally didn't believe it. He may have had friendships with individual soldiers who he had working for him – gathering information and so forth – but he wasn't the type to betray the UVF. He lived and breathed the organisation. There were some suggestions that he and Billy Mitchell had rubbed some of the more conservative elements in the UVF up the wrong way with their dialogues and intimacy with IRA factions. Although I wasn't fully behind the talks at the time, Jim and Billy were quite entitled to have these conversations and see if they could be of benefit to the loyalist working-class people who were desperate for the conflict to end. Then there was the simple issue of Jim being a strict disciplinarian. Certain people didn't like that, and it made him unpopular with them.

I stormed up to the UVF's headquarters, where I found Tommy West. Frenchie Marchant and Rab McAuley, both members of Brigade Staff, were with me. 'What the hell has happened?' I shouted as I kicked the closest object to me, a chair, across the room. 'Why was the Setter killed?' My mind was, uncharacteristically, a blur. Had the Provos killed Tommy? I didn't think so, and I was tormented at the thought that Jim had been shot dead by former comrades. Tommy was adamant that it was the work of republicans, and that the UVF wasn't involved.

'Ok then, Tommy, we have a list of six IRA targets, and we're going to hit each and every one of them right away.'

Tommy's face went white when he heard me say that.

'Tell me straight, Tommy, was it the Ra [PIRA] that shot the Setter or was it the UVF?'

His face creased, and I could tell he was in pain at the thought of what he was about to say.

'It was the UVF, Hutchie. Now, I don't want you going and doing anything stupid.'

I was crushed. Joe Bennett had been arrested at a house he was living in on Mansfield Street – the same street where the Setter was killed just a few days after. He had stored what one paper described as an 'arsenal' in the small house, which he shared with a local woman and her two kids. Revolvers, pistols, zip guns, two primed bombs and endless rounds of ammunition. Notwithstanding the weapons, he was quite literally sitting on a powder keg. Given the rumours surrounding the Setter, it is quite possible that some people put two and two together and came up with the wrong conclusion about him. It was common knowledge in the area that Joe Bennett had all of this stuff stashed in his house. Literally anyone in the vicinity could have tipped off the police, but because it happened two days before the Setter was killed, some people naturally came to the conclusion that Joe had perhaps ordered the hit.

***

Before Jim was killed, as the winter turned to spring, the military began to apply more and more pressure on me. One afternoon in March, I was in a car with a couple of other YCVs passing St Mary's church on the Crumlin Road. As soon as we turned right into Silvio Street, a squad of Paras surrounded us. I told the other two guys to run and I got out of the car and ran down a nearby alleyway. Almost immediately, a soldier appeared at the mouth of the alley and cocked his rifle and shouted, 'Stop or I'll fire.' As I raised my hands in the air, I saw a woman called Mary Douglas, who I knew well, and I shouted over to her to contact Mina Browne to notify her of my impending arrest. Mina had been a member of the Shankill Defence Association, and she worked closely with the UVF on matters of welfare. Mina would

then contact Jonathan Taylor, a solicitor who represented most UVF and RHC personnel at the time. This was part of the whole process when this sort of thing happened, and it was happening more and more regularly. On this occasion, however, I wouldn't be needing my solicitor.

One of the Paras grabbed me by my hair and flung me into the back of one of the Land Rovers. I was kept on my own while they arrested the other two separately. They had me on my stomach and were all taking turns to stand on me, beating the living daylights out of me with the butts of their SLRs. One of them said, 'Stop, he's already fuckin' submitted to us; he's been arrested ... we're gonna have legal people on ... watch what yer doin'.' One of them proceeded to handcuff me, and the other one blindfolded me. The Land Rover roared into gear and drove off.

I didn't have a clue where I was, as the Paras drove me all over the place, and of course I couldn't see a thing. I could feel the Land Rover being driven in a low gear, going up a steep and pretty rough incline, so I guessed that we were up the side of the mountain or somewhere like that, but for all I knew they could have been driving me into Ballymurphy or Turf Lodge. After what felt like an eternity, the Land Rover came to a stop. I was lifted from the floor of the jeep, where I had lay with the soldiers' feet on me, and was grabbed by both arms, thrown onto the ground and made to kneel. All of a sudden – BANG! I was totally disorientated. What had happened was that one of the Paras had hit me on the head with the butt of his rifle while simultaneously one of the others had fired a shot in the air. While I was kneeling, I heard trickling water, like the sound of a stream. As soon as I fell over from the impact of the rifle butt, I felt a splash on my face. Everything was damp. I didn't know whether it was blood or whether I was lying in the stream. I didn't know if I had been shot. After about five seconds I realised that it was

water rather than blood. All the Paras started laughing as they lifted me up by the arms before throwing me back onto the floor of the Land Rover.

I was driven back down the Shankill and into Tennent Street, where the Red Caps (Parachute Regiment) had a base. They were still chuckling away as they took my blindfold off. The daylight stung my eyes and my vision was completely blurred. I could see the blood that had trickled down from the side of my head and onto my shirt, which was now heavily stained. Two of the Paras grabbed me and dragged me into a makeshift gymnasium. I knew immediately that things weren't going to get any easier. One of the soldiers took down a punch-bag from its hook while another removed my hands from behind my back and tied my hands in front of me. They then hoisted me up and hooked my makeshift handcuff onto the punchbag hook. I was dangling a few feet off the ground as they took turns to beat me with their rifles.

I was in agony now and wanted to get the hell out of there. When they lifted me off the hook, I thought they'd had their fun and would let me go. Point made. However, as I lay there on the gymnasium floor with my hands still tied, I noticed out of the corner of my eye a squat young squaddie marching in. He sneered at me and barked, 'You and me? Fancy your chances you Irish bastard?' The others held me as this new tormentor went to work on me. I was in a world of pain that couldn't get any worse, so I just let him get on with it. 'Are you not going to fight back?' he spat. 'No,' I said, 'I can hardly fight back while my hands are tied.' Their laughter and mockery gradually faded, replaced by frustration and anger. They hooked me back up onto the punchbag holder and started beating the shit out of me again. Another soldier came in with an SLR. For good measure, he hit me in the ribs with it, cracking one of them; at the same time, another one of them smashed me on the side of the face, breaking my cheekbone. The doctor at the base had a look at me before I

was eventually released. Incredibly, he stated that I hadn't been injured, though my injuries were later confirmed when I went to one of the local hospitals.

Aside from the soldiers, this whole spectacle had an audience of two – my friends who had been in the car. The Paras made them watch the whole thing. I was physically tortured while my friends were mentally tortured. After this, the police and the army stopped me every time that they saw me in a car or taxi. They harassed me on the street. That was the army's aim – to try and scare us into conceding; to try and frustrate us. We would never give up, no matter what they did to us.

Given the extent of my injuries I was keen to raise awareness of what had happened. The Paras had become infamous because of Bloody Sunday, but they caused havoc and heartache on the Shankill as well. In December 1973, a UVF man who I knew well, Minto Howell, had been shot dead late at night across the road from Aberdeen Street by members of the Queen's Own Highlanders; the Paras had also killed two completely innocent Shankill Protestants, Richie McKinney and Robert Johnston, in September 1972. Hughie Smyth saw the significant currency to be gained in highlighting the episode to the press; it was brutality of the working class, pure and simple. Unsurprisingly, however, co-operation from mainstream unionism was not forthcoming. Hughie Smyth took me and the other two lads to the Ulster Unionists and wanted to do a story in the media with photographs of my injuries. Harry West, the leader of the Ulster Unionists at the time, said no. He claimed that if we went public, we'd only be reinforcing republican propaganda. Hughie was exasperated and said, 'This fella has been beat to a pulp by the army – it's nothing about republican propaganda.' His protests fell on deaf ears. Indeed, around the same time as this happened, Jim Kilfedder was floating the idea of curfews in loyalist areas while the Rev. Donald Gillies from the Presbyterian church in Agnes

Street had asked for the army to be given greater powers. The politicians, the churches – we couldn't rely on any of them for leadership anymore. They were completely out of touch with the mood music in communities like the Shankill as the social fabric rapidly continued to fall apart rapidly. The loyalist community was completely out on its own.

A significant manifestation of this alienation and frustration came in the form of the Ulster Workers' Council (UWC) strike, which began on 15 May 1974. The strike was a protest against the Council of Ireland included in the Sunningdale Agreement, signed on 9 December 1973, which had led to the formation of a power-sharing executive including unionists and nationalists. The loyalist paramilitaries provided some of the muscle for the strike, which saw Protestant workers in the main industries across Northern Ireland put down their tools and walk out, bringing the entire country to a standstill for almost two weeks. The strike eventually brought about the collapse of the executive and was regarded by loyalists as a victory against the imposition of an Irish dimension on domestic affairs. Although the UVF didn't have as high a profile in the UWC strike as the UDA, Ken Gibson, a senior UVF member who I had known for some years, was always very visible at public demonstrations during the period. The day-to-day events of the UWC strike passed me by as I languished in prison on a charge of car theft. In early April I had been involved in stealing a car for YCV business but had been caught and sentenced by Holywood petty sessions to four months in prison. Luckily I was able to serve a much shorter sentence in Long Kesh. I had plenty of time to think, and I realised it had been a careless thing to get arrested for. I was adamant that I wasn't going to get caught again.

The success of the UWC strike encouraged further exploration of a political route for the loyalist paramilitaries. The UVF was galvanised in its attempts to progress the Ulster Loyalist Front

into a more durable political machine with a long-term vision for the Protestant working class. In June, shortly after Merlyn Rees, the Secretary of State for Northern Ireland, had reversed the proscription of the UVF, the organisation launched the Volunteer Political Party. I was soon due for release, and although I was supportive of Hughie Smyth and his involvement in politics, I was unsure about the VPP. More specifically, I was uneasy about Ken Gibson's proposed role in it. Ken, who had been released from internment in Long Kesh the previous Christmas, was the chairman of the new political enterprise. The vice chairman was Billy Davison. In a statement published on the front page of *Combat* (a UVF magazine), they announced that the VPP had been formed with a two-fold aim: 'firstly to encourage all Volunteers to think both objectively and politically, as to the type of Ulster they want and secondly ... to ensure that the general public will easily identify that the voice of the Volunteer Political Party is also the voice of the Ulster Volunteer Force.' They understood that the rank and file, who had been on a war footing, would have to be attracted with some less-than-subtle militaristic rhetoric: 'We state that by forming a political wing in the Ulster Volunteer Force we have added a new piece of weaponry, which if used to its full potential can be just as deadly as the S.L.R. or the G.P.M.G., but like all weapons it must be used correctly and by the right people.'

The UVF was in friction during this period. On the one hand there was momentum toward a political movement. This had been galvanised by the success of the UWC strike. Shortly after the strike ended, Ken Gibson, John Falls, Tommy West and Stanley Grey met with James Allan of the Foreign and Commonwealth Office and Michael Oatley from MI6. In early April, just over a month before the strike commenced, Hughie Smyth, along with Ken Gibson and Billy Mitchell, met with the Minister of State, Stanley Orme, at the Northern Ireland Office (NIO) headquarters

at Stormont Castle. While the UVF delegation tried to address issues such as the internment of loyalists, Orme appeared keen to coax those present into the political project, stating that

> out of the shattered edifice of the Unionist Party, the working class Protestants and the working class Catholics were struggling to find some political leadership of their own ... at the next election there was no reason why the UVF might not have a number of members elected to the Assembly and indeed why they might not be a member of the Executive.

While this all sounded positive to those who wanted to go down the political path, the reality was that while these meetings were taking place, the IRA was still killing people. The UVF, which was supposed to be on ceasefire, was responding in kind with a crescendo of violence that culminated in the bombings in Dublin and Monaghan on 17 May.

In the weeks leading up to Jim Hanna's death on 1 April, there had been a lot of internal wrangling within the UVF leadership. I was first and foremost a paramilitary leader and felt that the military side of things should be kept separate from any political enterprise. My fears were confirmed when I discovered that Ken Gibson wanted to be in charge of the whole show. As leader of the YCV, I sat at Brigade Staff meetings with other UVF leaders. When I heard Ken outline his plan for the VPP, which included the bizarre proposal that one person should be in overall charge of all political manoeuvres and military operations, I was horrified. If Ken, or whoever else held this position of 'Operations Manager' in the UVF and VPP, was turned and began touting on the organisation, it would have been catastrophic for the security of the UVF. One man with all that sensitive information? No thank you. It could have

signalled the end of the UVF, and potentially a huge amount of jail time for many volunteers.

I'm not specifically saying that Ken would have done this, but anyone with that amount of power in their hands would have been potentially susceptible to being squeezed if the security forces had tried to turn the screw. The UVF kept military operations tight and on a need-to-know basis by necessity, and I felt that it should stay that way. If the lines became blurred between the military and political movements, it could cause a mess. I believed that there were a few people who wanted to reassert their authority on the organisation. There was a meeting of the senior leaders to discuss this new Operations Manager idea. I was invited and asked to put my view forward. My view was certainly the view of most of the people in the room, and it meant that Ken and his supporters narrowly missed out on implementing the position of Operations Manager. It was a common-sense decision made on the basis that it was diametrically opposed to the protocols of the UVF as a military organisation.

There was an individual on Brigade Staff at this time who ran a little differently to everyone else. He lived locally, but he just seemed to rise to the top out of nowhere. I never took to him and suspected from the off that he couldn't be trusted. I told people as much, but he had support. He was keen on this Operations Manager idea being implemented. On one occasion I was at a meeting in the Loyalist Club when this guy appeared over my shoulder. 'You can't do anything without telling me,' he said. I couldn't believe it. 'Who do you think you're talking to?' I replied. Frenchie and everyone else at the meeting were taken aback by the intrusion and looked at me to see what was going to happen next. 'I'm talking to you,' the man said. 'Well, you can talk to my arse. Do you think I'm going to be giving you information? The point of the opposition to your stupid plan [to implement an Operations Manager] is fucking simple. A number

of volunteers who go out on operations are working in close units and most of them don't know what the others are fucking doing. That means that we are looking after the security of the operatives.' The others in the room, led by Frenchie, shouted, 'Hutchie is making sense and that is how we were told from the beginning to conduct business. There will be no co-operation in this room, you are wasting your fucking time so do what the fuck you like. There is no support for it from us.'

This was all happening at the same time that Ken Gibson was trying to get back into a position of authority. My sense of unease and suspicion about Gibson's intentions was further exacerbated when I started to hear rumours that he wanted me out of the way because I wouldn't buy into his vision for the UVF. A YCV called Roy McCorkindale came to me to inform me that he had been approached by Gibson. Roy had been one of a group, including me, that used to meet in Gibson's home to discuss the situation in 1972; he came to me now to tell me that Gibson had been openly suggesting to him and others that I should be replaced as leader of the YCV. 'He said he had heard that you weren't happy with the idea of there being an operations manager,' said Roy. 'What does he think we're doing here, running a factory?' I replied. Apparently, Gibson said that it was necessary as part of the VPP experiment. 'Don't fuckin' mention that to Hutchie,' McCorkindale had apparently warned him. The political tail wasn't going to be wagging the military dog on my watch. Of course, when Gibson spoke so openly about me being 'replaced', such talk could be interpreted in a couple of different ways. There were very few bloodless coups in paramilitary groupings in the 1970s. I felt betrayed and angry. It would have been extremely easy for me to react on the spur of the moment and do something silly. I kept a clear head, retained my focus and told Roy to agree with what Gibson was saying but to feed back any further comment to me.

Shortly after this, I arrived early to another meeting of Brigade Staff that had been called to discuss this ongoing 'Operations Manager' issue. My patience was beginning to wear thin. Me, Frenchie, Rab McAuley, Tommy West and one other (who shall remain nameless for his own protection) were all sitting in the room before the meeting was due to commence. We were just casually chatting about things, but I was ready for another argument about this strategy that had been envisaged for the UVF. To this end, I had told a number of YCVs to search everyone coming in at the door. If a man refused to be searched, I had advised that he be turned away. It was common sense in such a volatile atmosphere. The others asked me how the YCVs were going to make sure people obeyed this order. 'Well, they have the most powerful men around here with them.' They looked at me, a bit confused. 'Smith and Wesson,' I said. 'I have never met them, but I hear they can be very persuasive.'

Unknown to the others, I also had my own protection. This wasn't abnormal at the time, and anyway, I figured that given the ongoing rumours about me being replaced, it would be better to be safe than sorry. As the meeting commenced, I asked Tommy what the meeting was about. I knew fine well but wanted to be sure. 'Well, this is the way it's going to be, Hutchie,' he said, 'We're implementing a new position entitled Operations Manager.' I decided to try a different tactic and said that that was ok but enquired as to who would be appointing this new person. Tommy told me that it would be Brigade Staff. I looked around the table and asked each of the officers to stand up, one by one, and tell me if they were supporting this new initiative. Tommy said that he didn't want to do that – that the UVF was a military organisation. I agreed and said, 'Exactly Tommy, that's why I don't want an operations manager!' This individual I didn't like stood up and started pounding the table with his fist: 'I'm. Fucking. Implementing. It. Now!' I asked him how he was going

to do that. 'I'm a member of Brigade Staff and the others will be supporting me,' he responded. A gun was produced, and I gave him a choice: was he going to insist we go with his idea, or would he walk away and drop the idea completely.

Suddenly, beads of sweat started to break out across his forehead, and each person around the table quickly stated that they wouldn't be supporting the appointment of an operations manager. Frenchie and the others told him that he was done, and to go home and put his slippers on. I told another senior individual at the meeting who had a similar attitude to follow him. These interlopers knew by this stage that they were being given the opportunity to walk away. They had no support from the floor. Three members of Brigade Staff were with the officers under their command. Unknown to the guy who wanted to implement the operations manager, I had actually spoken to Frenchie and the others before the meeting took place. Frenchie had asked how many of the Brigade Staff would support us if we rejected the idea of an operations manager. I told them that I understood three were with us and two against. Rab McAuley thought that my prediction would be borne out, and he was right.

As the tension around the room lifted, someone asked, 'What in the hell just happened there?' I said, 'You know what happened? That was what's called a bloodless coup.'

Hours after this, Tommy West ordered two UVF men to go up to the house of the guy who had been so adamant that we create and appoint an operations manager, and apprehend him. Word reached me that he had told them he'd be down at the Loyalist Club to present himself to Brigade Staff in an hour's time. I was flabbergasted at this naivety and asked the two guys to drive me up to his home, where I was determined to bring this now ex-Brigade Staff member back to Tommy in one piece to answer questions. As we turned into the street where he lived, we were met with a predictable scene. Furniture was scattered all over the

pavement and men, who were guarded by the army, were busily lifting it into a removal van. There was no sign of the man. He was probably back at his barracks being debriefed by military intelligence.

Ultimately, Ken Gibson's ambitions proved to be too lofty. He stood as a VPP candidate in West Belfast during the October 1974 UK general election and was annihilated, taking only 2,690 votes (0.4 per cent) and losing his deposit. After this humiliation, the VPP was dissolved and Gibson retired off the scene almost completely. The UVF called a special meeting of all officers above the rank of Platoon Commander on Tuesday, 22 October. The ceasefire was held by a narrow majority of 38 to 34 (though the UVF maintained that it reserved the right to attack republicans in response to IRA terrorism). At a press conference to announce the continuation of the ceasefire, UVF Brigade Staff members read a statement which, among other things, declared that 'Following the recent election campaign in West Belfast the results seemed to indicate that the ordinary people did not want the UVF outside of its military role ... the UVF must comply with the wishes of the people and revert to military action against the IRA.' Although I had other things on my mind when this statement was released, it proved that my cynicism had been well founded. I could hear the mood music, while Ken Gibson was trying to play an unpopular tune.

One day in late May 1980, I was sitting in my cubicle in Long Kesh reading the *Belfast Telegraph* when I came across a feature that carried interviews with several of the UWC leaders to mark the sixth anniversary of the strike. Gibson was one of those interviewed. He lamented the failure of the politicians who had been involved in May 1974, describing them, without a hint of irony, as 'back-stabbers'. I couldn't help but have a wry chuckle to myself as I folded up the newspaper and threw it on the bed.

***

On Tuesday, 22 October, while the UVF was having a meeting to discuss the ceasefire and other matters relating to the political climate, I was sitting in my mother's house in Jersey Street. My heart was thumping, my clothing saturated with sweat. There was suddenly a series of loud knocks at the front door. I stood up, straightened myself and walked down the stairs and toward the door. On opening it, I was greeted by exactly who I had been expecting – the RUC. The officers brought me to Springfield Road station, where I was questioned repeatedly about my movements on the morning of Monday, 21 October. The police told me that two Catholics had been shot dead on their way to work. They were half-brothers called Michael Loughran and Edward Morgan. Apparently I could help the police with their enquiries. 'I haven't a clue what you are on about,' I told them. 'I'm unemployed and just help out with the loyalist prisoners from time to time.'

There was a discussion, and I was eventually told that a police officer had spotted me in a car earlier that Monday morning; the officer said that he had also seen another person with me who he didn't know. Due to my reputation as an active loyalist, he logged my sighting when he clocked in at the police station to start his shift. I remembered having noticed an officer looking at me that morning. I just assumed he might have been a cop on his way to work. The YCV unit had been planning an attack on the Falls Road. Monday morning was when the attack had taken place, and the YCV had assassinated the two young men. Even though the evidence was clearly pointing toward my involvement in the shooting, I tried to maintain an air of defiance. I sat in the interview room feigning disinterest and told the police lie after lie.

First of all, I decided that an outright denial might work, so I concocted a story stating that I had woken at 8.30 a.m. and gone down to Studio 10 to put together clothes and food parcels for UVF prisoners. I had been roughed up by the army before

and had given nothing away, but this was intense. I knew that I had been spotted by a police officer climbing over the wall at Brady's Lane, where we had dumped the car used in the shooting. I thought long and hard about my training and all the techniques of anti-interrogation. I thought back to the early days of the YCV in 1972, when I was going around the country and showing volunteers how to deal with situations such as this. I thought about my beatings at the hands of the army, the stick I got for my long hair and the constant harassment my friends and I endured because of the path we had chosen. Never once did I crumble. But sitting in the police station, I now knew I was in an extremely difficult position. I had ducked and dived and talked my way out of situations before, but this was going to be a hard sell.

The police knew my story about being at Studio 10 was rubbish. It completely contradicted the physical evidence. I was given time to think things over, and I decided that I had to go for a damage-limitation approach. I wanted to assess how much information they really had about what happened. I believe that they had some information but certainly not all of it. They had the cop who spotted me in the car and my handprint on the steering wheel of the car. It was obvious they were putting the pieces they had together to build the story. I tried hard to make it appear that I was an innocent youth. I had to make sure they weren't going to get the truth, as it was of paramount importance that I protected any others who were involved. I was unaware that they had also arrested Tom Winstone, who was a close friend and someone who had my utmost respect. Eventually I was charged and remanded in Crumlin Road Prison, closely followed by Tom, who had also been involved in the incident.

Loughran and Morgan had been identified by the YCV as active republicans. How accurate the information was, I don't know. At 7.30 a.m. our active service unit spotted them on the Falls Road and assassinated the two men as they passed the

junction of Northumberland Street, just yards from the Shankill. The police had been alerted to the shooting and had pursued our car to Brady's Lane, a little cul-de-sac between Peter's Hill and Greenland Street where a clean car was supposed to be waiting for us. The police had given chase, and the safe car didn't pick us up. I made off on foot and spotted a police officer looking in my direction as I climbed over a wall.

We knew to keep our heads down and not to contact any others associated with the YCV or UVF. I always thought that the police and the army weren't clever enough to pin me down. It was youthful arrogance, I suppose.

As it stood, 1974 had been a tumultuous year with the death of Jim Hanna, the tensions with Ken Gibson and Brigade Staff, and my brief spell in jail for having a stolen car with false registration plates. As I became accustomed to my surroundings in the police station, I knew deep down that I would be returning to Long Kesh, and this time I would be there for a much, much longer period.

When word got around the country, people in the UVF were apparently surprised. Not only that I had been arrested, but that I was still a teenager.

I hadn't yet turned 19.

CHAPTER 7

IN THE COMPOUNDS

When Tom Winstone and I were being led from the dock, we went through the usual and expected ritual of acting defiantly, clenching our fists and shouting, 'Up the UVF!' We had to. This was important, as we had to show our families and comrades that we were not fazed by what was happening to us. In truth, I don't think I had properly absorbed what was going on. Like everything else up until that point, I was living in the moment. I was 19 years old and had always considered myself to be mature for my age. I had been involved with the ongoing Troubles for around four years at this stage, so I had had to grow up very quickly. I was still a young man – a teenager. I was full of bravado, perhaps – but in truth I was probably incapable of comprehending the effect my actions had on my parents. My mother remained stoic and didn't directly address what I had been involved in, but my father was more to the point. He came to visit me and would ask, 'Why did you get involved with this sort of thing?' Telling me that 'Those politicians will fight 'til the last drop of your blood.' I think my father found it particularly difficult, as he had spent a lot of time in the company of Catholics, many of whom were good friends and work colleagues. I'm sure he must have worried about what they would think of him and the way he had raised his son. He just wanted a good future for me, and he reminded me that while my friends and I were spending our twenties and thirties in Long Kesh, the children of

those politicians who had been crying blood and thunder would be going to university and getting well-paid professional jobs.

My parents had separated by this stage, and I think my mother was in a difficult place, although she never showed it. While I was in Long Kesh, a Catholic was killed by the UDA after visiting the Royal Air Force club off Clifton Street, where my mother did some part-time bar work. During a visit, she told me about this man and his wife and how lovely they were; she asked me why the UDA would have done such a thing to a totally innocent man. I told her the truth: that I didn't know anything about the UDA or why they would have done something like that. However, I often think that was my mother's way of indirectly asking me the big question she was struggling with. She never asked me any other questions like that, and as time went on I realised that she was more of a prisoner than I was. She was without her youngest child and had to struggle with a lot of unanswered questions. Long Kesh had changed a bit since the last time I had been held there, in 1974. The fire of October that year, when PIRA prisoners had burned Long Kesh to the ground, allegedly in protest at the heavy-handedness of some prison officers, led to a bit of hasty rebuilding work, and a significant number of prisoners had transferred to other places like Magilligan on the north coast. It was still a place where I felt a sense of familiarity, as I knew so many people. The loyalist cages had the feel of a small town, and I could feed off other people who were in a similar situation to me. My mother was at home, alone, having to go to bed every night and accept that I was in prison – unsure whether she would see me walk the streets of the Shankill ever again.

Shortly after I had been sentenced, a UVF volunteer from East Belfast who was a couple of years older than me was also incarcerated. David Ervine had spent time on remand in the Crum while I was there, having been arrested a few weeks after me.

Little did I know it then, but he would become a close friend and a political ally as we embarked on a journey that was unthinkable in the dark days of 1974.

As I became accustomed to my surroundings in Compound 18, I was reunited with a familiar face. Gusty Spence was the C.O. of all UVF/RHC prisoners, and almost all volunteers who were imprisoned in Long Kesh had to go through the 'Gusty Spence interrogation'. Gusty had once said that 'When the young lads came in it was gun, gun, gun. Our first task was to wean them off it – people had to know what they were fighting for.' He also asked volunteers why they were in Long Kesh. This was classic Gusty psychology, whereby he would use a stimulus, or a challenge, to elicit a response from an individual. I had used this tactic on the outside and knew the motivational benefits of it. Of course, for some guys who didn't know Gusty or the way he operated, this approach rubbed them up the wrong way and they found him to be arrogant. However, I knew exactly what he was doing. Young guys who might not have considered why they had lifted a gun were now in a position where thinking was going to be a large part of their daily lives.

Once I had settled into my new home, I began to realise that life in the compounds was a mixture of study, political debate, sport and kinship. We were all in the same boat, and while some were serving longer sentences than others, we had all ended up in Long Kesh because of our commitment to the UVF or the RHC. Some guys were serving indeterminate sentences, not knowing when they would be released. Others had benefitted from remission and were getting out halfway through their time. The UVF/RHC compounds were a reflection of the working-class neighbourhoods we all hailed from. Despite what people think, and the way the media have tried to portray us, we weren't a bunch of psychopathic sectarian thugs. We were young guys who had got caught up in a conflict not of our making. We had to

support each other and ensure that there was no bullying and that the more vulnerable lads didn't get too low in mood.

After a while we all transferred over to Compound 21, which became the headquarters. Compound 21 had been home to Official IRA prisoners, but as Long Kesh was being separated into 'phases' of loyalist and republican prisoners of war, it made more sense for all UVF/RHC and UDA prisoners to be in one phase while republicans were in the other. It was in Compound 21 that I began in earnest a voyage that would set me up for a life in politics and community work. I liked the system there. Gusty was a bit like Brian Clough. He knew how to manage men and use psychology to challenge and motivate. He wasn't heavy-handed, but he understood that if guys transgressed, they had to be punished in some way. It didn't mean going over the top, and no one was ever physically punished; similar to when I had given people door duties if they were caught drinking, Gusty's forms of punishment in Long Kesh would have been to clean out the ablutions or brush out the compound. He was also able to put an arm around people when necessary and promoted self-improvement of the individual.

Self-development would become a large part of my life in Compound 21, but there was still time to mess about and enjoy the company of friends. My old mate Trevor King was always raking around and making up names for people. On one occasion he was delighted when he managed to get a pet cat into the compounds. Trevor's cat wasn't the first to appear in the cages, but he got a bit of a surprise when she produced a litter of kittens. He loved these wee cats, and to ensure that the screws (prisoner officers) didn't get wind of what had happened, he put them into Jimbo Tipping's locker. Suffice to say, Jimbo wasn't best pleased when he went to get his belongings and discovered they had been turned into a temporary feline hotel! They all started running around the cubicles one night after the screws had

locked up. Trevor hushed everybody and told someone to turn the telly down. We all thought he was going to make some big announcement in relation to the UVF or something, but instead he walked round every one of us before solemnly declaring, 'Youse have to be careful with the wee kittens, they're only tiny.' As he finished his oration, Trevor tip-toed backwards before clumsily standing on one of the poor animals. He was devastated by what had happened. The whole cat episode had provided a bit of light relief up until the unfortunate kitten's tragic demise.

A lot of the lads, whether they were loyalists or republicans, spent time in Long Kesh playing football. Some of the inter-compound games between loyalists were tasty affairs, notorious for the sometimes intense rivalries and tough tackles. Although I was a massive football fan, I preferred to run. One of my favourite non-fiction works was Alan Sillitoe's short story 'The Loneliness of the Long Distance Runner'. I could relate to the young protagonist named Smith, a Nottingham teenager who finds solace in the isolation of long-distance running. Through his running, and the reflection he engages in while enjoying the freedom to think clearly, he begins to gain clarity about the class divide in Britain. I was undergoing a similar process of self-education and self-reflection, and running provided me with a canvas of space and time to get lost in my own thoughts.

Each morning I would run around the perimeter of the wire, and I eventually began to clock up around 15 miles a day. Running became an obsession as well as a means of dealing with incarceration. It was as much a mental challenge as a physical one, and some of the other guys also became involved. One of my main running companions was William Mitchell, a young YCV member from the Rathcoole estate. I had known William before incarceration, and like me, he had a talent for running over long distances. Nothing stopped me and William doing our daily run, even the most severe weather conditions. One winter

in the early 1980s, an intense freeze descended on Northern Ireland, and with Long Kesh being in a valley, the extreme cold turned the whole prison into something reminiscent of Ice Station Zebra. Knowing that it was likely to be cold the next morning, William and I gritted the ground outside the huts where we would normally run. On the sides of the huts, there were window boxes where we normally kept food and drink that needed to be chilled. When we woke up the next morning, we were astounded to see that eggs which had been left in one of the window boxes had cracked and exploded, with the yoke freezing on its way out of the shell. Likewise, our Coca-Cola cans had burst with the extreme cold. None of this deterred us, and we went out in minus temperatures to do our daily run. It had become an obsession and a form of self-discipline [see Appendix for an original copy of my training stats from this period].

***

In 1974 Magilligan prison had opened eight full compounds to accommodate the growing number of prisoners with convictions relating to the ongoing conflict. There were four republican and four loyalist compounds, with two full compounds of UVF personnel. By 1977 the compounds at Magilligan were being phased out due to declining numbers, and in October of that year many prisoners were transferred to Long Kesh. Among them were several UVF and RHC personnel. The Magilligan lads arrived by Wessex helicopter on a Sunday and included quite a few familiar faces, none more so than their C.O., Joe Bennett. For several weeks Frankie Curry had been excited by the prospect of joining up with Bennett again, and he was constantly on at Gusty about how Bennett was a brilliant ATO and a superb all-round loyalist. Gusty was a little bit more circumspect about

the prospect of having Bennett introduced into the Sandhurst-like culture that he had tried to cultivate in the UVF cages of Long Kesh. Discipline was key, and while not everyone liked the ethos, it was nonetheless the prevalent culture in the UVF and RHC compounds. To us, Magilligan sounded a bit like a holiday camp, and Bennett probably made for an adequate C.O. in those circumstances.

However, it is important to remember that not all UVF/RHC personnel who ended up incarcerated were supporters of Gusty and the way he did things. I can't write with authority about Magilligan, but it is an important part of the UVF/RHC prison history. My friend and comrade Robert Niblock, an RHC prisoner of war, told me about his memories and how feelings that were fostered in Magilligan transferred over to Long Kesh when eventually UVF/RHC prisoners were forced to return in 1977:

> Magilligan Camp in County Londonderry, right on the edge of the Foyle, operated as a special category prison – housing both republicans and loyalists from July 1974 until closure of the Compounds in October 1977. In comparison with Long Kesh it was much smaller and had a very simple layout. The original reason for the emergence of Magilligan as a prison camp for special category prisoners was due to rapid overcrowding in Long Kesh as well as the need to house many prisoners who came from northern areas of the province closer to home.
>
> By mid-October 1974 the situation in Long Kesh had reached breaking point. Each of the twenty-one cages were full to capacity; the courts were still sentencing record numbers of prisoners and for much of the year the jail was the focus of unprecedented protests. Something had to give. It did, in the shape of IRA prisoners burning the jail to the ground. In the weeks that followed, an increased

number of prisoners were being sent to Magilligan rather than the Maze. There was simply no alternative. Indeed, in the wake of the fire, when only two loyalist cages were left untouched, hundreds were forced to share accommodation originally intended to house eighty prisoners. UVF camp commander in Long Kesh Gusty Spence offered some prisoners the opportunity to relocate. Many did. These men were more than relieved to get away from a regime they found restrictive and unwarranted. At the same time, this was a master stroke by Spence as he unburdened himself of those who were seen as disruptive or 'persona non grata' to the militaristic culture he fostered among UVF/RHC prisoners of war.

By this stage there was already a command structure in place at Magilligan which was based on the prototype in Long Kesh. In reality this duplication was loose and not enforced in the same manner it had been in Long Kesh. For many of those who endured the discipline of Gusty Spence's regime it came as a welcome reprieve. Gone were the drill, the lectures, physical training, weekly muster parades and hut inspections. This new regime was relaxed and gave a freedom of sorts that suited the majority of guys. In fact, saying the regime was more relaxed would be a gross understatement. Whereas in the UVF/RHC cages of Long Kesh routine and discipline was the order of the day, those in charge in Magilligan applied a more liberal approach. Laissez faire by-the-sea if you like.

The blatant reality is that Long Kesh and Magilligan were worlds apart. It was common knowledge that Magilligan had a lifestyle that would have endeared itself to young prisoners in particular. 'Butlins without the Redcoats' was a description of it that I have heard many times. Obviously word reached Long Kesh of the less

than militaristic approach to imprisonment in the cages of Magilligan. It's true to say though that this lifestyle didn't appeal to everyone, there were some prisoners who applied to return to Long Kesh, but by and large I think that the majority of those who served there at that time enjoyed the relative freedom.

By late 1975 committals to the jails were slowing down and not many new faces were coming through the gates of Magilligan. By March 1976 this virtually ground to a standstill with the abandonment of Special Status. In mid-1976 Gusty exiled a number of prisoners from Long Kesh to Magilligan. Some of these men were classed as 'mixers' or those who were seen to have a strong but bad influence on the younger UVF prisoners. It was all about Gusty exerting his authority and trying to control the situation.

The numbers in all of the cages in Magilligan were dwindling by early 1977 and for many months it became obvious that a return to Long Kesh was inevitable. This duly occurred in October 1977. We were given less than a weeks' notice – for security reasons, I would imagine. The move took place on a dull Sunday. We were removed from cage H – the only UVF one left. Small groups at a time were escorted in minibuses to hangars at a nearby airfield and then subsequently transported (handcuffed to screws and escorted by heavily armed soldiers) by Wessex helicopter to Long Kesh.

In the lead up to the move many were apprehensive and fearful, some openly stating that they feared the Spence regime so much that they would rather relinquish political status than comply with his authority. The O.C. of Magilligan at the time was Joe Bennett. In the days before the actual move we as a group had many meetings. The mood at the meetings ranged from acceptance,

opposition and even threats of insurrection. The lead and most vociferous form of opposition came from the Bennett himself who threatened mutiny if we as a group weren't housed in a cage of our own under our own autonomy. Fighting talk indeed but it was never likely to happen despite the bluff and hyperbole. On admission to Long Kesh there was a required induction during which we (around thirty of us) were separated into three different cages – 18, 19 and 21. [...]

The next morning – a Monday – we were herded into the canteen to receive a 'welcome' from Gusty himself. We duly lined up in ranks of three; the usual routine for the Long Kesh guys, but somewhat unorthodox for many of the Magilligan men. Gusty paraded in front of us, basically laying down the law and at times reading the riot act. There were heated exchanges including threats and counter-threats and a seriously ominous mood. It was during these exchanges that I first heard the word 'maggots' used to describe the Magilligan prisoners. It wouldn't be the last.

Relationships between many of the Magilligan influx and the Long Kesh guys were strained. From a personal point of view I heard many times from different prisoners that were seen as renegades, disturbers and of course, maggots. In the early days of resettlement I personally recollect many cases of friction and hostility. There were fraught moments. [...] There were also some strong and at times hostile feelings towards some of Gusty's staff, though not all. There were cases of ones who hadn't been in Magilligan, but who held negative views towards the Long Kesh command, taking sides with those who had arrived. Through time many of these views softened. Those who hadn't left the cages and remained more or less fell into line, citing the need to retain

> political status as the most important reason. Ironically by the start of the 1980's there was a less militaristic approach to imprisonment within the UVF cages of Long Kesh. Perhaps because by then there were no new prisoners coming in (we were down to one cage only, cage 21) the population was virtually lifers or 'twenty-year men', many of whom had enrolled in the Open University and were embarking on a study path that would last for seven or more years. Whatever the reason prison life was much more appealing, if that can be true, and although the label of 'maggot' would never be forgotten, it was sliding further into the background.

I recall the Wessex helicopter arriving and vividly remember Joe Bennett disembarking, where he was heard to say, 'I'll not be taking any fucking orders from that bastard Gusty Spence.' I don't know what his problem was, but unbeknown to Bennett, Gusty already had a strategy in place to deal with any attempt at subordination. A few days prior to the arrival of the Magilligan lads, Gusty had asked to meet with me. He understood that I also knew Bennett from the early 1970s and wanted to get a feel for the sort of person he was going to be dealing with. I told him straight that Bennett was a great and inventive ATO, but he was also a fantasist and a loudmouth, who was, in my opinion, susceptible to corruption and compromise through vices such as gambling.

After talking to me and others, Gusty devised a plan. He told us that he would offset any dissent from Bennett by giving him a false rank – this was classic Gusty psychology. True to his word, Gusty took Bennett aside on his arrival in Compound 21. He had been in high spirits and was horsing around with the other arrivals from Magilligan, and despite his previous promise that he wouldn't be taking orders from Gusty, he was suddenly

humbled to be on the receiving end of an offer from a senior officer. 'Young Joseph Bennett, it's good to have you and your men here in Long Kesh. It's been a long time since our paths crossed, but my nephew Frankie and Hutchie both assure me that you are the real deal. The command structure is different here, but I know you held the rank of C.O. in Magilligan. Well, here I am C.O. of all UVF and RHC personnel, but I am going to give you rank that is equivalent to that which you held in Magilligan. I'm going to make you my 3IC. It's a very important role.'

Me and the others were in stitches when we heard about this. Bennett fell hook, line and sinker for Gusty's charismatic charm. There is no such military rank as 3IC, of course, but Bennett was so blinded by his own ego and the attention he had received from Gusty that he still felt like the top man, even if everyone else knew differently. It worked in the long-term, and Joe Bennett ended up becoming a decent person to have around the place. Later, he was given proper rank, though he had become unpopular with the comrades whom he had arrived in the helicopter from Magilligan with, as he didn't take Gusty on as he said he would. He wholly capitulated to Gusty's mind games and didn't recognise that his ego had been massaged to get control of those volunteers who were threatening revolt on their arrival in Long Kesh.

***

On 12 July 1977 Gusty made a bold oration to the UVF/RHC prisoners in which he advocated defending the rights of all men in Ulster, no matter their political opinion. He also lambasted the bigotry of senior unionist politicians, describing them as 'fascists' and going on to ask, 'Do they not realise that the IRA was a natural manifestation of Catholic fears just as the UVF/UDA were born from loyalist fear?' This was a statement that took a lot of courage, but it was one which had emerged from intense political

debate within the compounds. Those on the outside, who still had their 'war head' on, more than likely couldn't understand where Gusty was coming from; in fact, to make a comparison between the UVF and the IRA was plain heresy to some. However, we in Long Kesh were facing up to the realities of the socio-economic and political factors that had influenced young men and women on both sides of the sectarian divide in their decision to take up arms. Volunteers who were serving long and often indeterminate prison sentences had thought about and discussed at length the ongoing situation in Northern Ireland. While we were never going to become republicans, we were able to begin to understand and analyse why the IRA had launched their campaign of violence in the first place. Had there been inequality against the Catholic community? Most certainly. Had we been any better off than those Catholics? Definitely not.

In his oration, Gusty went on to describe the unionist politicians, whose rhetoric had often given young loyalists the green light to take up arms, as 'witch-hunters – Ulster's Senator McCarthys', stating that 'If one does not agree with their bigoted and fascist views then one is a "taig lover" at best or a "communist" at worst. They are adept at labelling those who disagree with them.' Gusty had become used to debating the issues of the day with republican paramilitary leaders in the Camp Council at Long Kesh (a council formed at Gusty's behest and consisting of the C.O. of each paramilitary organisation housed in the prison) to discuss issues of common concern in the prison, and in his 12 July speech he advocated that the paramilitaries take the initiative where the politicians had failed:

> The politicians seemingly cannot or will not give us the peace we so earnestly desire, so I therefore call upon the paramilitaries – all the warring factions – to call a universal ceasefire, to open dialogue with each other in order to pursue

> ways and means of making such a ceasefire permanent. Eventually loyalist and republican must sit down together for the good of the country if we claim to be patriots.

The politicians didn't take any notice of any of this of course, but Gusty was sincere in his statements. He had come to realise that when people use political violence, their message is drowned out by the guns and the bombs. He always said that wars were created by politicians and solved by soldiers. The 12 July speech came on the back of the arrest of the guys who had been involved in what the media had termed the 'Shankill Butchers'; their actions had caused disgust among most ordinary working-class loyalists. At around the same time, in May 1977, Ian Paisley and the United Unionist Action Council (UUAC) had tried to replicate the 1974 UWC strike in what became an embarrassing charade. He had hoped to press the Secretary of State for Northern Ireland, Roy Mason, into taking action against the IRA. The UDA allowed itself to be sucked in, but the majority of workers decided against going on strike. The UUAC was lambasted by the UUP, Vanguard and the Orange Order. It was a further fragmentation of unionism, and a humiliation that Paisley should never have recovered from. Gusty's argument that the paramilitaries should show leadership looked even more relevant in the wake of Paisley's unpopular May strike action. He hit the nail on the head about Paisley and others like him when he said:

> No fascist or bigot can expect sympathy or understanding in the UVF compounds of Long Kesh. The sooner we realise that our trust has been abused and the so-called political leadership we followed was simply a figment the sooner we will attempt to fend for ourselves politically and to commence articulation in that direction. We can do without the immature, emotionally unstable and bigoted element

> within loyalist circles. As a political leadership they are a sick joke – a mixture of inane hacks and power-hungry clerics who would not recognise the truth if it kicked them in the face. These are the men who have cunningly and purposefully fused religion with politics and festered fear amongst the loyalist community for their own designs and to regain power.

A couple of weeks after Gusty's speech, Billy Mitchell and I issued a letter supporting him. We felt that Gusty was right and that his plea should be 'commended to all true patriots who wish to see the present crisis in Ulster brought to a speedy end without a loss of principle'. Furthermore, we pondered on the 1974 era, when the VPP was formed. Undoubtedly, we had missed an opportunity to seize the moral high ground and take the initiative in a political direction. Of course, hindsight is a wonderful thing, but we were engaged in a deep process of self-analysis in the light of Gusty's speech and we wrote:

> Some of us held similar views as long ago as early 1974 but, to our eternal sorrow, did not have the moral courage to pursue these policies ... Instead we espoused the policies of 'populism' for fear that we would be branded as disloyal by the vast majority of super-Prods who have so much to say and so little to offer concerning the violence and bloodshed that has ravaged our fair Province ... The forces of modern-day enlightenment are shaking away old prejudices and uprooting ancient myths. An age of upheaval is undermining and toppling long-established systems of political and sectarian tribalism, status and belief. An older order is dying, with all the ugly brutality, turbulence and bloodshed that has attended other throes of change in the past.

In 1978 Gusty Spence stood down as C.O. of UVF/RHC prisoners in Long Kesh. To those like myself who were close to him, it came as absolutely no surprise. He had become disillusioned with the leadership on the outside and was keen to distance himself from the organisation so that he could concentrate on communications with his family in preparing for his eventual release. He was also tired and felt that he had probably brought the men in Long Kesh as far as he could. He had left a legacy, but he had also been in jail since 1966 and was keen to return to his family. There had been correspondence with several influential people, mainly politicians, who were being asked to fight Gusty's corner. I'm sure Louie was keen that he spend more time campaigning for his release than worrying about the men under his command in Long Kesh. No one begrudged him choosing to concentrate on himself after many years spent as C.O.

To ensure that things transitioned smoothly after Gusty's retirement – that the prison authorities continued to hold the UVF prisoners in high esteem – someone with a similar mindset had to take the mantle and drive forward the ethos that Gusty had implemented. Bobby Spence, Gusty's brother, and another UVF veteran from the Shankill, Jackie Mahood, who was in Compound 19, took over as part of a combined leadership system. Bobby, who was in Compound 21, was a great man who had served in the navy as a gunner and was a veteran of the Malayan and Korean wars. Like most former members of the armed forces, he was very principled. Bobby and Jackie continued in the same vein as Gusty, so the transition was relatively seamless. I had been very close to Bobby on the outside and held him in high esteem, so I felt pleased that the UVF/RHC would retain the same disciplined system in Long Kesh that Gusty had worked hard to implement over many years. Little did I know that discontent among the UVF/RHC prisoners of war would eventually lead to this system being overthrown.

In March 1980, things changed in the compounds. The disciplined and militaristic culture that Gusty had implemented was resented by some volunteers, and there was a coup in Compound 19 against Jackie Mahood. I sensed that some people were getting 'gate fever' and that there was a sense of restlessness coming from wives and girlfriends, as well as parents who had gone to the Eagle (the UVF headquarters on the Shankill Road) and complained about the military-style system that had been maintained after Gusty stood down. This atmosphere on the outside obviously began to infect some of the guys in the compounds. There was no release procedure in place for indeterminately sentenced prisoners, so some of the parents of those prisoners who were being held at the Secretary of State's pleasure began to apply pressure for their release. This was supported by the Northern Ireland Association for the Care and Resettlement of Offenders and the Quakers.

When Brigade Staff approached me with these concerns, and the complaints about the rigid system, I was adamant that running the UVF/RHC compounds the way Gusty had – and Bobby, Jackie and I had – was best for everyone. I told them that if the structure was taken away, then the place would go to the dogs. There were three approaches required in any assessment of this situation: psychological, political and militaristic. I believed if we did away the system that had been in place since the 1970s, then the prison officers would be in control, not the UVF and RHC prisoners of war. They would fight hard to criminalise us.

The writing was on the wall, but I told them to work away. The decision was taken to appoint people. There were suggestions of having a vote, which I thought was ridiculous; the UVF is a military organisation, and orders must come from the top and then be strictly adhered to. Before things were changed, Brigade Staff provided me with the opportunity to revise my decision to retain the old system. They asked me would I be changing this,

that and the other, to which I firmly responded 'No', 'No' and 'No'.

A meeting was called in the canteen, where a vote was taken for Brian Moorehouse to take charge as C.O. All volunteers in the UVF/RHC compounds had a vote. I refused to take part in the charade. Voting wasn't something that should have been part of a paramilitary setup; it was something I had made abundantly clear during the heated meetings in the 1970s. One prisoner stood up and looked at me: 'Hutchie, is there anything that you're going to change?' My response was a simple 'No'. That was the nail in the coffin, and Brian Moorehouse won the vote and became C.O. Brian had become part of loyalist folklore in March 1971 when he removed a tricolour from the funeral hearse of a Belfast republican, the events all caught by television news cameras. For several years, the anonymous 'lad who stole the flag' was celebrated in a song sung in shebeens and clubs, as well as on the terraces at Ibrox.

I felt that things had been quite relaxed since Gusty had stood down. Certainly, the intensity of the 'mini-Sandhurst' had been phased down to a slightly more laid-back culture; it crucially retained the physical and mental discipline he had implemented while giving volunteers a bit more flexibility to develop independently. No one was being given a hard time under my watch in Compound 21, as I couldn't abide bullies, but what annoyed me most was the compound being a mess and people not making their beds for three or four weeks. This became the norm after the coup, and it was bad for people psychologically. I was also worried that the UVF/RHC compounds would become like a regular prison, where it was survival of the strongest.

Another one of the reasons why I had long embraced the Gusty system was that it kept volunteers away from screws unless they held rank as a UVF officer. The rationale for this was simple. Some of the screws were constantly spoiling for a

fight, or for a reason to get their batons out. With lots of men serving indeterminate sentences, who were separated from their families and didn't know when they were going to be released, there was always the possibility of people losing the head and getting involved in physical confrontations. The mindset of the UVF in Long Kesh was that we were ambassadors for the UVF and the wider loyalist community while we were incarcerated. When Gusty, Bobby and Jackie had held the position of C.O., prison officers came to the door of each hut to do a count of the men, who then stood obediently outside their cubicles allowing whoever was on duty to do their count from the door.

When the new regime took over, some guys lay in their beds during the count, which meant that the prison officer on duty could walk down the middle of the hut and enter cubicles. I and a few others stood at our doors, as we had always done, to prevent prison officers from entering our living quarters. It was a matter of personal choice now that there was a new leadership, but moreover, when we did it, it was designed to show the screws that we were in charge, not them. The new system may have given volunteers autonomy, but it weakened the UVF as an organisation in the eyes of the authorities. If the governor could have seen the huts at this point in time, I have absolutely no doubt he would have been rubbing his hands with glee. Fortunately, I had a group of good comrades around me who shared my vision. Eddie Kinner, Marty Snodden, Gusty, Tom Winstone and a few others were of like mind, and we continued to demonstrate a firm allegiance to the old militaristic regime of self-discipline and self-improvement.

As 1980 progressed, it was proving to be a hugely difficult year; the solidarity that had been carefully cultivated by the special category (political status) UVF/RHC volunteers in the compounds was dissolved. However, things got much worse when, in late February, just as the new regime was about to

take control, my mentor Billy Spence died suddenly. Billy was a strategist and a deep thinker, and a lot of his personality rubbed off on me. His passing affected me greatly. No matter how devastated I was by Billy's death, it must have been a hundred times harder for his family. In a cruel twist of fate, tragedy struck the Spence family again that year when Bobby Spence died. On 12 October, while he was jogging around the wire, Bobby collapsed and died after suffering a massive heart-attack. We were all devastated.

During the research for this book, I discovered a document that was written in November 1980 by the Governor of Long Kesh. The so-called 'progress report' on me was for the attention of the Northern Ireland Office Treatment of Offenders Branch. Some of the governor's comments contained highlight my defiance and refusal to accede to the new regime:

> Up until March 1980 Hutchinson acted as second in charge of Compound 21 and was to become O/C/ at the time. The remainder of his UVF peers decided that they wished to follow a policy of non militarisation in the Compounds e.g. no parades, early rising, continual cleaning etc. Hutchinson however, still wishes to be associated with the old regime and the small group which still remains of that regime.
>
> Hutchinson whilst acting as spokesman always did so in a polite and courteous manner, putting forward suggestions forcefully, but at the same time always prepared to accept 'no' as an answer and was always prepared to recognise the problems of others.
>
> Hutchinson still continues to be polite to staff and does on occasion have conversations with his Compound gate Officers. Does get on well with other inmates in the Compounds ...

> Unfortunately Hutchinson's own personal refusal to be interviewed demonstrates that he still sympathises with the old UVF regime which disappeared in March this year.

The Moorehouse leadership continued for around five years, when eventually the UVF contacted me to admit that the whole thing had gone wrong. They had been consulting with people in the prison service who had been asking the organisation what on earth was going on. Prison authorities told the UVF that the compounds were a tip, and that there was also a group around me who wouldn't co-operate with the prison officers. I and the group around me were upholding our values and behaving like political prisoners. We were no threat to the prison service unless they tried to criminalise us. If they tried to do so, then we would react to show that we had special category status, which had been bestowed on us and republicans back in 1972. We were political prisoners and had political status, and that's how we, as UVF/RHC prisoners, behaved. This set us apart from others, such as ordinary criminals.

At the time I believed, along with others, that some of the UVF men in the compounds wanted to go to a life sentence review board to ensure that their release was on the horizon. I knew that Brian Moorehouse was one of them, as he told me as much. His argument to me was that I was being punished because of my position in Long Kesh. I pointed out that there was no evidence of that, as there was no way for the prison officers to actually measure our progress. I pointed out that the screws were not trained to give a professional opinion and that they didn't spend enough time with the volunteers to make any assessment. He accepted my analysis but still thought it would be harmful for a volunteer if they held a political position. I explained that the authorities were using information they had obtained that related to the period in which we were involved in the UVF and RHC on

the outside, and that we couldn't change that. Brian didn't accept that part of my argument. He also didn't accept my point of view that as a political prisoner I could not be rehabilitated as it was society that was wrong, not me. Brian suggested to me that being C.O. wouldn't look good at his interview, and he seemed keen to resign his position.

The idea of giving up rank and towing the line to please the whims of those in charge of the prison system was anathema to me and others who had retained their military status; it was something that should have been rejected as a point of ideology by all UVF/RHC prisoners of war. A life sentence review board was something used for criminals. I wasn't a criminal – I was a political prisoner. Society was to blame for the Troubles occurring, not me. I was proud of being a UVF prisoner of war and was quite content to get on with doing what I felt a volunteer should be concerned with in Long Kesh, such as studying and exercise to ensure mental and physical development. After all, these were just some of the principles that the YCV had been founded on all those years ago, before the First World War. I certainly wasn't going to dance to the tune of the prison governor or faceless bureaucrats.

The prison regime tried to portray me and those who stood with me as the renegades, making it out that we were the ones in the wrong. We were viewed as intransigent and hard-line militants. This was a classic example of mind games, and it was designed to make people paranoid. Once paranoia creeps into that type of atmosphere, where people are separated from their families, men become more malleable to the authorities. That was obviously the aim of the system, but I wasn't going to let it beat me.

After Moorehouse stood down, Tom Winstone and I took charge of all UVF/RHC prisoners in the compounds and tried to reverse any decline that we felt had set in. A Gusty-lite system

was introduced that was designed to bring order back to the way things were. I stayed as loyal as possible to the ethos of Gusty, with a little more flexibility to make life easier for volunteers. On foot of being the new C.O., I was contacted by the life sentence review board. They knew that I didn't recognise their legitimacy or authority over UVF/RHC prisoners of war, but they were keen to try and stir things up and notified me that my release date had been put back by five years. I was never sure what this tactic was meant to achieve. Was it intended to destroy people's morale in the hope that they would conform to the system implemented by the government whereby political prisoners were criminalised? My response was simple: 'As a member of the Ulster Volunteer Force, I do not recognise this system.' When I was put on 'the boards' – meaning that I was sent to a cell by myself with no mattress as a form of punishment – I replied, 'I do not recognise the governor's authority. You have no authority over me. The only organisation that has authority over me is the Ulster Volunteer Force.' It was all about trying to find a non-aggressive way to challenge the system and not allow the system to break our spirit.

Sometimes my reading came in handy, and I was once able to infuriate a screw without resorting to violence. A screw with a Protestant background started verbally abusing me, calling me all the names under the sun. He obviously hoped that he could provoke a physical reaction from me, so I asked him to stop what he was saying. His frustration increased; his response was to give me more abuse and remind me that he would say whatever he liked to me, as he was in charge. I told him, 'It's true what George Bernard Shaw said – that a screw married a prostitute and brought her down to his level!' After this altercation, I was hauled into the governor's office and accused of calling this screw's wife a prostitute! Once we had cleared things up, the governor said, 'On you go.' I turned to him and said, 'Here, don't talk to me like

that. I'm not on trial.' He threatened me with the boards again, to which I responded, 'Oh, the boards? Don't tell me you have lions down there now?!' and walked out.

On one occasion in July 1983 the governor was walking round the compound, heading toward my hut. He asked to see me in the bunk: 'I've got something to tell you.' I followed him and stood, unsure of what to expect. 'Don't be asking for parole because you're not getting it. Your father is dead.' With that, he just took himself off. It was cold and clinical. Another UVF man, Davey Allen, had absconded while on compassionate parole to attend a funeral and that meant none of the rest of us could get out, even to bury our parents. I could have thrown Davey Allen's name into the conversation, but there was no point. It was an issue for the UVF on the outside to resolve.

It took strong mental resolve to survive each day in Long Kesh, and as leader of all UVF/RHC volunteers I like to think I did a good job of keeping people on the right path.

***

Many column inches were spent writing about the loyalist prisoners in Long Kesh, mainly by people who had no experience of what our lives had been like on the Shankill and other loyalist areas. These middle-class commentators in the local newspapers felt confident in criticising us, labelling us as ignorant and oafish. One of the main culprits was Patrick Riddell, a curmudgeonly contrarian who would have argued that a white door was black. In the early summer of 1977, Riddell wrote a typically condescending piece in the *Sunday News* in which he strongly criticised the educational standards of young loyalists like me. I was beginning to develop my ability to articulate the loyalist working-class point of view and felt that it was important to challenge the ignorance of these middle-class commentators. In

response to the constant condescension of Riddell and others like him, I decided to write a letter, giving the perspective of a young loyalist. It was my aim to highlight that our perceived ignorance and underachievement were not fully our own fault. The letter was published in *Combat* as well as the *Sunday News*:

Compound 21,
Long Kesh Prison,
Lisburn,
County Antrim

4th July 1977

Dear Sir,
As a loyalist prisoner encaged at Long Kesh Prison Camp I feel compelled to reply to Patrick Riddell's unfair criticism of the educational standards of loyalists – especiallly with regards to the subject of Irish history. Loyalist youngsters, like myself, from the working class ghettos are the product of a State educational system which has, for its own peculiar reasons, deemed it necessary to exclude Irish History from the classroom. Instead of directing his criticism at young loyalists like me, Mr Riddell would be more reasonable if he were to condemn the State educational system in Ulster. When I left school, which was just six years ago, the only history I was taught was British History (mostly about the monarchy). Never once was I ever taught about the social, economic, cultural or political life of Ireland.

I am a long-term loyalist prisoner sentenced as a result of my support for the Ulster Volunteer Force; and since I have been incarcerated I have been engaged in educational studies in all aspects of Irish History and in Irish Culture and Language. Our classes run from September to June and

> in that period we are permitted a teacher for one single hour each week, usually at night. It is obvious that a single hour per week is insufficient for the tuition required for examinations. Not only so, but it is almost impossible to obtain the necessary text books required for the courses. I would also point out that the Examining Board does not provide for examination in Irish History above C.S.E. standard; hence there is no encouragement for us to take in-depth studies in Irish History. We have, however, on our own initiative, and with the support of our own UVF officers, been able to pursue such studies in private.
>
> So please, Mr Riddell, don't criticise the youngsters of today for the sins of your own generation.
>
> Yours, etc.
> William Hutchinson

I wanted to point out that we had come through an education system that didn't teach us Irish history properly. People like Riddell couldn't hope to understand the socio-economic conditions that people like myself emerged from; they had never experienced poverty and hardship. Without a sophisticated or even basic understanding of our past, young loyalists of my generation were perfect cannon fodder for the politicians, who worked people into a frenzy. David Ervine later asked a famous rhetorical question: 'What came first: the polluted politics or the paramilitaries?' The toxic political atmosphere had always been there, and the young men who ended up in jail in the 1970s were the culmination of years of rabble-rousing by clean-handed orators. Don't get me wrong; I accept responsibility for my actions, but I wasn't going to take lectures from the Riddells of this world, who knew nothing of the fear that had stalked the streets of the Shankill and other loyalist areas in the early 1970s. It was always a case of keeping

the working class ignorant and suppressed, using them when things were difficult and then blaming them when the situation exploded. Just as we had been fodder for factory owners and landowners in previous generations, so too were we collateral for the politicians in the war against the IRA.

In 1979 an excellent educationalist by the name of Dominic Henry moved from Magilligan prison to Long Kesh. He transformed the education system and fought a long and hard battle with the NIO to introduce proper formal education into the jail. This education would include Open University courses. The main issue was that the prison authorities didn't want us to be educated, they wanted us to be punished. They saw us as a problem to be dealt with. Despite this attitude, many of us persisted toward gaining a formal education. With Gusty Spence's foresight in the UVF compounds at that time, there was a participatory approach to education. I decided that I wanted to further my knowledge of Soviet history and politics by studying it in pursuit of an 'A' Level. I made enquiries, and Dominic came back to me to say that unfortunately it wouldn't be possible; that I would need 'O' Levels before I could do an 'A' Level. I was determined to go down the education route and took 'O' Levels in English and maths, both of which I passed with the help of a tutor from Armagh, a lady who was friendly with the Social Democratic and Labour Party (SDLP) politician Seamus Mallon. Subsequently I reapplied to do the 'A' Level in Soviet history that I had been keen to undertake and was informed by the prison authorities that I wouldn't be allowed to do it, and that they weren't going to give a reason.

I was despondent about this, as I had worked so hard to prove the authorities wrong. One day I was walking along the wire beside Compound 20, where Official IRA prisoners were housed, when I heard a guy calling to me. It turned out to be Liam 'Bumpy' McAnoy. I went over and exchanged pleasantries

with him. After a bit of small talk, he said, 'Hutchie, are you sure you weren't brought up on the Falls? You sound very socialist, the way you talk.' I told him that I didn't like labels, but that when I was a youngster I spent a lot of time with my dad at Dunville Park and the cinema in Clonard; I saw people from the Falls and knew that the people on the Shankill weren't any better off than them. I went on to point out that I was British and a unionist, and I reminded him of the welfare state and the NHS that existed in the UK. After a bit of good-natured debate about the definition of a socialist, McAnoy said to me, 'I'm doing this essay and I'd like for you to have a read of it for me. Just to give me some feedback.' The essay was on the social sciences, and although I couldn't give him any feedback from an academic perspective, I was interested in the subject enough to understand the broad concepts; I said that I would get back to him with my thoughts. I thought the essay he had written was very good, and when I went back to him, he said that it was for the Open University and asked whether I would think about trying my hand at a similar piece of work. He told me that his tutor was a lady called Jenny Meegan and that if I did the essay, she could mark it. Eventually I got myself together and wrote a paper, thinking nothing more of it. A week or so later, it was returned to me and Jenny had given it a B plus. Not too bad for a first attempt, I thought!

The excellent grade and the positive feedback I had received from Jenny whet my appetite to explore the possibility of an Open University degree in social sciences. I had always been fascinated by human behaviour and the structures that underpin society, so it seemed like a natural thing to do. I had seen the Shankill slowly changing in the early 1970s before I went to jail. Developers and planners were engaged in slum clearances, and there had been plans for a Belfast Urban Motorway, which were later implemented. A short time after I arrived in Long Kesh, in 1976, I came across a book entitled *The Rape and Plunder of*

the Shankill by Ron Wiener. I read it from cover to cover and it was a revelation. It was the first time I had read a book that spoke directly to me about the community in which I had grown up. Wiener was an academic who had come to the Shankill in the mid-1970s to do some action research on urban planning. Wiener's research was the foundation rock upon which Jackie Redpath, a Shankill community activist, had built the 'Save the Shankill' campaign, which protested the ill-judged ideas of outsiders who had no knowledge of the area and the importance of its kinship network and community spirit. People who had lived cheek by jowl in terraced streets were now being shifted into 'Weetabix' style flats while the Westlink dual carriageway was driven through part of the Lower Shankill. Locals had little to no power in stopping the redevelopment and reading more about it in Wiener's book opened my eyes to the devastation that this had caused to the community.

I spoke to Jenny Meegan about the developing interest that I had in urban planning, and she strongly encouraged me to pursue social sciences. Accessing formal education through the Open University was a natural extension of the system and culture that Gusty Spence had created and fostered in the UVF/RHC cages in Long Kesh. The UVF had an education officer – two memorable ones being Flint McCullough and Billy Strain – and we also had a study hut. In the study hut, we were surrounded by books of all descriptions: novels, science fiction, reference books – anything you could think of. If there was something that we wanted to read which wasn't available, we could approach the education officer, he could go and order it in the library, and we could have it in ten days or so. This was particularly important when it came to accessing Open University course materials, books or book chapters that had been recommended by a tutor. Just knowing that there were like-minded people around me who wouldn't put obstacles in my way helped me greatly in my quest for education.

It was vitally important for us that the Open University tutors could come in and engage with us in the compounds. Some of the tutors were nervous – they had probably been told that we were monsters and that sort of thing – while others didn't seem to be fazed in the least. This system of supported open learning was crucial for people like me. Distance learning was all well and good, but to have these brilliant teachers coming in and pushing me to develop – to go that extra mile with my education – was priceless.

All the hard work paid off when I later gained my degree in social sciences. Given my vocal interest in the work of Ron Wiener, I had been encouraged by some of the tutors to go on and do a diploma in town planning. To then go on and achieve a degree was quite something for a guy like myself who had left school at the age of 15. I wasn't the only UVF/RHC prisoner to gain a qualification. There were many others.

Education was also a form of resistance. Though the UVF/RHC leadership in Long Kesh was amenable and supportive of volunteers seeking to pursue education and knowledge, the prison system would often create obstacles. There were always restrictions and censorship of what we could and couldn't read, and sometimes it would become a battle between the UVF/RHC prison leadership and the prison authorities as the censors clamped down on our access to books, magazines and learning materials. Dominic Henry was really upset by this, as it meant that some of the Open University set texts were banned for a period. On many occasions I was forced to petition the governor for access to educational facilities so that I and others could continue our Open University education [see letter dated 8 July 1985 in Appendix].

***

'These men will spend thirty years in here, just to make sure that the Provos don't get out!' These were the sabre-rattling words of Cecil Walker, the Ulster Unionist MP for North Belfast, when he brought a delegation of British politicians to see UVF prisoners in Long Kesh in the mid-1980s. This was, of course, absolute rubbish, which was typical of the sort of blood and thunder rhetoric of so many unionist politicians in the 1970s and 1980s. I told him straight that he was wrong: 'We are soldiers and we will bring about peace. Your comments suggest to me that politics is too important to be left to politicians.' He certainly wasn't expecting that response, but studying through the Open University and engaging in the debates that Gusty had encouraged had emboldened me to formulate principles and values, communicating them with confidence.

Anyway, it was always the intention of loyalist prisoners to escape the confines of incarceration. I and others in the UVF/RHC compounds did not believe that we should have been in Long Kesh, or indeed in any other prison. What use were soldiers if they weren't in the thick of battle? Numerous attempts were made by loyalists over the years – some successful, some not so successful. In October 1972 two Shankill UVF men escaped from Crumlin Road Gaol in separate incidents. Tommy Cull walked out the front gates, having pretended to be another prisoner who was due for release, while later in the month Danny Strutt got over a wall to find himself free. After Strutt's escape, the UVF released a statement which declared that the organisation regarded itself as being in a war situation and that its incarcerated members, as prisoners of war, had a duty to attempt to escape from whatever prison they found themselves in. On 7 April 1973 Robert Niblock and Billy Neill escaped from Long Kesh by hiding themselves in a garbage truck. Later, in 1976, Stevie McCrea made an audacious attempt to escape by concealing himself under a van that was used for mobile X-rays. All three were intercepted in their ventures,

with Stevie not even making it out of Long Kesh, but the point is that they tried; loyalists were as keen to escape as republicans. The idea that we weren't is simply a myth.

So desperate were some men to escape, in fact, that in August 1984, one of the loyalist escape attempts ended in tragedy. Two UDA life sentence prisoners attempted to leave Long Kesh by concealing themselves in the back of a departing bin lorry. The lorry's loading mechanism was activated when Benny Redfern jumped in and he was crushed, dying a day later in the Royal Victoria Hospital. Soon after this I wrote to the human rights lawyer Kevin Boyle. Boyle, who was from Newry, had been one of the People's Democracy marchers attacked by Protestants at Burntollet back in 1969, when he was a lecturer in Law at Queen's University Belfast. In 1984 he was a lecturer at University College Galway. Prisoners have always written to politicians, academics and lawyers to see if they could get someone to champion their cause, but I felt that it was important to outline a coherent picture of how life sentence prisoners who had become embroiled in the conflict during the early to mid-1970s felt about their plight. Many of the life sentence prisoners who had become involved in the UVF and RHC had done so during a period of extreme social and political turmoil, when men who would never previously have become involved in violence, or even have come to the attention of the police, became killers. In the late 1990s, speaking to the journalist Peter Taylor, Billy Mitchell described this phenomenon when he said:

> Someone didn't fly over Northern Ireland and drop some sort of 'loony gas' and suddenly people woke up one morning as killers. We didn't go to bed one night as ordinary family men and wake up the next morning as killers. Conditions were created in this country whereby people did things they shouldn't have done. While I'll accept responsibility for

what I have personally done, I won't accept responsibility for creating the conditions that allowed me to do it and that allowed other people to do it.

As was almost always the case, Billy had hit the nail on the head. In my correspondence with Kevin Boyle, I was articulating the same case for the men who found themselves behind the wire with no prospect of release on their horizon. Along with my brief letter, I included the following thoughts in a short paper, which are indicative of my thinking at the time:

Special Category Life Sentence Prisoners

The attempted escape (Thursday, 9/8/84) by two life sentence prisoners, resulting in the death of one (Benny Redfern), highlights clearly the level of desperation felt by such prisoners, living from day-to-day with no hope for release in the foreseeable future. The intention of this paper is to summarise the views of a number of life sentence prisoners (hereafter referred to as L.S.P.'s), who are at present imprisoned in the compound section (loyalist) of Long Kesh of the Maze prison. The purpose of this paper is to inform the reader of the great concern felt, not only by the L.S.P.'s but also by their families, about the indefinite period of time in which they might have to spend in prison.

Before the paper goes on to expound the uncertainties and injustices felt by L.S.P.'s it is important that the reader should be reminded of the circumstances surrounding the involvement, and hence the imprisoning of, the above mentioned L.S.P.'s.

During the early 1970's sectarian conflict, due to political instability, had engulfed most villages and towns throughout N. Ireland. It was because of, and due to, the bellicose rhetoric of demagogic leaders that young men then

became the L.S.P.'s of to-day. The L.S.P.'s originating from that period in the early seventies when sectarian conflict was at its height, feel somewhat betrayed and aggrieved by the margin of support given for them now to that of the encouragement and support giving [*sic*] during the period mentioned above. The Protestant community then felt vulnerable to attack from republicans. Due to what they believed to be the unwillingness of the Government and lack of security forces on the ground to deal effectively with the situation at the time, and at the instigation of elected representatives, they formed their own defence groups from young men and respected community leaders.

In the late sixties the prison population in N. Ireland was approximately 600 – this has now more than trebled into the largest prison population per capita in Europe. Of the numbers presently incarcerated in N. Ireland approximately 420 are L.S.P.'s and of these there is in the region of 170 in the Special Category compounds of Long Kesh. Some of these L.S.P.'s were sentenced in the early seventies and were subsequently transferred from Crumlin Road prison to Long Kesh with the introduction of the compound system. The average length of time spent by special category L.S.P.'s is 8–10 years.

The emphasis on the compound system is on containment rather than on rehabilitation or reforming. No one can deny that during the early years of the compound system confrontations took place, practically on a daily basis, between the relevant factions and those in authority (i.e. prison staff). It was because of, and due to, such confrontations, that the label 'university of terrorism' became synonymous with Long Kesh and the compound system. However, in recent years there has been relative stability within the compounds. This can be interpreted to

such an extent that the special category prisoners within the compounds are now regarded, by both prison staff and governors alike, as conforming to the established procedures as laid down for them.

A vast amount of the credit during this period of transition must go to the prisoners for liberating themselves from the prejudices, fears and illusions which became instilled in their minds from the advent of the troubles. This can also be attributed to the prisoners taking maximum advantage of the facilities available. In particular, such fields as education, sport and handicrafts have met with considerable success during this period. Varying from yoga to theology; from athletics to health and community studies; from football coaching to general subjects at 'o' and 'A' level and from boxing to degrees with the Open University. Not only do the L.S.P.'s partake of such studies to gain qualifications that would stand them in good stead for the future, but a great deal of time and skill is also spent in the making of handicraft items such as leathercraft, woodwork and design-painting on glass. The application of such skills as handicrafts can be regarded not only as constructive, but also as a satisfactory means of employing one's time.

Having noted the background of the L.S.P.'s involvement in the present 'troubles', and made reference to the exemplary manner in which they have conducted themselves while incarcerated, the paper will now look to the main concern felt by the L.S.P.'s – that of release.

There is a general consensus of opinion amongst compound L.S.P.'s that they have become somewhat forgotten. This cause of anxiety is as a result of a lack of initiative by the N.I.O. for not pursuing steps towards granting, or even towards giving, an indication of release dates for L.S.P.'s.

We have often heard mention of the suggestion that one must meet what is termed 'the criteria' for release. What, we ask, does this criteria entail? Does it mean: (A) serving a period of time to suit the offence and: (B) does it concern the risk of re-offending? If this be the case, surely then compound L.S.P.'s meet with such criteria. As stated earlier in the paper and in answer to both demands, the average period of time served by L.S.P.'s is from 8–10 years and during this period they have come to recognise that peaceful co-existence achieves more than violent confrontation.

This paper also wishes to point out that contrary to media reports L.S.P.'s are also human beings and recognize the suffering caused as a result of their actions. Although the L.S.P.'s cannot hope to erase all the suffering which resulted from their actions, they do hope that some form of compassion can be shown to alleviate the burden of suffering which their sentences have thrust unwittingly upon their families. Compassion as portrayed in this context is the need to end this 'state of limbo' that the families of L.S.P.'s have to endure.

The aims of this paper were to give the reader an insight into how L.S.P.'s have managed to cope in an environment that exacts everything but compassion and understanding. The implications of a life sentence are not entirely clear to the general public and since it does not affect them their concern is minimal. However, what they fail to perceive is the suffering and hardship which such a sentence (with no release date) inflicts upon the families of those prisoners concerned. In conclusion the paper would like to stress that because of, and due to, indefinite sentences, there is a serious risk to the stability of the most fundamental unit in our society i.e. the family. What this paper seeks is a positive response from the N.I.O. that they will give their

> attention and concern to the families of L.S.P.'s so that they might look forward, with some certainty, to the day when they will be re-united with their loved ones.

I didn't take part in any of the review bodies in the prison, but I was beginning to understand the human rights of the families on the outside.

Boyle responded and encouraged me to keep up my correspondence and written protests [see copy of letter in Appendix]. Communicating with Kevin Boyle was important. We may have come from different sides of the sectarian divide, and experienced the early Troubles in very different ways, but I knew there was no point in existing in an echo chamber. Prison, with its access to education, had ironically broadened my horizons. The physical horizon may have been one-dimensional and bleak, but I was beginning to embrace the medium of conversations and dialogue as the best possible means of changing the way things were, both in prison and in Northern Ireland as a whole. While I hadn't become a peacenik, I was certainly coming to the conclusion that peaceful methods were probably more beneficial than solving differences with a gun or a bomb.

***

In early 1974 Gusty had been behind the formation of a 'Camp Council' in Long Kesh. It was a way of ensuring that we had a 'no conflict' policy when prisoners from opposing factions found themselves in neutral areas, such as the minibus to take us to the visiting area or prison hospital. Gusty was engaged, through the council, with PIRA leaders like Billy McKee and Frank Card (Proinsias Mac Airt) and UDA guys such as Ned McCreery and Jimmy Craig. The Official IRA and the INLA also had their C.O. representatives. It brought enemies together to talk over issues

of common concern in Long Kesh. After the PIRA prisoners set fire to Long Kesh in October 1974, the authorities rebuilt the phases in such a way that there was less chance for direct contact between us and the Provos. Subsequently, the council fizzled out.

On 1 March 1976, Merlyn Rees, the Labour politician and Secretary of State for Northern Ireland, had announced that there would be a phasing out of special category status for paramilitary prisoners. This decision was based on recommendations made by the Gardiner Committee in its publication entitled 'Report of a Committee to consider, in the context of civil liberties and human rights, measures to deal with terrorism in Northern Ireland'. This was due to come into effect on 31 March. This meant that any UVF/RHC volunteer (or IRA, INLA or UDA volunteer) who was convicted after that date would have to go to the new Maze H-Blocks, be treated as a common criminal and be forced to wear a prison uniform. In terms of the republican side of things, this criminalisation brought focus toward blanket and hunger strikes in the H-Blocks in the late 1970s and early 1980s. Loyalists who were housed in the H-Blocks also protested against criminalisation and engaged in a clean blanket protest, but it didn't endure to the same extent that the republican hunger strike did. Several prominent republicans, most famously Bobby Sands, carried their strike through to their deaths, and Sinn Féin and the whole republican movement subsequently received a huge boost in its support within the nationalist community. Meanwhile Sinn Féin, on the back of the election of Bobby Sands to Westminster, had devised the 'Armalite and ballot box' strategy – a twin-track of violence and politics.

The population of the compounds subsequently declined as a result of less prisoners coming in and short-termers being released. Most of the guys left in the compounds were life sentence or indeterminately sentenced prisoners. As the numbers shrank, the Provo prisoners started to come back into the same phase of the

compounds that we were in. The unspoken principles of the Camp Council, with its non-aggression pact, were soon resurrected to ensure that there was no conflict between Provos and UVF/RHC prisoners.

On one occasion I refused to be strip-searched on the way through visits and ordered all of my men to do the same. This really angered the authorities and I was put on the boards, again. The screws gave me a hard time over this and kept needling at me. I told the Provos that we were planning a big protest in the compounds against these strip-searches and asked would they support us. The blunt answer was 'No'. When I asked for elaboration, I was told that if the Provos encountered any issues with prison officers, then the army (IRA) on the outside would deal with it. I understood their position, and it was obviously based on an order that had been given by the PIRA Army Council, which many people believe also had a role in choreographing the hunger strikes.

There always seemed to be a lot of interest in what was going on in Long Kesh and the H-Blocks, and I think that the focus brought on the prison system by the hunger strikes made people even more keen to understand what was happening. Consequently, we became accustomed to a regular stream of visits from different political delegations and government representatives. As C.O., I had a problem with this and approached the governor. I told him, 'Look, either people come in here and talk to us in a constructive way, or they don't get in at all. We're not animals in a zoo for the great and good to gaze at.' Structure had to be brought to the whole system. I would welcome people coming in with specific questions, but I was fed up with faceless bureaucrats coming in to get a frisson when they saw what life was like behind bars, and I was certainly fed up with people like Cecil Walker coming in and banging his drum to try and play the big man in front of British government ministers.

After this, visits became a bit more focused and guys from Whitehall would often arrive with specific questions that were obviously designed to gain intel for policy formulation. On one occasion in the late 1980s, an Australian diplomat arrived, and as was custom I gave him a presentation on life in the compounds under my command. I also had statistics on recidivism and other pertinent issues for UVF/RHC prisoners who would eventually be released back into society. He was clearly impressed, and he asked me what I thought was happening on the outside – was this all going to end soon? I told him that the UVF/RHC prisoners would certainly be advocating that and drawing up strategies for how to bring the conflict to an end. He then went and met with Pat Thompson, the Provo commander in Long Kesh. Before he left, he told me that he was having dinner with Whitehall officials that evening and did I mind if he raised some of the issues I had outlined? I told him that I didn't, as long as he put everything in context.

The next day Pat Thompson approached me at the wire and asked what I thought about what the diplomat had said. I suggested we build on the momentum and that an approach should be made to some trusted church leaders, who would act as linkmen to the organisations and stakeholders on the outside. I made contact with a Church of Ireland minister, Will Murphy, and Pat did the same with a Catholic priest, Fr John Murphy, who had been close to the hunger strikers before they had died. These were people we trusted implicitly. The PIRA on the outside had been talking to Redemptorists from Clonard Monastery in West Belfast. Jim McDonald had also been talking, on a very informal basis, to these Redemptorist priests, and he was feeding back information to the UVF leadership. There were no negotiations, but Jim was able to give the Redemptorists a flavour of the UVF's thinking. That meant that the Redemptorists were privy to a

parallel process and could get a good idea of where the main paramilitary groups were heading.

As the 1980s progressed the numbers of UVF/RHC prisoners of war in the compounds began to dwindle dramatically. Many guys had been released, and there was only a small number of us by the late 1980s, all housed in Compound 21. The compound system was beginning to cost too much – for the government in terms of money and the prison in terms of manpower. The writing was on the wall: we knew that we would be moving over to the Maze cellular prison, better known as the H-Blocks. As C.O. for the UVF/RHC prisoners, I had to make clear to the prison authorities the terms on which we would make such a move from the compound system. We were political prisoners with special category status. I had to make sure that the governor always understood this so that we couldn't be weakened in any way. On one occasion, in the summer of 1987, I discovered that we had temporarily lost our special category status if we were transferred to the prison hospital as patients. It was protocol that any special category prisoner who was hospitalised was kept on a communal ward that was segregated from other prisoners. Importantly it meant that we also retained privileges such as a television in the ward and one food parcel a week. I petitioned the governor and safeguarded our rights as political prisoners. If the authorities felt that they could take away our rights when we were in the prison hospital, then where might it end? Any attempt to change our special category status when we moved to the H-Blocks, for example, would be resisted firmly. I outlined this in dialogue with both the prison governor and senior UVF/RHC personnel in the H-Blocks. I was told that this was one of the key reasons why I was chosen to be the C.O.; I could negotiate with those in authority and didn't back down easily. I was a coherent and level-headed ambassador for the UVF/RHC POWs.

On 5 June 1988, the compounds finally closed and all the remaining UVF/RHC prisoners moved from the place we had called home for so many years to the Maze 'blocks'. We were located in H8, which meant there were now two full UVF/RHC blocks.

For many of us who had been incarcerated in the dark days of the 1970s, there finally appeared to be a light at the end of the tunnel.

CHAPTER 8

RELEASE AND REGENERATION

I was finally released in June 1990. I hadn't been institutionalised. No political prisoner should allow themselves to become institutionalised. Having said that, there were some things to adjust to. Since 1975 the only horizon I had had was the barbed wire and sky. I couldn't see anything else from the compounds. When I arrived back on the Shankill, everything seemed magnified. Black Mountain, where I had played as a child, looked vast, like it was sitting on top of the Shankill. It reminded me of the big jelly trifle version of the Hollywood Hills on the cover of the American rock band Little Feat's *The Last Record Album*. If that seemed strange, then nothing prepared me for seeing the Castle Court shopping development that was on the site of the old post office building on Royal Avenue in Belfast city centre. With all its metal and glass, it could have been mistaken for something from *Star Wars*. Walking through the city centre, I couldn't understand why people were walking toward me; for years I had been surrounded by people walking round the wire in the same direction so that we wouldn't bump into each other. Millfield, an old part of Belfast that runs along the bottom of the Shankill and Falls, had been completely gutted, and where there had once been old Belfast housing with half-doors that always seemed to be open, there was now just a big road connecting to the Westlink. It was impersonal and surreal.

Everything had changed so much since I had gone into jail a decade and a half previously. My perceptions were heightened as I became accustomed to this familiar but strange environment. When I went into Long Kesh, I had developed a coping mechanism to deal with incarceration; now that I had been released, I had to call on my mental strength to deal with the massive sensory changes that came with freedom.

Despite the redevelopment of the inner city that bordered the Shankill, and that lovely and familiar skyline, the area itself had changed dramatically since 1974. I had been back on the road on parole and for Christmas visits in the run-up to my release, but I hadn't had a chance to fully absorb the destruction that the planners had wrought on the place I loved and called home. There were large desolate spaces where buildings had been knocked down and hadn't been replaced. Derelict buildings and boarded up houses dotted the streets. It was depressing to see a once-great community decimated by the hand of developers. Some things were, thankfully, familiar. My mother had moved to Riga Street, another traditional little Belfast street tucked in off the main Shankill Road. Riga Street was just around the corner from our previous houses in Matchett Street and Jersey Street, so it felt like a real homecoming when I left prison and went to live with her. Many of the houses had been knocked down and rebuilt, but there was still a sense of place, a sense of home.

It was great to be back with my mother. I still felt a sense of guilt at what I had put her through, but she never asked the questions that I am sure had been playing on her mind for the previous sixteen years. If she had asked, I would have talked to her about it, but she never did.

We had plenty to catchup on, but I kept to a similar routine to that which I had become accustomed to in Long Kesh. I got up early in the morning and ran for five miles. Despite this, I was

constantly full of energy, and it wasn't long until I was straight back to trying to help my community. In 1990 I was able to use the education I had attained in Long Kesh to do this, rather than the old methods that I had used before I went to prison. I got a job with Farset, an organisation based on the Springfield Road that served as a base for social initiatives between interface communities, and I was based in the Shankill Activity Centre, which was being run by Gusty Spence and Ken Hagan on a voluntary basis. The activity centre provided jobs for prisoners returning to the Shankill who might otherwise have found it difficult to gain employment. I set to work on examining the possibilities for social and economic redevelopment in the Greater Shankill, with specific focus on the responsibilities of those who had ownership of derelict land in the area. I started to build up quite a number of contacts across Belfast. This was boosted by my work alongside a number of the Belfast Action Teams – groups of community workers who promoted and worked on the interests of their respective areas. It was great to get out and about, and to put into practice the education I now had; then, after meeting with various new people, I could head back to the centre and tie in with Gusty and Ken.

There was one occasion when I became quite friendly with one of the guys I had been working with. He was from a Catholic background, but we never talked about politics. I was guarded about my past and didn't want to shock him by telling him what I had been involved in. Nowadays you can just type someone's name into Google to bring up information about them; in those days, it was word of mouth. Someone told this fella about Billy Hutchinson, and from that day on he never looked so much as sideways at me again. The old defence mechanisms I had relied on in the past, when I had kept myself at a distance from people to keep things simple, were harder to sustain when I was out working with different people, but often – particularly when

things like that happened – I wished I could just fall back on them and protect myself and others.

Not long after I was released, I applied for a job as director of Springfield Inter-community Development Project. I was successful and was tasked with co-ordinating inter-communal activity, devising a programme that would implement a new community development strategy, and researching the problems of interface communities. This meant that I was working from the Shankill and Farset with people in Springmartin, Highfield, Whiterock and all along the Springfield Road. The project had been developed as a means of trying to create a neutral environment whereby we could harmonise relationships between the two communities while ensuring that investment was brought into some of the most deprived areas in West Belfast. I set up funding for a women's group to develop a dialogue around issues specific to the women in these communities, and in 1992 we were awarded funding to employ somebody from a republican area in West Belfast to act as a development worker on the nationalist side of the Springfield Road interface. Interviews for this post were held in the offices of Outward Bound, a cross-community programme, which included among its staff a young Catholic man by the name of Terry Enright* whose father I knew very well. Tommy Gorman was one of those whom we interviewed for the post. Tommy was a former PIRA prisoner, and he became famous in January 1972 for escaping, along with other IRA prisoners, from HMS *Maidstone*. The *Maidstone* was a prison ship that was moored in Belfast Lough.

Despite knowing of Tommy due to his escapades, I had never met him before – but I instantly liked him. He was an interesting guy, and when he got the job we worked really well together. He would run projects in republican areas, and

* Terry Enright was killed in January 1998 by the Loyalist Volunteer Force.

I would concentrate on the Shankill and its outlying estates. Then we would meet up on a regular basis to compare notes.

Throughout 1993 and 1994, republicans were having all sorts of meetings about the way forward, and on one occasion Tommy invited me along to one in Conway Mill. He was cynical about the leadership of Gerry Adams and thought that it might be entertaining to go along and make mischief. Adams was talking about how republicans would eventually become the majority community, and that it was through that demographic shift and the politics of Sinn Féin that Ireland would be reunited. Tommy stood up and challenged Adams, stating that if he had known at the outset of the Troubles that it was simply a case of outbreeding Prods, then he wouldn't have had to spend so much time in jail. He needled Adams and generally made it awkward for him.

I tried to keep a low profile, but Tommy's orations had obviously drawn attention to where we were sitting and on the way out of Conway Mill I got a hard time. Terence 'Cleeky' Clarke, a veteran Provo who had spent several spells in prison, was waiting along with another guy at the bottom of the stairs. As I came down with Tommy, they started giving off to me. I told them to fuck off and tried to walk on, but Tommy stopped me. 'Hold on, Billy.' He turned to Cleeky Clarke's mate: 'Did I fucking hear youse two right there? Billy is four times the man you are. Sure, you wore the uniform in prison. You broke. Billy didn't, he fucking ran the jail.' Looking back, I'm sure Tommy did all this for badness, but I liked him and enjoyed the time I spent working with him. Unfortunately, Tommy later had to leave Belfast and move to Donegal because the people he had disagreed with during the peace process started causing him a lot of stress, sending fire engines and food takeaways and all sorts to his door.

While I was fortunate enough to be able to use my education to get a job that interested me, and which meant that I could

put my learning into practice, many other loyalist and republican prisoners who were being released weren't able to get a break in the same way that Tommy and I had. A lot of political prisoners who had served long sentences were beginning to be released in the late 1980s and early 1990s and found that due to the Hurd Principles – a policy designed to ensure that funding was not made available to community organisations which were suspected of being 'fronts' for paramilitaries – they weren't able to get work within their communities, never mind in the traditional job market. This led, in 1990, to the setting up of the Progressive Release of Political Prisoners (PROPP). PROPP was a venture whose foundation was facilitated by Marty Rafferty, a Quaker and social worker who was employed in the Quaker Family Centre at the Maze. Loyalist and republican former prisoners were able to find common ground, and PROPP provided a positive forum for them to discuss issues of mutual concern and interest. These conversations were a natural extension of some of the dialogue that had taken place through the wire in Long Kesh in the 1970s and 1980s. Unfortunately, PROPP later fell by the wayside when republicans replaced guys like Tony Catney, who had developed a rapport with loyalists, with more ideologically rigid representatives who weren't prepared to deviate from the Sinn Féin party political message.

I was really enjoying my work with Springfield Inter-community Development Project, but I was increasingly being drawn to politics. If prison had given me the tools to work across the divide on issues such as deprivation and inequality, then it had also provided me with the skills to make coherent and convincing political arguments. Like Gusty Spence and David Ervine after their respective releases, I found myself being drawn toward the Progressive Unionist Party. The PUP had been formed in 1979 and it continued where previous UVF-linked political experiments such as the ULF and VPP had left off. The driving forces behind

the PUP's formation were Rev. John Stewart, Jim McDonald and David Overend. Rev. Stewart was a Methodist minister from the Woodvale area, while Jim had been involved in the welfare section of the UVF for several years. Like Jim, David Overend had a background in the NILP. In the March 1966 Westminster election, David had stood in North Belfast, canvassing heavily on the Shankill, and eventually won 42.6 per cent of the votes. It was almost enough to unseat the Unionist Party's Stratton Mills, but he fell short. The UVF had always had a strong pro-Union and socialist element, and in the past the Shankill had voted for independents who challenged the status quo.

After the UWC strike, a lot of UVF rank and file began to see the unionist politicians for what they were – empty vessels who whipped the loyalist working class into a frenzy when some paramilitary muscle was needed. In the five years since the strike, this analysis had gained momentum, and with the 'Ulsterisation' policy (encouraging recruitment to the local Ulster Defence Regiment and RUC; the introduction of Diplock courts) that had been championed by the Labour government's Secretary of State for Northern Ireland Roy Mason in his tenure between September 1976 and May 1979, support for the UVF had declined in loyalist areas. The UVF was all well and good when Ulster was under threat, but with some of the stuff, like the so-called 'Shankill Butchers' being arrested in 1977, people were horrified to discover what had been happening in their community. For those of us who were incarcerated in Long Kesh during this period, we had the space and time to develop political arguments and experiment with freely expressing ourselves. That's what Gusty had advocated as he realised that we needed to take the mantle of politics when we were eventually released. However, the picture on the outside was different, where the UVF was fighting a war. Now that their campaign had been made more difficult by Mason's security clampdown, the leadership of

the organisation, which had been isolated from contact with the government, required a stake in any future political negotiations.

The PUP provided that vehicle, and it meant that if there were issues with prison conditions or anything like that, the party could bring people in to meet the NIO or government representatives under those auspices.

However, the PUP was more than a party about prisoners. In Long Kesh we had discussed the possibility of loyalists sharing power with nationalists. Of course, the UWC had collapsed the power-sharing executive in 1974, but in our analysis, that was due to the Council of Ireland rather than a fear of democracy. We understood that one of the largest and one of the most rapidly growing demographics in Northern Ireland was the Catholic middle class. We knew that they would vote for the SDLP, who loyalists would be happy to talk to. In our discussions in the compounds, we figured out that if we wanted the Union to remain safe, then we would have to appeal to those middle-class Catholics. I don't mean in an electoral sense; it was never a vision of ours that we would suddenly be embraced by people who hated and feared the UVF, but we knew that if we politically advocated a vision of the Union and Northern Ireland's place in it as economically stable, then very few middle-class Catholics would want that status quo to change. After all, they were doing well if they had a house, two cars and a couple of foreign holidays a year.

Ideas that might have seemed like heresy in 1972 were being spoken of in serious tones by the late 1970s and early 1980s. We felt that it was a rational approach to politics; and that is what was needed after years of bloodshed Unfortunately, perhaps, our thinking was too far ahead of its time, as outside the confines of Long Kesh the loyalist community was faced with the reality of the ongoing Anglo-Irish Agreement crisis in the mid-1980s. Only a month before the Anglo-Irish Agreement

was signed in November 1985, the PUP had been forceful in promoting an equitable vision of a potential future Assembly for Northern Ireland, which included suggestions for a North–South committee to discuss areas of mutual concern rather than constitutional issues. In the document of proposals entitled *Sharing Responsibility*, the party also recognised that there were 'two legitimate aspirations' relating to the constitutional issue in Northern Ireland. The PUP stated that in producing the proposals, it wanted people in Northern Ireland to realise that although these constitutional issues were important, political parties and society had, throughout the years of violence and inequality, ignored fundamental aspirations such as 'freedom from fear and violence [and] social deprivation in all areas'. The PUP further noted that in producing an updated version of proposals which had been published in various iterations under the title *Sharing Responsibility* since the party's formation, 'We have concentrated on the sharing of responsibility rather than the sharing of power ... The task of everyone in this region is to bring a halt to the violence and ensure that power politics is not allowed ever again to breed communal violence.'*

By the time I had been released from incarceration, the PUP had stood candidates in various elections and they were strong in ensuring that any inward investment into Northern Ireland didn't jeopardise or exploit the local workforce.

On 25 March 1991, the UUP, DUP, SDLP and Alliance agreed to arrangements for political talks in an attempt to find an alternative accommodation to the Anglo-Irish Agreement. The preliminary talks, which became known as the Brooke/Mayhew talks, commenced on 30 April (Peter Brooke and Patrick

---

* *Progressive Unionist Party, Sharing Responsibility* (Belfast: PUP, 1985); see also Tony Novosel, *Northern Ireland's Lost Opportunity: The Frustrated Promise of Political Loyalism* (London: Pluto Press, 2013), pp. 179–205.

Mayhew were Northern Ireland Secretaries of State who served under Conservative Prime Minister John Major). The loyalist paramilitary organisations – the UVF/RHC and UDA – had come together to form the Combined Loyalist Military Command (CLMC) with a parallel political entity, the Combined Loyalist Political Alliance (CLPA). The political alliance comprised the PUP and the Ulster Democratic Party (UDP). This meant that there could be multilateral agreement between the main loyalist paramilitary organisations on any potential ceasefire or political manoeuvres, rather than one organisation trying to pull everyone in a specific direction. The UVF had understood the need for both the CLMC and CLPA to ensure that they had a clear vision of what was occurring politically with the British government and the main parties in Northern Ireland. While the umbrellas of the CLMC and CLPA made for some uneasy alliances given the history of bad blood between the UVF and UDA, both sides understood that it was better to be united than divided when it came to negotiating with the British government and other stakeholders.

In the late 1980s and early 1990s the UVF had begun to identify and target known republicans and members of their families in a bid to put pressure on the PIRA and Sinn Féin. Despite this, the CLMC declared a ceasefire on 17 April 1991 to commence on 30 April in order to give the preliminary talks between Peter Brooke and the four main political parties a chance to progress. After a number of false starts, the talks commenced on 17 June – a whole two months after the initial ceasefire announcement. With no tangible developments in sight, the CLMC called off its ceasefire on 4 July, a day after Peter Brooke had announced the end of the initial stage of political talks. In declaring the end of its ceasefire, the CLMC stated that 'We have proven that we have a desire for peace, which can be seen as genuine, and have no vested interest in the continuation

of violence.' There were certainly seeds of hope for the future if political progress could be made, and an atmosphere conducive to a more long-term ceasefire was created. However, a number of challenges still lay ahead.

CHAPTER 9

Ceasefire, Negotiations and Challenges

On Saturday, 23 October 1993, while the people of the Shankill were busy shopping along the road, two PIRA bombers masquerading as fishmongers walked into Frizzell's fish shop near Berlin Street. As one of them placed a holdall on the counter, the bomb went off and exploded in the small shop, turning it to rubble. People rushed down to the site of the bomb to try and help those who had been injured or trapped under falling debris. As time went on, there was a horrible realisation that many people had died. When Trevor King arrived at the bomb site, he was incandescent. I said, 'Trevor, this is shocking. It takes us back to the early 1970s. I understand that people will want to retaliate, but you need to allow people to mourn before listening to the calls for retaliation.' I could tell that he was torn, as he said, 'To me this is so close to home. The innocent people murdered will be known personally by many volunteers. It is going to be difficult for me, but I cannot make a decision other than an emotional one.' I said, 'Trevor, but we're so close to a breakthrough with the negotiations.' Both myself and Trevor would have had the same gut instinct after atrocities on the Shankill in the early 1970s, so it felt a little strange for me to be standing there, outside Frizzell's, trying to ask him to think long and hard before responding. I knew it was an impossible position to be in, thinking about the options he had to juggle in his head. He finally stated, 'I'm not

A group picture from Long Kesh. Me (on the left), Martin Snodden (red hair, background) and Tom Winstone (foreground, black hair).

At a so-called peace-line in West Belfast before the 1994 loyalist ceasefire was announced. Image courtesy of Pacemaker Press.

On the campaign trail for the June 1998 Northern Ireland Assembly elections. The loyalist people needed a voice other than big-house unionism to represent them. The PUP provided that alternative. Image courtesy of Pacemaker Press.

Me and David had been friends since we were both on remand in late 1974. In politics we were the typical 'good-cop/bad-cop' partnership, and it worked. Image courtesy of Pacemaker Press.

Considering a question from the floor at the PUP annual conference in October 1998. We may have reached an Agreement in April 1998, but there were plenty of challenges ahead. Image courtesy of Pacemaker Press.

The 2001 loyalist protest at Holy Cross School was counter-productive and further served to demonise loyalism in the eyes of the world's media. I do think that some of the locals had genuine grievances which were manipulated by nefarious elements within loyalism. Image courtesy of Presseye.

On 27 June 2009 my role as interlocutor between the UVF/RHC and IICD came to a conclusion when the process of decommissioning was completed. My old friend Hughie Smyth and Brian Lacey (PUP chairman) are stood behind me. Dawn Purvis is beside me, while Winston Rea, on the left – a former senior figure in the RHC – holds a statement. Image courtesy of Pacemaker Press.

Talking to Eamonn Mallie on 27 June 2009 after I had attended a press conference in East Belfast to announce UVF/RHC decommissioning, which concluded my work with the IMC. Image courtesy of Presseye.

At the 2012 PUP annual conference. I was positive that the PUP could make a difference in the stagnant political landscape at the time. Issues with flags and parades were around the corner and would provide obstacles to the party's long-term growth. Image courtesy of Pacemaker Press.

At a protest against the limiting of the flying of the Union flag at Belfast City Hall, December 2012. A flag isn't the most important thing in the world, but when people are deprived of a stake in the socio-economic fabric of society, its removal becomes their focus. I saw the protest as a means of bringing people into the PUP and educating them. Image courtesy of Presseye.

Handing in a letter of protest to Chief Constable Matt Baggott after news broke that members of the PIRA who were 'on the run' had received letters of comfort informing them that they would not face prosecution for historic offences. In the meantime, loyalists had been rearrested and jailed after investigations by the Historical Enquiries Team (HET). Image courtesy of Pacemaker Press.

After topping the poll in the Belfast City Council elections of May 2014. It was a bittersweet victory, coming as it did only a matter of days after Hughie Smyth, the incumbent and one of my closest friends, had died. Image courtesy of Presseye.

At the launch of Conor's Corner in September 2015. A statue of the 'people's painter' William Conor was erected at the corner of Northumberland Street and the Shankill Road. I was proud to unveil it. The bronze statue was made by an Irish-based German sculptor called Holger Lönze.

fucking listening to you, Hutchie.' I could understand his feelings. He was a UVF commander, after all.

When Trevor had cooled down a bit, he came back to me and said, 'Look, there's no way I can hold this back. Something must be done. We need to do it quick and finish it.' I understood it was a difficult position to be in, but I was concerned that he was going to be influenced by his own people and others who would, at the same time, have been talking to members of civic society about a UVF ceasefire. Obviously, I was familiar with that thirst for vengeance that informed Trevor's decision, but I knew that those not involved, on the inside, would be calling for calm. I didn't think that reprisal would be valuable at this time because it was a kneejerk response informed by anger at the killing of innocent people. In responding like this, the UVF would be carrying out a revenge attack while the families and the people affected were still mourning, and the world's media was camped out on the Shankill awaiting something happening.

One of the bombers was killed and the other severely injured as the device went off in the crowded shop. The Provos cravenly stated that they were attempting to wipe out Johnny Adair and the UDA leadership, who supposedly met in rooms above Frizzell's, but the people of the Shankill saw that as a cynical attempt to limit the potential damage done to Sinn Féin's support outside Northern Ireland. Why, if they were trying to kill UDA leaders, did they do it in such a way that so many innocent Protestants would be killed or injured at a time when the offices used by the UDA were closed?

The UVF carried out several killings in the aftermath of the Shankill bomb, while the UDA was involved in the Rising Sun Bar shooting in Greysteel. Just as it had appeared that progress was being made, the latter part of 1993 looked as if it would lead to absolute oblivion.

Loyalist paramilitaries felt out in the cold by the end of 1993. The UVF felt that nobody was listening to them, while on the other hand Irish America was supporting Sinn Féin and trying to boost their profile internationally. Although the reaction to the Shankill bomb had been brutal, it was the way in which organisations like the UVF spoke. Violence was their language. I had been a purveyor of that language in the 1970s, but I knew that we had the potential to go down a different route. Actions like this by Provos, which seemed intent on drawing loyalists into conflict, only served to diminish our political message.

On 15 December, Prime Minister John Major and the Irish Taoiseach, Albert Reynolds, presented what would become known as the Downing Street Declaration. As they stood outside No. 10, the two men told the press that Northern Ireland could only be transferred into a united Ireland if it was the wish of a majority of the people. The declaration was, they hoped, a chance to 'foster agreement and reconciliation, leading to a new political framework founded on consent and encompassing arrangements within Northern Ireland, for the whole island, and between these islands'. The British government no longer had any 'selfish, strategic or economic interest in Northern Ireland'.

It was obvious that we were being presented with the option of solving the problems in our own country ourselves.

The Downing Street Declaration was a significant mark of progress in the series of talks that John Hume, the leader of the SDLP, had been having with Gerry Adams since 1988. Sinn Féin's reward for this engagement came when Gerry Adams was granted a visa to enter the United States. Adams had been meeting with Congressman Bruce Morrison, an old classmate of President Bill Clinton.

Despite our fears of isolation, the PUP and UVF had not been sitting idly on their hands. In early 1993 we were approached by an Irish trade unionist by the name of Chris Hudson. Chris was involved in the Peace Train, a movement set up in 1989 to protest the ongoing PIRA bombs and bomb scares on the

Belfast–Dublin railway service. He developed contact with the UVF leadership after attending a conference in Dublin, and from that point onward Chris was able to act as a conduit between the UVF and the Irish government. He was a straight-talker and got on particularly well with David Ervine. I think on a few occasions, particularly after the killings at Loughinisland, Chris felt like throwing the towel in. It would've been difficult to blame him, as it often seemed like he had a completely thankless task. Despite this, Chris persevered with the UVF leadership and was eventually able to bring Gusty Spence and Dick Spring, the Tánaiste under Taoiseach Albert Reynolds, together for discussions later in 1994. Although there was no direct contact with the British government, the Irish government was slightly more accommodating and Albert Reynolds met representatives of the UVF to lay out, from his perspective, what the Irish position was. Things were slowly falling into place in a manner conducive to a loyalist ceasefire.

The Protestant clergy played an important role in debating with the CLMC. The Rev. Roy Magee and Archbishop Robin Eames attended a series of meetings in the run-up to the ceasefires. I had learned by this stage the importance of civic society and the influence that members of the clergy, for example, had with the UK government. Although I was a devout atheist at that stage of my life, I still felt that these men were important voices who spoke on behalf of quite a few people in the Protestant community. They reflected attitudes and opinions that we needed to consider when deciding how to bring about the ceasefire. Importantly, it also demonstrated a reengagement by the Protestant church leaders, many of whom had disappeared from loyalist working-class communities during the early Troubles when people needed their counsel most. Robin Eames, in particular, was able to make contact with John Major on behalf of the CLMC and get assurances that we weren't walking into a trap.

However, despite expending so much energy on often tortuous negotiations and meetings, it sometimes seemed that the guns would never fall silent. The CLMC had originally planned to announce a ceasefire in July. They had wanted to pre-empt the IRA and not be seen to be on the back foot. The months leading up to the summer of 1994 were, however, some of the most difficult for loyalism since the peace process had begun. On 16 June Trevor King was shot down by the INLA as he stood on the Shankill Road. Two other guys, Davy Hamilton and Colin Craig, were also shot during the incident. Hamilton died almost a day later; Craig, who the UVF was investigating due to rumours that he was an informer, died at the scene. Trevor died a few weeks later, in hospital on 9 July, after fighting on a life-support machine.

Although some perceived these killings as a case of the INLA trying to settle old scores, there was something even more sinister at play, in my opinion. For example, almost a month after the INLA shot Hamilton, Craig and King, the IRA killed Ray Smallwoods. Ray had been a key figure in the UDA side of the CLMC and was regarded as one of the leading lights of the new political voices emerging in loyalism as part of the UDP. I felt that the IRA – perhaps even in cahoots with elements of the INLA – wanted to make sure that any planned loyalist ceasefire fell apart. This would allow Gerry Adams to be serenaded around the world as a peacemaker while loyalists shed blood in retaliation for the killing of prominent guys like Trevor King and Ray Smallwoods. We would have been pushed into the corner that so many people around the world wanted us to be condemned to. It would have suited the agenda of so many if we had imploded at this point.

The UVF leadership was trying to keep a lid on things, but the killing of a popular and long-serving volunteer like Trevor meant that it was inevitable somebody would look to exact revenge. In the early 1990s the UVF strategy had become more refined, with the organisation targeting known republicans and their families. However, in response to Trevor King's death, it seemed like it didn't matter who the UVF killed. On 18 June 1994, a UVF unit killed six innocent Catholic men in O'Toole's bar in Loughinisland, Co. Down. This sort of shooting wasn't UVF policy, and it made life extremely difficult for us in the PUP as we were trying to carve a political path for loyalism.

By October 1994 things had fallen into place for the CLMC to the extent that they were confident in declaring a ceasefire. The PUP and UDP were encouraged by the informal dialogue we had with the Irish government and representatives of Irish America and knew that we wouldn't be left out on a limb if we went public. On Thursday, 13 October 1994, the CLMC announced its intention to call a ceasefire from midnight that evening. I stood at the back of the room in Fernhill House as my mentor, Gusty Spence, read an immeasurably genuine statement in which he directly addressed the grieving families of those innocent people who had been killed by the UVF during its armed campaign: 'In all sincerity, we offer to the loved ones of all innocent victims over the past twenty years abject and true remorse. No words of ours will compensate for the intolerable suffering they have undergone during the conflict.' A shiver ran down my spine when I heard those words from Gusty. The CLMC had gone further than the PIRA by directly addressing innocent victims of loyalist violence. It was a key part of the statement, which was genuine and described how all of us felt. Gusty also paid tribute to those in the UVF/RHC and their families who had sacrificed so much since those dark days of the late 1960s when he stated:

> In the genuine hope that this peace will be permanent, we take the opportunity to pay homage to all our Fighters, Commandos and Volunteers who paid the supreme sacrifice. They did not die in vain. The Union is safe.

> To our physically and mentally wounded who have served Ulster so unselfishly, we wish a speedy recovery, and to the relatives of these men and women, we pledge our continued moral and practical support.
>
> To our prisoners who have undergone so much deprivation and degradation with great courage and forbearance, we solemnly promise to leave no stone unturned to secure their freedom.
>
> To our serving officers, NCOs and personnel, we extend our eternal gratitude for their obedience of orders, for their ingenuity, resilience and good humour in the most trying of circumstances, and, we commend them for their courageous fortitude and unshakeable faith over the long years of armed confrontation.

Toward the end of the statement, Gusty spoke directly to what I was hoping to achieve with the PUP:

> Let us firmly resolve to respect our differing views of freedom, culture and aspiration and never again permit our political circumstances to degenerate into bloody warfare.
>
> We are on the threshold of a new and exciting beginning with our battles in future being political battles, fought on the side of honesty, decency and democracy against the negativity of mistrust, misunderstanding and malevolence, so that, together, we can bring forth a wholesome society in which our children, and their children, will know the meaning of true peace.

As Gusty finished speaking, I was feeling very emotional. When I talked to some of the journalists who had turned up, I had a tear in my eye. The first thing I thought of was the courage of the leadership of the UVF/RHC in terms of getting us to the ceasefire in conjunction with their partners in the CLMC. My thoughts turned back to the early days of the conflict, and its dark days and bloody nights when we thought that the Shankill would be decimated by the PIRA's campaign of sectarian violence. I thought about the sacrifices my mother had made during the long years of my incarceration as a political prisoner. I remembered all my friends who had been killed, whether they were civilians or fellow comrades in the UVF. Charlie Logan and Frenchie Marchant way back, and more recently, Trevor King, whose family was still coming to terms with his brutal murder. Then I thought of my young son, then aged ten. It felt like we had reached a bright new dawn, and I looked forward to him being able to enjoy a youth that I had never had.

The loyalist ceasefire had been called because people like me, who had been at the coal face of the conflict, knew that a solution could not be found down the barrel of a gun. The dreadful and stressful period of active service in the 1970s and my subsequent experience of political debate and education in jail had provided me with two potent tools: harsh experience and knowledge. I was determined to use these tools to create a better society for everybody who lived in Northern Ireland. It had only been a few months since the CLMC had declared its historic ceasefire, but there was a strong sense of positivity within the PUP – a sense that we could provide a genuine class-based alternative to the previous generations of big-house unionism.

In the days after the announcement of the ceasefire, I monitored the reaction to it. Overall, it seemed that people were relieved that the CLMC had called a halt to its campaign. Just as some loyalists on the Shankill had described the Provo ceasefire as a 'surrender', so too did some people misread the intentions behind our ceasefire. The PUP had been floating the idea of a ceasefire and its potential ramifications as far back as 1986, when we were developing a political model whereby all citizens of Northern

Ireland would be involved in sharing responsibility for a better future for the country. There had been the 1991 ceasefire, and the CLMC had also been the actual forerunner of the 1994 ceasefires until republicans began killing prominent loyalists throughout the summer.

Less than two weeks after the ceasefire was announced, Gusty, David Ervine and I, along with a few UDP representatives, travelled to the USA for a five-day visit, taking in New York, Washington and Boston, which allowed us to explain to people there what our position was. I had been in the States previously, to run in the New York marathon, but up until the eleventh hour it seemed that I wouldn't get a visa for this important trip. Thankfully, Bill Flynn, an Irish American businessman who was also president of the National Committee on American Foreign Policy, intervened during a trip to Northern Ireland shortly before we were due to fly out. In fact, Bill had turned up at the CLMC press conference in Fernhill House and was quickly diverted to another room. Unknown to him, he was being hidden out of the way so that he couldn't lay claim to any involvement in the ceasefire. He was behind the initial invite we received to go out to the USA. After Bill met with the US Consul General, Val Martinez, I was granted the required visa.

Bill's role working with the CLMC cannot be underestimated. He was part of a group of Irish Americans, which included Bruce Morrison, Niall O'Dowd and Chuck Feeney, who had visited Northern Ireland before, in September 1993. During that visit they were perceived by loyalists as being very close to the Sinn Féin leadership and sympathetic to their cause. Before they were due to fly back on that occasion, Jim McDonald arranged an early breakfast meeting in Duke's Hotel, near Queen's University, with them. Gusty, David and I, along with a couple of UVF leaders, were present and we told these Irish Americans that they would have to be impartial in the peace process. Loyalists were sick to their back teeth of hearing about fundraising events held in the USA for the 'cause' in Ireland. We felt that some of the Irish Americans had this glamorous notion of the PIRA's campaign that airbrushed out the human suffering. This meeting began a process of mutual understanding and demonstrated the power of dialogue. We had expected these guys to be very pro-Sinn Féin and dismissive of our position, but that wasn't the case. What they were really worried about was the rise of Islamic fundamentalism; this was seven years before the horrific events of 9/11. In turn, they couldn't believe what we were saying. They thought that all unionists and loyalists were intransigent, obstructive and unwilling to share power with nationalists. They soon learned that this was the antithesis of the PUP position.

When we arrived in the USA in late October 1994, we talked to a range of people across the country, and we were able to demonstrate that our position as loyalists in Northern Ireland was as legitimate as Gerry Adams and Sinn Féin believed their position to be. During a meeting with Bill Flynn and some colleagues in New York, Gusty and David were putting across their views in a back-and-forth dialogue. At one stage I interjected and stated what I thought needed said, and then I remained quiet for the rest of the meeting. I was of the belief that talking for the sake of talking was of no benefit, and it was better to choose words carefully and convey a concise message. As I took notes and set to work on the complimentary Coca-Cola and biscuits, some people at that meeting assumed that Gusty and David were the clever ones and I was just the military representative with nothing to say.

After the meeting, which had taken place in one of Flynn's portfolio of huge commercial properties, finished, we all walked out to the lift. The final three people waiting for the lift were me, Bill Flynn and his head of security. Bill said to his man, 'It's ok, me and Billy will take this other lift – you go on down.' I was wondering what was going on. When we entered the lift, Flynn started a conversation that struck me as being a bit strange. 'You're more than you let on to be,' he said. I replied, 'I don't let on to be anything. I'm very straightforward. You ask me a question and I'll tell you what I think. There's no back doors with me; what do you want to know?' Flynn replied, 'I was watching you in the room, and I was listening to everybody. David gives me the impression that he's leading the political stuff and Gusty is leading the UVF side of things; but I don't believe that.' 'What bit do you not believe?' I asked. 'None of it,' Flynn responded. 'You're the man that was sent here to keep an eye on them.' I told him I wasn't babysitting anybody, and that if they had come here by themselves, they would have said exactly the same things that they had said in the room a few minutes ago. As the door opened, Flynn said to me, 'There's more to you than meets the eye.' I liked Bill; like me, he didn't mince his words and got straight to the point. He couldn't work me out on that occasion, but I found his generosity and willingness to engage in dialogue to be important in our attempts to build legitimacy.

The picture back home was different. Only two months after the ceasefire, the British government was making grim noises which suggested that the PUP and UDP had served their purpose in delivering the loyalist ceasefires, and that our representation at round-table talks would be minimal if we were allocated any at all.

On 15 December 1994, members of the PUP and UDP were invited to Parliament Buildings Stormont to engage in exploratory dialogue with representatives of the Northern Ireland Office. Sinn Féin had already had similar meetings, and we were consequently dipping our toes in the water to see if any progress could be made in promoting our mandate as representatives of loyalism. It was expected that David might lead the PUP team, but Gusty insisted that I take charge and represent the delegation on this occasion. He knew very well what Bill Flynn had discovered. I was good at holding my nerve and had learned from an early stage in my life in the UVF that it was often more important to listen than talk.

In fact, the real reason that Gusty had asked for me to lead the delegation was very simple when he explained it to us. Gusty said, 'The reason for Hutchie leading is due to who the government appointed as the chair of their delegation of civil servants.' Gusty went on to point out that the chair and I had history from negotiations in the prison, and he pointed out that we came out on top on those occasions. Gusty claimed that, in his opinion, this would give our delegation an advantage.

The UDP team consisted of Gary McMichael – the son of the late UDA South Belfast commander John Michael – David Adams and Joe English (all of whom had been in the USA with us), and Tommy Kirkham and John White. The PUP delegation was me, David Ervine, Jackie Mahood, Lindsay Robb and Plum Smith. I didn't know much about Lindsay Robb other than someone had told me that he was a journalist from Lurgan who had a good reputation down there as a loyalist. It seemed a bit odd that he had risen to this stage so quickly, but I was driven in my desire to make progress, and so long as I had David, Jackie and Plum alongside me, I felt confident that we could articulate a range of issues. Little did I know it then, but Robb, who turned out to be a printer rather than a journalist, was more than likely a plant who had been choreographed into place by people in Mid-Ulster who were sceptical of the ceasefire and wanted an inside track into what the PUP would be talking about.

It was strange being at Parliament Buildings. For so long, it had lain empty and was a haunting physical reminder of the genesis of a lot of the problems and injustices that had led to so many years of violence. It was the site of several huge loyalist rallies in the 1970s and 1980s, but now we, the former paramilitaries, were here to put across the loyalist point of view to those who operated the machinery of government.

On arrival at Parliament Buildings, we were greeted by another civil servant who I knew from meetings I had with him in Long Kesh. He welcomed us and commented to me that it had been a while since we last talked. He then said, 'Mr Hutchinson, just to let you know, we have changed the way the chairs were originally laid out. We thought it would be more comfortable for everyone if we didn't put you up against your old adversary.' I hadn't read as much into the situation as they had and replied, 'I am sure it will make no difference whatsoever.' It was interesting that they had been thinking so deeply about our reaction to the meeting and the psychological implications of it all.

During the meeting it was made clear to us at the outset that this was regarded as merely exploratory dialogue and should not be mistaken for negotiations. For my part, I told the members of the NIO that I was honoured to be present, reiterating that the PUP had a role to play because the government could not afford to marginalise any section of the community at this delicate juncture. I stated that we had done some of the hard work by talking with the UVF/RHC to ensure a ceasefire, and that it was now up to the government to assist us in ensuring that it remained stable. I then laid out the PUP's position, stating that any future alterations to the constitutional position of Northern Ireland would need the consent of loyalists; that responsibility would need to be shared in any potential devolved administration; that the release of political prisoners should be included as part of a settlement; that there should be a full debate on the future of policing; and that there should be a strategy for decommissioning paramilitary weapons, and economic regeneration. From our perspective, these were the key factors in moving things along in future.

After a short break in proceedings, Gary McMichael became quite animated. He was frustrated at what he perceived to be the government's constant implications that the UDP and PUP were 'one issue' parties with a small mandate, and that our involvement in any future process would be limited compared to that of Sinn Féin's. Gary told the officials that the UDP had a 'latent mandate' within the loyalist community and should not have any restrictions placed upon the parameters of its involvement in attempting to find a peaceful solution. I agreed with him, and David Ervine concurred. David noted that the government seemed to be posing a veiled threat that once the usefulness of the PUP and UDP had been exhausted, we would be cast aside. David reminded the officials that the CLMC had influenced the loyalist paramilitary rank and file into supporting the Downing Street Declaration through exhaustive dialogue with members across the country. To many loyalists it had appeared to be a backdoor deal between Sinn Féin and the British government, but the CLMC had tempered fears and edged the UVF/RHC and UDA toward the October ceasefire.

This idea that we had no mandate had been playing on my mind for some time before 15 December. I had rolled it over in my head as a possible challenge that the government and media would throw at our feet. Shortly before the Stormont meeting, I had a conversation with Billy Mitchell and told him of my concerns. Hughie Smyth was a Belfast City councillor, and had been lord mayor, but that was about the height of it. Billy was a deep thinker and had read widely. He was able to quote from a range of books but his paucity of words on this occasion summed up our raison d'etre extremely well. 'Just tell them that our mandate is the silence of the guns.' It was a soundbite that encapsulated why the PUP was central to any political negotiations and settlement.

When David, Plum, Jackie, Lindsay and I came out of the meeting and descended the front steps of Parliament Buildings, we were faced by the press. I was asked about the government's statement that the PUP did not have a sufficient mandate to be given a full role in future roundtable talks. 'That is something the government is saying,' I stated, 'but we are not certain. We feel that our mandate is the silence of the guns.' It wasn't meant as a threat. It was just a fact. The hard miles that the PUP and the UVF/RHC had put in since 1991 were to ensure that the gun would be taken out of society in Northern Ireland. To that end, we had succeeded, so our mandate was clear and could be built upon if we were given the opportunity. After all, Sinn Féin's mandate at that stage was much the same; together we had a collective responsibility to analyse and coax our respective paramilitary colleagues in a positive direction. Unfortunately, our detractors in the DUP decided to spin my line, stating that I had told the press that the PUP mandate was solely the silence of the UVF guns. It was a simplistic interpretation and a gross contradiction of what I had actually said and what was correctly reported in the newspapers – it was designed to make David and I look like a front for gangsters.

This exploratory dialogue continued into January 1995, when I optimistically referred to the loyalist ceasefire as our 'hunger strike moment'. The Provos had used the hunger strike of the early 1980s as a means of launching Sinn Féin as an electoral force. I felt that the ceasefire could be a platform on which to build a confident, forward-looking PUP that would attract the support of the loyalist working class and other unionists who were seeking a fresh way of doing politics. The difference was that when Bobby Sands was elected as an MP in April 1981, the Provos and Sinn Féin were in the midst of the hunger strike. They were able to seize the momentum created by events in the Maze. In early 1995, when I made this comparison, there was a possibility that we might not have another local election for eighteen months or so. In the meantime, anything could happen; the buzz that followed our ceasefire could become flat, and all the positivity we had generated could potentially fizzle out. By the time that the PUP was able to relaunch itself into the electoral process, people might have forgotten who David Ervine and Billy Hutchinson were, or what we and the PUP had done for peace.

During this period the British and Irish governments were in discussions that would result in the Framework Documents, published on 22 February 1995. The Framework Documents were established to assist negotiations between the parties in Northern Ireland. The feedback we were receiving from some people during the talks between the British and Irish governments apparently suggested we would find it positive. What did this really mean, however? I warned the PUP and the UVF/RHC that if we didn't have a direct input, then how would they know whether we would be pleased with the document or not. The second point I made was that I was hearing that others, such as Sinn Féin, were being told the same as us. If we had different objectives and desired outcomes for the Framework Documents, then how could it be workable if everyone, republican or loyalist, nationalist or unionist, was being told the same thing? I made the point that we needed to see what was in the document before even thinking it would be good for us. I had heard this language being used in the prison, and it was never good for us – it was only good if we had an input. There was no point in promoting something that had been agreed above our heads, particularly if we were being told we had no mandate.

We always had to be cautious. We couldn't go too far for those people we spoke on behalf of – the UVF and RHC, and also those who we hoped would vote for us in any future elections. Many of these people had suffered directly at the hands of the PIRA. At the same time, it was necessary for the PUP to promote the loyalist narrative to republicans and nationalists. We had to be visible as a political party with a political message, rather than just as a proxy for the UVF. In January 1995 I was invited to speak at Pilot's Row community centre in the heart of Londonderry's Bogside. I was there to talk on the subject of 'Unionist/Loyalist Perspectives on the Peace Process'. In my speech, I stated that as a result of debate and analysis that had taken place, the CLMC had issued a comprehensive statement that contained six principles which, in my opinion, were extremely pertinent to the advancement of an egalitarian and pluralist society:

1. There must be no diminution of Northern Ireland's position as an integral part of the United Kingdom, whose paramount responsibility is the morale and the physical well-being of all its citizens.
2. There must be no dilution of the democratic procedure through which the rights of self-determination of the people of Northern Ireland are guaranteed.
3. We defend the right of anyone, or group, to seek constitutional change by democratic, legitimate and peaceful means.
4. We recognise, and respect, the rights and aspirations of all who abide by the law, regardless of religious, cultural, national or political inclinations.
5. We are dedicated to a written Constitution and Bill of Rights for Northern Ireland wherein would be enshrined stringent safeguards for individuals, associations and minorities.
6. Structures should be devised whereby elected representatives, North and South, could work together, without interference in each other's internal affairs, for the economic betterment and fostering of good neighbourly relations between both parts of Ireland.

This was a common-sense way forward, and I told the audience that I was adamant that the war was over. No one community in Northern Ireland had a monopoly on deprivation, I said, 'Poverty was not peculiar only to the Creggan or the Bogside. In all working class areas poverty was endemic, as was the lack of opportunity and the scab-waged jobs. All of this wretchedness was carefully planned and executed because that is the way of the class system. Our politics were left to others.' I pointed out that the collapse of Stormont in 1972 had 'freed the working class loyalist who no longer felt obliged to keep quiet and remember his/her place'.

I hadn't entered the Bogside that day in the hope of converting people. I wanted to explain the loyalist experience from a personal perspective. I felt that on class issues in particular, there was a large degree of common ground. After I completed my speech, it became clear that the crowd had a very mixed reaction, not just to my presence on the platform but also to the very idea of my invitation by the organisers. There were people in attendance who didn't want to understand anything about Britishness. One man told me I couldn't be British, as I was born on the island of Ireland. I replied that I was actually born in Northern Ireland, which is part of the UK. I pointed out to him that the reality was that he was born in the UK; however, that being the case did not prevent him from saying that he was Irish. One other person told me that their family were vehemently anti-British and wouldn't allow the *Radio Times* into the household. Although it seemed like a very petty thing to boycott, I tried to understand his position – but to be quite honest, I didn't see how that position would work against the British in any way.

***

Throughout 1995 we kept pushing forward, and in early September the PUP accepted an invitation to have talks with the Irish government in Dublin. Obviously, this was a big step, but given the communications that the UVF had had with Dublin through Chris Hudson, we were confident, as a political party, that we could go there and put forward our position as loyalists.

At the beginning of February 1996, I spoke to some Irish newspapers who were sceptical about the stability of the IRA ceasefire. My analysis was that there was no appetite to go back to violence, and although Sinn Féin were frustrated by their perception of a lack of political progress, it was likely that the IRA would keep its powder dry. Unfortunately, I was proved horribly wrong. On Friday, 9 February 1996, the IRA issued a statement to RTÉ declaring that its ceasefire was to end at 6 p.m. that evening. Just over an hour later, a massive explosion occurred in the London Docklands and Canary Wharf. Two men were killed outright, and hundreds were injured, while hundreds of millions of pounds worth of damage was done to local prestige businesses.

I was in the Liverpool Club in Disraeli Street when the news filtered through on the television. There was an air of despondency that slowly gave rise to an atmosphere of anger and tension. Someone shouted, 'That's it fucking over then.' Deep down inside, I felt that it probably was over; that the UVF would undoubtedly break their ceasefire. I just kept quiet and left the club. A few minutes later, David Ervine rang me to arrange a meeting with the UVF Brigade Staff. When we met with the leadership, I was pleasantly surprised to discover that their attitude was more circumspect than I had anticipated. They weren't planning any military response and were keen to keep the loyalist ceasefire intact. They understood and appreciated that we had to be given the opportunity to try and make things work politically. Responding to this provocation could have led to a spiral of bloodshed. The UVF kept its counsel, and the leadership held back those volunteers who were itching for revenge. The IRA were also trying to provoke a response closer to home. A day after the bombing in London, the RUC arrived at my door and told me they were moving myself and my family for our safety. 'Why?' I asked. 'There's been a credible threat made to your life by the Provos, Mr Hutchinson.'

Through gritted teeth I tried to play this latest threat down so as not to exacerbate any anger within the ranks of the UVF. The UVF leadership were clear that the onus was on the Irish and British governments. They communicated to the Irish that they had to give an assurance that the Provos could not use the Republic of Ireland as a refuge. In turn, the UVF was clear that the British also had to impose strict sanctions on Sinn Féin. Word was sent to the UVF from John Bruton, the Taoiseach, and John Major, the British Prime Minister, that there was agreement on this but that it was imperative that the UVF leadership held the line. There was multilateral condemnation of the bombing by the British, Irish and American governments, but Gerry Adams and Sinn Féin showed little remorse and, as usual, blamed everyone else. This time it was the fault of John Major and the British government as well as the leaders of unionism for refusing to 'enter into dialogue and substantive negotiations'. The process was heading toward negotiations, so the perception was that the IRA was just flexing its muscle. I had been threatened before, so I had to treat this like the proverbial water off a duck's back and get on with working toward the bigger picture.

Despite all the backchannel guarantees with the Irish and British governments, it was ultimately up to the Provos to prove that they could commit to peaceful methods. We were all hostages to fortune, and there was an inevitable and tangible fear within the loyalist community that the IRA would now engage in a sustained campaign of violence. If they decided to go down this path, then it meant that people within my community would eventually suffer. In those circumstances, the loyalist ceasefire could not hold, despite what the UVF had said. The day after the Docklands bomb, I wrote up a statement that was published in the Dublin newspaper, *The Sunday Tribune*. I felt that it was important that the loyalist perspective was heard loud and clear in the Irish press. I reiterated the PUP's commitment to the democratic process and condemned the IRA's attack as demonstrative of an aversion to that very process. I stated that 'we must not permit them to remove hope'. I admitted, however, that a fresh, prolonged IRA campaign could be deleterious for the UVF's commitment to peace: 'Whilst it would be our hope that violent republicanism would remain isolated and exposed, the reality is that the loyalist ceasefire could conceivably become increasingly fragile, and then our task becomes extremely difficult.' I warned that if the IRA were to revert to their 1970s tactic of bombing the mainland in an attempt to force the British government to 'coerce' the unionist people, 'ignoring the principle of consent', there could be extreme danger for peace in Northern Ireland as well as the Republic of Ireland.

> Can republicanism not yet come to terms with the fact that we the unionist people in Northern Ireland are the British presence. Their attempts to present the conflict in terms of British colonialism, ignoring our presence, have failed in the past. Having called their ceasefire, acknowledging this fact, there is no logic to Friday's act.

I further called on all shades of constitutional nationalism, including Irish America, to 'focus on the malignancy within the republican movement, rather than using their threats to direct pressure onto the British government'. Neither the UVF nor the PUP would be dancing to the IRA's tune. It was either conference or conflict; the IRA couldn't have it both ways anymore.

The UVF didn't respond to the provocation of the Docklands bombing, and the PUP was able to continue on its course. There was no reward for the UVF leadership. They weren't being bought – they took the stance they did because they felt that it was the right thing to do. They could easily have been swayed by people's passions, but they stood firm. This was a huge relief for me, David, Hughie and others who were involved in trying to negotiate toward a peace settlement. The UVF leadership deserved massive credit for acting as a restraining influence on its personnel during what was an extremely unstable time. There were people who wanted to go back to war; the guys in the Eagle successfully curtailed that.

It wasn't just the Provos that were throwing obstacles in our path toward a peace settlement. Ian Paisley and the DUP were a persistent headache for pro-peace unionists and loyalists at this time. Paisley seemed to gloat in an 'I told you so' way after the Docklands bombing. His outdated brand of politics – the politics of fear – was becoming a thing of the past, and he had to cling on to any thread of negativity he could to keep the pot boiling. Of course, over the year and a half since the IRA had called its ceasefire, the DUP had done next to nothing to progress any opportunities for peace. After the bombing, Paisley criticised me and David, stating that we feared an election. The opposite was true, of course; in fact, we were determined to keep any positive momentum alive so that we could eventually stand for election when the circumstances were right. Paisley knew that while the IRA's terror campaign continued, he would always have something to shout about. He was afraid that if the violence stopped for good, then people would seek out parties to vote for who didn't just offer doom and gloom, two things that those who had voted for him had been fed on for years. The DUP certainly wasn't doing the hard graft that I was. I was negotiating with and advising the UVF leadership during a time of crisis, whereas Paisley was whipping up old fears as usual.

In the aftermath of the Docklands explosion, the CLMC released a statement that read:

> We see the overall picture in relation to our common enemy, the IRA, and an escalation into sectarian civil disorder will give them 'on a platter' the excuse to go back to violence in

this Province by portraying themselves as defenders of the Catholic people. This could have disastrous consequences.

***

The summer of 1996 was no less challenging a time than the first quarter of the year had been. Orange marches had become a huge issue. A year prior, in July 1995, Drumcree had been the site of major tensions when, for the first time in 188 years, the Orange Order was prevented from proceeding to Portadown on its way back from an annual church service at Drumcree. It seemed obvious that despite the positivity that had surrounded the 1994 ceasefires, the Provos were beginning to fight a cultural war with the setting up of 'concerned residents' groups which protested at Orange marches that had taken place for decades.

In 1995, tensions arose in Portadown when an Orange march was stopped from proceeding along the Garvaghy Road (in a Catholic area) toward its destination, Drumcree church. Violence broke out a year later, in July 1996, which spread to Belfast. On this occasion Sinn Féin had been quick to make political capital from it. Their language was filled with the rhetoric of fear – pogroms were mentioned. It all harked back to the summer of 1969. We couldn't let the politics of fear win. In the then-Protestant Torrens enclave between the Cliftonville and Oldpark roads, the few Catholics who lived there were complaining of intimidation while the Protestant residents were adamant that Provos from nearby Ardoyne were exacerbating the situation. My mind went back to August 1971 and May 1972 as I heard news that a large number of Ardoyne republicans had descended on Torrens to 'evacuate' the Catholic families. The Protestants were outnumbered, and women and children fearfully stayed in their houses. A local UVF unit took a car to an arms dump, returning with an AK-47. Fortunately, I arrived at just the same time, and before one of the UVF men could retrieve the Kalashnikov from the car boot, I reached him. I knew how he felt; I had been that young man twenty-four years previously. I had wanted to defend Torrens against republicans. I told him what the consequences would be if he opened fire on these people. For him, for the peace process. It worked, and the UVF backed off. If the ceasefire had broken in Torrens that night, there could have been bloodshed for days.

Tragically, blood would be spilled outside Belfast. In the form of the Drumcree crisis, Billy Wright and his rogue UVF unit in Portadown had found the perfect vehicle for boosting their own nefarious agenda. Wright had been involved in the Mid-Ulster UVF for a number of years and had been supportive of the 1994 ceasefire. Despite his initial positivity about what the UVF/RHC were trying to achieve, it started to become obvious that Wright was involved in drug-dealing, something that I felt no volunteer should be mixed up in. It was anathema to the principles that I and many others agreed to when we joined the UVF in the early 1970s.

Throughout the early summer of 1996, Wright's men went heavy on the attack against the PUP, and in a communique phoned in to a television station, claimed that the peace process was tied to a nationalist agenda aimed at weakening the link between Northern Ireland and the UK. Given the increasingly tenuous support for the process in some loyalist areas, particularly outside Belfast, the declarations coming from elements of the UVF in Portadown made life difficult for representatives like myself and David Ervine. Any UVF or UDA members who felt disillusioned by the very concept of the peace process could gravitate to Wright. There was also a growing frustration among volunteers that the IRA had reneged on its ceasefire after only sixteen months, when it bombed Canary Wharf earlier in the year and Warrington in early summer.

On 8 July a young Catholic taxi driver from Lurgan called Michael McGoldrick, who had just recently graduated from Queen's University Belfast, was shot dead by Billy Wright's UVF unit. This was a clear breach of the ceasefire and had obviously been carried out in contravention of what Brigade Staff was working to achieve through the PUP and the talks process. Wright's anonymous articles and propaganda against the PUP had morphed into bloody sectarian violence against a purely innocent Catholic.

This was an extremely delicate time for loyalism. The IRA was back bombing England while pressure groups had formed in protest at supposedly contentious Orange marches in areas such as Drumcree and the Lower Ormeau. The UVF, for its part, had lost its patience with Billy Wright. On 2 August 1996, the UVF Command Staff published the following press release:

> As a result of a Preliminary Investigation into a Portadown Unit attached to the Mid Ulster Brigade of the Ulster Volunteer Force, a decision has been taken by the Command Staff of the UVF to disband this Unit as from 2nd August 1996.
>
> There will be ongoing investigations by the Internal Affairs Section of the Ulster Volunteer Force into the activities if [*sic*] this particular Unit.
>
> Captain William Johnston.

The statement was read out for television cameras by a UVF man in a balaclava who was flanked by five heavily armed volunteers. During the talks at Stormont, we had been under pressure from the UUP to tackle the issue of decommissioning, and there was a feeling that this press conference by the UVF could cause the PUP embarrassment. I told the *Belfast Telegraph* that it didn't cause us any embarrassment: 'No, it's our job to keep the guns silent. Peaceful dialogue is the way forward.' I further stated that, in my opinion, the reason the UVF had staged the press conference with balaclavas and weapons was to 'show that there's no one unit bigger than the UVF, and the UVF was stamping its authority. They have given their word on the ceasefire which means no one unit will decide (about the truce), it will be decided by the UVF.'

Wright and a UDA leader named Alex Kerr were ordered to leave Northern Ireland under pain of death by the CLMC. Wright was resistant, and in early September he staged a rally in Portadown in defiance of Brigade Staff. He was joined by the DUP MP for Mid-Ulster, Rev. William McCrea, who defended his appearance by stating that he was supporting 'free speech', suggesting that 'Within unionism and loyalism, a person should be allowed to differ without the threat of having to leave your country, or being told you will be put in a coffin.' Billy Wright probably felt on top of the world after his stage show, but the reality was that he was only the leader of a fiefdom he had helped to form around his own ego. He had little to no support outside the confines of Portadown and a few tiny outlying areas. His oration to the people who had gathered to hear him was little more than an echo chamber for a cult leader whose UVF career had ended in ignominy.

Shortly afterwards, I told BBC television news that 'the support shown by ordinary people to Mr Wright doesn't matter one iota to the CLMC or to any of those organisations; what matters to them is that he doesn't have the support of people who have got the guns.'

In their statement of 2 August, UVF Brigade Staff had made it clear that there would be an internal investigation into Wright's rogue unit. There was plenty to investigate. I had, for a long time, been suspicious of Billy Wright and some of the people who he associated with. Lindsay Robb emerged as one of these nefarious individuals. In July 1995 Robb, who had been part of the PUP team involved in the exploratory dialogue with the NIO in late 1994 and early 1995, had been arrested in Scotland as part of an undercover police operation into UVF gun smuggling. He was held at Maryhill police station in Glasgow. After Robb was arrested, Plum Smith travelled to Scotland to visit him. Plum was the PUP's prison spokesperson, and it was his job to go over and get a feel for what had happened, as well as to check on Robb's welfare. When Plum returned to Belfast, he reported that things seemed strange and told us that Robb felt that he had been set up. I began to become really suspicious about what was going on when a PUP delegation subsequently spoke to Robb and asked him to elaborate on his fears. He was evasive and wouldn't commit to his original story. It seemed clear to me that somebody had got to him between Plum's visit and the second contact, and he was now treading more carefully. Who that somebody was is anybody's guess, but I am almost certain that Billy Wright was involved; even if he didn't have a face-to-face with Robb, Wright must have paid someone or applied pressure to a screw to have a word with him.

I had been in England when Robb was arrested, and when I arrived back in Belfast, Jim McDonald and I arranged to meet Billy Wright at Jim's home to try and work out what was going on from his perspective. Wright told us that shortly before Robb's arrest, while they were over in Scotland, he had met him in a café, and although he didn't directly state that Robb was involved in an arms deal, he was skirting around the issue enough for me to deduce that that's exactly what had been planned. 'Who told Lindsay Robb to get involved?' I asked Wright. He looked unsure, hesitating for a moment, 'He wanted to – he wanted to get involved in it himself. Nobody cajoled him into it.' I was astounded. Apparently, Billy Wright had left this meeting with Lindsay Robb by himself and just travelled back home on the ferry without once being stopped. All the while, a sting was in place to snare those involved in a UVF arms deal – the one Robb had allegedly involved himself in. Billy Wright, a prominent UVF figure who had spoken to the media on several occasions, was able to get from Scotland to Northern Ireland without being stopped or hassled by any authorities? At the same time, I was coming back from London, where I had been on political business with the PUP, and I was pulled in at the airport and questioned for fifteen to twenty minutes about what I had been doing.

Nothing was quite adding up for me. I probed Wright a bit more. 'Billy, why do you think you weren't stopped? The police obviously knew this arrest operation was going down. They were watching Lindsay Robb, so they must have seen you as well. You're a leading loyalist, and you weren't even stopped.' I could see that he was squirming, but he tried to retain his composure. The next thing he said left me gobsmacked. 'Well, now that you say it, Hutchie, I was sitting on the boat and this man and woman came and sat down beside me and we got talking.' I asked him what the conversation had been about. 'Ah, they were asking me where I'd been and what I was doing and all that sort of stuff.' I said to him, 'Did you not find that suspicious? That two strangers planted themselves down beside you and started asking you all these direct questions? There's a saying on the Shankill, Billy: "The peelers wouldn't even ask you that."' Wright continued to play dumb. 'Now that you mention it, Hutchie, they were maybe cops or something.' I told him that when I went over to the football, I was stopped and questioned at the airport nearly every time; when I had gone over to Dundee via Glasgow to do one of my exams after I had been released from Long Kesh, the police trailed me all the way to my boarding house and called me all the names under the sun, warning me to do my exam and get out of Scotland and never come back. They waited outside my exam room and then called me a 'UVF bastard' and 'murdering scum' as I reached the ferry terminal at Stranraer to go home. Yet Billy Wright was immune from all that hassle?

Wright could not answer the questions properly. He was all over the place, falling back on repetitive phrases in an unnatural tone to calm himself. Eventually I told him to just stop. He appeared shell-shocked. I looked across at him and asked, 'Have you ever read *The War of the Flea*?' I could tell he didn't know where this was going and he replied, 'No, why?' I told him, 'It's about guerrilla warfare and interrogation techniques. I'm sorry to tell you, Billy, but you're using the kind of language used in that book here. So, if you didn't read *The War of the Flea*, where did you get this language from?' He tried to brush it off, saying that it was just the way he talked. 'No, Billy, it sounds to me like somebody has briefed you. If you haven't been briefed, you're certainly working for somebody.'

At this point, Jim McDonald, who had been quiet during the meeting, stopped me. 'You have to be careful, Hutchie, you're making allegations here.' I told Jim that if Billy Wright felt that I was accusing him of something, then he should just come out and deny it. I asked Jim did he not find Billy's answers strange. He said that he hadn't until I mentioned it. 'It's not about the line of questioning, Jim, it's about the type of answers he has given us. To me his language sounds like that of somebody who has been working undercover. It's all very technical.' Wright stood up and told us that he wasn't stupid, reemphasising that he always talked like this. 'You're far from stupid, Billy,' I said. Throughout the whole conversation, Wright didn't sound like a guy who led a paramilitary organisation; he sounded like somebody who had been well trained by British intelligence services or Special Branch.

By this stage in my life, I had years of experience of cross-examining people to discover if they were telling the truth. Talking to Wright was like talking to a machine. He wasn't defending himself; he was placing scenarios in my way like he had pulled them from a textbook. He tried to remain cool, calm and collected, until eventually he lost his temper and stormed out of Jim's house before making his way back to Portadown.

As for Lindsay Robb, I began to feel that there must have been more to his involvement in the PUP than met the eye. Talk emerged that he was a plant whose task was to get information from our talks with the NIO and British government and feed it back to anti-peace process unionists such as the DUP. He and Jackie Mahood were both close to Billy Wright, and both eventually defected to the Loyalist Volunteer Force (LVF).

Despite the distractions that Wright and his cronies had caused, the PUP's primary concern was forging a political path forward. As summer turned to autumn, the PIRA would take their turn to try and create obstacles to progress. On 7 October, the Provos once again decided to flex its muscle and drove two car bombs into Thiepval Barracks, Lisburn, which was the British Army's headquarters in Northern Ireland. A soldier, Warrant Officer James Bradwell, died four days later from the injuries he had sustained in the explosion, while scores of other people, military and civilian, were injured. The second car bomb had been detonated in the military medical centre, where the injured from the first explosion had gone to receive treatment.

This was another callous provocation by the Provos, and was, I feel, designed to provoke a reaction from the UVF. On the day that the bombs exploded, the Conservative Party conference had commenced, but more significantly for the PUP and me, we had just gone into the Maze prison to consult with UVF/RHC volunteers about the ongoing political process and the UVF/RHC ceasefire. There had been hardliners itching to get back to the old ways after the Provo bombing of the London Docklands in February, and the same emotions reared their heads again after Thiepval was targeted. We were inside the Maze, a few miles away, when the bombs went off, and we felt the reverberation of the explosions. There was real anger, but that is a natural reaction in the heat of the moment; the UVF/RHC prisoners were supportive of what the PUP and the UVF was trying to achieve. Importantly, like they had in February, the UVF leadership stood firm. David and I had discussions with the guys on Brigade Staff and there was no resistance or counterargument to our desire for the guns to remain silent.

Later that day, I told the *Belfast Telegraph*, 'It is no coincidence the bombs went off when the PUP was consulting with UVF prisoners. But we will endeavour to do all in our power to make sure that loyalists run to our own agenda and not that of others.' It was important that while the Provos were causing carnage, we weren't cowed by their aggression. We had to keep winning hearts and minds through words. In late November a PUP delegation and Jackie Redpath, my friend and a veteran community activist, flew out to Boston for meetings with Irish America. I was among the delegation and was shown around the city by John Cullinane, a multi-millionaire who was a leading figure in the Irish Catholic movement over there. We knew that he was friendly with Gerry Adams, and that he had feted Sinn Féin, but he appeared to be genuinely impressed by the restraint shown by militant loyalism in the wake of the Docklands bombing. We attended the American Ireland Fund's black-tie dinner at the Copley Marriott. I felt vindicated by the hard graft we had put in to encourage the UVF not to react to IRA violence, but I was also proud of the progress the PUP had made as people who would not normally entertain the thought of speaking to a loyalist queued up to shake my hand and complimented me on the work I had been doing back in Northern Ireland. It felt great, and I was quietly reassured that Irish America didn't have a singular view of the conflict through the lens of Sinn Féin any longer. Our initial visit in late October and early November 1994 had obviously paid off, and the good impression we had made had endured. Having a good guy like Jackie with us this time only strengthened our credibility.

We had weathered the incredible storms that had come our way throughout 1996, but further obstacles lay ahead. On a personal level, my increasing public profile put me in the frontline and exposed me to danger. Up until 1994, I had been able to work anonymously. Now I was a prominent face in loyalist politics. In the middle of March 1997, loyalist gunmen broke into the home of a Catholic father-of-nine, John Slane, who lived off the Falls Road, and shot him dead. A few days later the INLA responded by warning representatives of 'fringe loyalist or unionist parties' to stay out of nationalist areas and to cease working on cross-community projects. I couldn't help but feel that the INLA's threat was directed at me. I certainly wasn't aware of any other loyalist involved in cross-community activity. They were basically saying that the blood of John Slane was on my hands. It was ridiculous, and I felt that it was a cynical attempt to use the murder of a Catholic man to excuse threats on my life. These guys were bloodthirsty sectarian throwbacks with unsettled scores that remained long after most other factions had laid down their arms and articulated their cause through dialogue.

Days later, I had my suspicions confirmed when I was leaving a meeting in North Belfast to drive down to the BBC in Belfast city centre for an appearance on Radio Ulster's *Talk Back*, a popular current affairs radio phone-in show that was presented by the late David Dunseith. Throughout the morning, the station was broadcasting a trailer for the show, which was due to start shortly after the midday news. They announced that I would be in the studio to take part in discussions and answer calls. Nothing peculiar in that: I was obliged to appear in the press and media quite a bit to talk about the PUP's position on the loyalist ceasefire and where they stood in political talks. As usual, my mobile phone had been on silent mode during the meeting, and I'd forgotten to turn that off when I got into my car. I was driving along the Shore Road into the city centre, and as I reached the technical college near Wellington Place, I noticed a couple of police cars. An officer in one car was trying to draw my attention by urging me to wind my window down. I was a bit alarmed and shouted across, 'What's wrong?'. The officer yelled back 'We've been trying to phone you for the past 20 minutes, Billy! Everybody's phoning you!' I pulled in and a couple of the officers took my car and drove it off in a different direction while I was ferried to the BBC in a police car. 'Why weren't you answering your phone? There's been a threat to your life. Where are you going?' 'The BBC,' I said. 'Exactly – that's where the attack is supposed to take place.' I discovered that it was the INLA, and it didn't surprise me. The INLA was a purely sectarian organisation that had no interest in the peace process, and they obviously viewed me as a big scalp.

I couldn't let this distract me from what my real purpose was, and that was to move things along politically. All of the PUP's hard work paid off when the results of the council elections came in on 22 May. Hughie Smyth retained his seat in Court, while David Ervine and I were elected to Pottinger and Oldpark, respectively. This was a huge victory for both me and the party. We had dug in during what was a tumultuous period for loyalism. With the collapse of the IRA ceasefire in February 1996, and the controversies surrounding Billy Wright and Drumcree that summer, we were afraid that with no election to contest, we could potentially be consigned to the dustbin of history. That would have placed the peace process in a very dangerous position. With the IRA off their ceasefire, the UVF/RHC would have been denied political analysis and a voice in the ongoing project toward a peaceful solution. When Sinn Féin did reengage after any IRA ceasefire, the Protestant working class would have been at a strong disadvantage if the PUP hadn't been in the democratic process fighting their corner. We all had a feeling that the council elections were going to be a good news story for us. David had stood in South Belfast for the Westminster general election in which Tony Blair became prime minister. Although Martin Smyth won the seat for the UUP, David's campaign was a relative success, as he won 5,687 votes and ended up in third place, pushing the SDLP's experienced Alasdair McDonnell all the way before McDonnell ended up winning the seat.

As we left Belfast City Hall in a motorcade after the council election count, we were jubilant, but I knew that there was still hard work to be done. When all the car horns had stopped beeping and the waving of the flags had stopped, we had to ensure that we did what we were there to do: represent the people who had voted us into Belfast City Council. Unionist voters in Belfast had put their faith in myself, David and Hughie. David and I were the new kids on the block, but winning those seats gave the PUP a big confidence boost that we sorely needed during a period of stasis when grassroots loyalists were unsure of what the PIRA's next move would be.

David and I had developed a strong rapport and understanding since our time on remand and throughout the years of political debate in Long Kesh. He was an East Belfast man who supported Glentoran, and I was a Shankill man who supported Linfield; he liked a drink, whereas I was teetotal. David was at ease with the hustle and bustle of socialising in the Raven or the Cosy, two small bars in the East; I preferred the solitude of long-distance running. He was good with the media and had a broad appeal, while I liked to do things in the background as much as possible and probably came across as a bit prickly to people who didn't know me. We became a veritable 'good cop, bad cop' partnership, or to put it in a more appropriate context, perhaps, he was the dove and I was the hawk – and that suited me just fine. During the peace process period, David was being interviewed on American news television and was asked how he got away with being so verbose given that he had emerged from a relatively conservative paramilitary organisation. His answer involved perhaps the biggest compliment he could ever pay me: 'Billy has this big rope which he keeps tied around my waist, and whenever I go over the pier, he pulls me back.' David was able to be all things to all people, while I was the link with the UVF and the decommissioning body. Brian Rowan, a local political correspondent, once described me as the 'authentic voice of loyalism', and in her autobiography, Mo Mowlam, the Secretary of State for Northern Ireland from 1997 until 1999, hit the nail on the head when she stated, 'Billy Hutchinson ... There's a lot of energy there ... I think he was more focused than David and, while less good in public, he was more influential within the loyalist camp.' We were opposites in so many ways, but the dynamic was perfect, and it worked extremely well for the PUP during the crucial period when we were feted as peacemakers.

***

On 18 July 1997, Sinn Féin released a statement urging the IRA to call a ceasefire. The very next day, in a neat piece of choreography, the IRA did just that. Although it was a move that had to be welcomed, there was no jumping for joy or jubilation. This was the IRA's second ceasefire in just under three years, and the previous one had only lasted eighteen months before Sinn Féin spat the dummy out when things weren't going their way. Sinn Féin knew that they and the Provisional movement were going to be left behind when all-party talks resumed in September if they hadn't called the ceasefire. Time was clearly running out and the newly elected prime minister, Tony Blair, wanted peace talks resolved by May 1998.

The IRA ceasefire also provided the UVF with the degree of confidence it needed to liaise with the Independent International Commission on Decommissioning (IICD). The UVF weren't going to be led by the IRA, but there was no way that the PUP could advocate for decommissioning if the Provos were still actively engaged in their violent campaign. The IICD had been established on 26 August 1997 and was agreed upon by both the British and Irish governments. The commission required points of contact with the various paramilitary organisations, and the UVF/RHC appointed me as their interlocutor in October 1997. The IICD was chaired by a formidable former general in the Canadian Armed Forces, John de Chastelain. General de Chastelain was supported by Brigadier Tauno Nieminen from the Finnish Army and Ambassador Donald Johnson; Johnson was replaced by Andrew Sens in 1999. Between 1997 and 2009, I was in regular contact with the IICD on behalf of the UVF/RHC.

One of the most disappointing aspects of this 1996–1997 period was the noticeable gravitation of Jackie Mahood toward the LVF, where he had become one of Billy Wright's close acolytes. He had been the Brigade Staff's liaison with Wright, and somewhere along the line Jackie had become enamoured with the cult that surrounded him. Jackie had been a good UVF man going right back to the early 1970s, and we had been through the compounds together. To see him side with a bunch of criminals masquerading as loyalists upset me greatly. Jackie became disillusioned with the direction that the PUP and the UVF was going in. This was fair enough, but the thing that really set him in the UVF's crosshairs was when it became apparent that he was trying to start a campaign of dirty tricks to discredit the Shankill leadership. In Ed Moloney's *Voices from the Grave*, my late colleague David Ervine addressed this in an interview with a Boston College researcher:

> He [Billy Wright] certainly achieved support within the UVF, [but] thankfully I don't think it was widespread, I think that there were a number of people who were probably nervous because the leadership of the UVF in their mind had gone down the wrong road [...] I think there was a risk of a major challenge, but they weren't clever enough for it. I think the attempt came with the murder of Michael McGoldrick when a weapon was taken from Belfast and offered to Billy Wright ... and I think that not only was it meant to suggest that it was the UVF [who killed McGoldrick] but that the weapon was a Belfast weapon. However, it seemed that they picked a weapon that had no forensics; had the weapon any forensics that were related to the Shankill it would have given the illusion that the degree of support that Wright had was larger than the case [...] One of the people who went Billy Wright's direction was quite highly placed in Belfast and you could argue was close to the leadership, and I would have to assume that was more of an ego [thing] ...
>
> Q. Jackie Mahood, I assume you're talking about?
>
> A. Yeah, absolutely. I wouldn't doubt it was him provided the weapon.*

According to what David said the agenda was then clear: if the weapon was traced back to the Shankill, then observers could say, 'Well, there you go, Wright has the support of the Shankill and the UVF isn't really on ceasefire.' It didn't work and was a pathetic attempt to destabilise the UVF and the PUP during a period in

* Ed Moloney, *Voices from the Grave: Two Men's War in Ireland* (London: Faber and Faber, 2010), pp. 457–8.

which both the organisation and the party were standing firm in the face of extreme provocation from the Provos.

Such transgressions aren't generally forgotten or forgiven in paramilitary circles, and on 27 November 1997, Jackie Mahood was shot and seriously injured while operating a radio in a popular taxi depot he owned on the Crumlin Road. It was only in the weeks before he was shot that Mahood had finally resigned from the PUP. A year and a half later, in March 1999, my old associate Frankie Curry was shot dead as he visited his mother in the Hammer area of the Shankill. Frankie, like Jackie, had supported Billy Wright and had gone in a different direction to those of us who were seeking a political alternative. I can't speak for Jackie, and we'll never know with Frankie, but I can imagine that if they were given the chance to reassess their decisions to go rogue, they might have done things differently. At that point in time, in the 1990s, they obviously felt that the direction the UVF/RHC was going in wasn't for them. I still respect them both for the men I knew in the 1970s, when they were prepared, like me, to defend Ulster against the IRA. In the 1990s they went down different paths, which they thought were right for them.

Unlike Jackie Mahood, Billy Wright didn't get a second chance to ponder his decisions. In early 1997 he was arrested and imprisoned for making threats and intending to pervert the course of justice. On 27 December 1997, news came out of the Maze prison that he had been shot dead while awaiting a visit with his girlfriend. It transpired that the INLA were responsible. It didn't surprise me. If Wright had been working for someone – and I am certain that he was – and had become expendable, then who better to get rid of him than members of another organisation that was riddled with touts and drug dealers. Tragically, Wright's demise led to the wheels of misery turning once again like clockwork in Northern Ireland. As the bells rang to celebrate the dawn of

1998, the UDA, conspiring with the LVF, sought bloody revenge; throughout January 1998, a number of innocent Catholics were murdered.

Any time I think of this episode and the dark forces that had obviously choreographed Billy Wright's life right up to his death – and the subsequent sectarian carnage that was wrought upon innocent people – I am reminded of David Ervine's famous quote that it was often a 'dirty, stinking, little war' in Northern Ireland.

CHAPTER 10

Agreement

The end of 1997 and the first few weeks of 1998 were an extremely depressing and dispiriting time. It appeared that elements of the UDA that were in cahoots with the LVF were intent on dragging things back to the bad old days. It was understandable that the public was concerned and frustrated, and on Friday, 30 January a rally was held at the front of Belfast City Hall to reiterate the ongoing desire for peace among the vast majority of people. It was organised by the Northern Ireland Committee of the Irish Congress of Trade Unions. This should have been an opportunity for all right-thinking people to come together and make their disgust at the recent killings clear.

Unfortunately, some republicans saw it as an opportunity to go on the offensive about loyalists and collusion. Official banners that read 'End All Killings' were handed out and held high; however, there were also a significant number that had messages such as 'End Unionist Killings Now' and 'British Army Loyalist Death Squads'. Some of these banners mentioned the PUP. Some of these were held by Sinn Féin members and republican community activists. I was absolutely furious. The PUP had tried to take part in the rally; after all, David Ervine and I had been among the most outspoken critics of those loyalists who had perpetrated the killings of the previous weeks. We had put our necks on the line. I was working on a cross-community basis under a very real and constant threat of death from republicans, yet here were republicans using the name of the party I was proud to represent to attack what they described as 'unionist death squads'. The same people would never have described the IRA as a 'republican death squad', even though Protestants knew that's exactly what they were. The PUP was passionately committed to the peace process, and David and I, and those who supported us, had spent long, often tortuous hours trying to win hearts and minds within our communities. When the IRA broke its ceasefire, we ensured that the UVF and RHC maintained theirs. Sinn Féin's rhetoric felt like a slap in the face. I spotted Gerry Adams walking by the front of City Hall with some of his men. I immediately confronted him. 'You should be ashamed of yourself. Those banners are designed to make a political point. This isn't about republicans or loyalists, it's about all the people who have suffered in society. Youse are dancing on the graves of every innocent Protestant who was killed by the IRA.' Adams was obviously shocked at being challenged like this; he probably wasn't used to it. He tried to make some sort of argument, but before he could finish his sentence I had stormed off. I was sick to my stomach.

This seemed to be the clear agenda now that the IRA was back on ceasefire – to make loyalists out to be the villains of the conflict, while republicans were just innocent bystanders who were targeted as part of some big conspiracy by the British government. I had friends in the Catholic community; I worked with Catholics on a regular basis. I understood the tangible fear they were living under, particularly in areas such as North and West Belfast, but I couldn't understand why these republican elements had to stain a peace rally with their political message. Why couldn't they have done this on the Falls Road, or in Ardoyne, before setting the banners aside and marching to the City Hall in common cause with their Protestant, unionist and loyalist neighbours?

***

As winter turned to spring, progress began to be made in the talks process. On the evening of Thursday, 9 April, there was a buzz around the PUP negotiating office at Castle Buildings. It was a mixture of excitement and hesitation. At some stage later in the night, Ian Paisley and his crowd appeared at Stormont. He had whipped his followers into a typical frenzy, and when he spoke to the press, he shouted and guldered about the supposedly treacherous goings-on between the parties. To Paisley and the DUP, the talks were another sell-out and a step on the road to the doomsday scenario of a united Ireland. It was a throwback to the worst rhetoric and scaremongering of the 1960s, 1970s and 1980s. I could feel that we were close to something, and we had to keep our nerve. During Paisley's oration to the television cameras, some members of the PUP began to barrack and shout down Paisley. Although I understood their strong feelings about Paisley and the deleterious effect that he had had on the loyalist working class throughout the Troubles, I felt that it wasn't the sort of behaviour we should be seen to be engaging in when we were on the verge of a breakthrough unlike any of those we had seen previously. I immediately went in and dragged them out of the press marquee. You should make your case and stand over it; don't shout other people down when they're speaking. They were just aping Paisley and relegating themselves to his level. As far as I was concerned, Paisley was taking the easy option as usual and throwing stones from the outside rather than coming into the process and putting his point across with dignity.

This was the kind of distraction I just didn't need. My brain was working overtime as I mulled over what was on the table. I was part of history in the making, but I wasn't entirely sure of everything that was being agreed upon. To put it plainly, I had reservations. I went for a walk around the outside of Castle Buildings with a senior UVF man. I needed to get things straight. It started to snow as we walked. Only on Tuesday, two days prior to this, the mood around the negotiating tables had been bleak; I had even told Henry McDonald (a respected local journalist) that people were talking about the possibility of going back to war. I spoke openly about the options being compromise or conflict. David Trimble, the leader of the UUP, had faxed Tony Blair to tell him that he was rejecting the deal. The UUP wasn't happy that Sinn Féin could serve in an executive government without the prerequisite of IRA decommissioning. There was talk of the deal being a Sinn Féin wish-list. Things then swung positively, with Blair making a personal intervention to reassure Trimble. At the eleventh hour, Blair, rather than Mo Mowlam, met with Trimble and tried to placate him by indicating that although the text of the agreement could not be changed this late in the day, he would pen a letter with personal reassurances about IRA decommissioning. Of course, we knew nothing of all of this until later.

Things were happening so quickly as things were that I had to stop to absorb what was occurring, and what the implications of any agreement would be. Like Trimble only a few days before, I had concerns about the issue of cross-border bodies. More specifically, I was concerned that if we harmonised with Dublin, we would be leaving the loyalist community prone to a fast-tracked united Ireland. I also had a concern about a discussion that Sinn Féin had put on the table. Gerry Kelly was adamant that prisoners be released after six months. Everybody in the PUP was concerned about this, not just me.

We had a clear mandate from the UVF/RHC prisoners, who were now being commanded by the veteran Shankill UVF volunteer Sam Austin. They had told us that this deal should be about the union with Great Britain and not about the release of prisoners. They didn't want to be used as pawns in negotiations. Indeed, earlier in 1998, when Mo Mowlam made her famous visit to the Maze to speak to the UDA and IRA prisoners, she asked myself and Plum Smith about the UVF/RHC prisoners. We told her plainly that while she could have access to them, there would be absolutely no negotiations with them. They weren't up for it, and they wanted to keep their communication channels purely focused on the UVF and PUP. After her visit to our prisoners, Mo confirmed what we had told her: that the UVF/RHC prisoners in the H-Blocks were singing off the same hymn sheet as the UVF and the PUP, and they had informed her that any agreement should be about safeguarding the Union, not about their early release.

Of course, many life sentence prisoners had been released under the radar through the Life Sentence Review Board's guidance. In December 1994 there were over three hundred former life sentence prisoners on the streets, and we had negotiated the release of 173 UVF/RHC prisoners since original discussions took place in 1988. But the PUP felt that releasing so many prisoners in the gaze of the public so soon after an agreement had been reached could sap people's confidence in what we were putting on the table. The PUP wasn't a party that was just about prisoners and guns. We wanted a better society for all the people of Northern Ireland. That meant taking into consideration how society, and victims in particular, felt about issues such as prisoners being released. It had to be done gradually and sensitively.

I also began to consider that we had been used by the UUP. Of course, I had always been aware that there was no way the UUP could ever have entered talks with Sinn Féin without the PUP or Gary McMichael or David Adams (of the UDP) providing them with the backup they needed from those with an ear to the ground within working-class loyalist communities. Something else about the UUP's attitude that evening concerned me. There was something incredibly insincere in the way they were behaving, and I just wasn't comfortable. There were a lot of Provos around the place, and although I couldn't put my finger on it, I felt that something ulterior was going on. Years later, my gut feeling would be proved correct.

Despite all of this, I returned from my walk-and-talk with the senior UVF man and re-entered the PUP's negotiating room adamant that I would show no dissent or rancour and go with the consensus. I had a cup of tea and talked to David Ervine and Plum Smith. Throughout this discussion I continued to work some of the doubts I felt out of my system. I began to feel that what we were doing was the right thing for both the Union and the loyalist people. I was never going to walk away at this point, but I did consider distancing myself. After I had cleared my head, I realised we had come too far. We couldn't allow this to go down the drain.

As we were due to go out and face the press, I pulled David aside: 'I know in my gut something has happened here tonight, but I can't say for certain what it is.' David just brushed this off as nerves and we went outside. Almost immediately, as the press scrum started, Eamonn Mallie came to the front and said, 'David Trimble has a letter to say that decommissioning is going to happen straight away. He and the Prime Minister have agreed it.' I had a clear message for Trimble and Blair – the letter wasn't worth the paper it was written on. I felt that we first had to decommission the mindsets of the people who had the guns, and that full decommissioning could only occur when it was right for the whole of society in Northern Ireland. For example, I had been the interlocutor for the UVF with the IICD for around five months, and I knew that the UVF (and indeed, the IRA) wasn't going to decommission its armoury based on a letter written by Blair to make it easier for Trimble to sell the agreement to those within the UUP ranks who were not on board. Decommissioning had to be done at a time that was right for all of the people in Northern Ireland; it couldn't just take place because Trimble didn't want Sinn Féin involved in an executive while the PIRA had its arsenal.

You can't negotiate an agreement and then, after it has been done and dusted and everyone has left the building, add something on to the end of it to please one person. Like a lot of the gestures made by Blair during his tenure as prime minister, it proved to be thin and empty. Decommissioning could not be a prerequisite for parties entering an executive. If it was, then we and Sinn Féin would be on the outside for a long time. This was all about Blair pushing things through so he could take the glory that came with it. He stated that he 'felt the hand of history' on his shoulder, but it was all hot air and empty rhetoric designed to make people feel special. Blair had little knowledge or understanding of the cultures from which the UVF or indeed the IRA had sprung. The military-minded men at the top of these organisations weren't just going to hand over weapons to ensure that David Trimble remained UUP leader. There were two processes ongoing at the time – the political and the paramilitary. Each had to be dealt with delicately. I felt that the best way to deal with Sinn Féin was to bring them so far into the political establishment that they had little to no wriggle room. The PUP would face up to its democratic responsibilities in the Stormont chamber. Sinn Féin could be challenged through political debate. That was the future.

Eventually Blair would decide that the PUP was too much hassle and we would be demonised as loyalism imploded after 1998.

CHAPTER 11

Post-Agreement Problems

Although we had put in the hard yards by reaching the agreement on Good Friday, it still wasn't a given that the PUP would automatically win seats in the new legislative assembly, or that there would even be an election. Elections were due to take place on Thursday, 25 June 1998, but before that could happen there was the not insignificant matter of a referendum to gauge the public's support for the agreement. People in both the Republic of Ireland and Northern Ireland were to be given the chance to vote 'Yes' or 'No' on 22 May. I wasn't the only person having reservations, and within both the so-called green and orange constituencies, people were wavering over some of the details of what had been agreed. Peace was there for the taking, but not at any price, it seemed. The euphoria that infected some people on Good Friday had begun to peter out and the chance to run a 'No' campaign breathed new life into Paisley's anti-agreement rhetoric. The UK Unionist Party, Bob McCartney's latest project, were aligned with the DUP on this, and there were several prominent Ulster Unionists who were digging their thumbs into Trimble as the pressure increased on his credibility as UUP leader.

In the end, 71.1 per cent of people voted 'Yes', and the elections to the Northern Ireland Assembly proceeded as planned. I put in a huge amount of hard graft in the weeks leading up to it; the PUP, myself included, realised that this was our best chance ever to have a say in the machinery of government in Northern Ireland. With society galvanised by the overall positive result in the referendum, I knew that the PUP stood a decent chance of making inroads in the assembly election. We decided to run twelve candidates, and we hoped to build on the success of the previous year's council elections and David's good performance at the Westminster count in South Belfast. Much to my delight, David and I were both elected in North and East Belfast, respectively. For those who had been advocating a progressive brand of loyalism, there was some disappointment when the UDP didn't get a single seat. All the effort put in by people like Gary McMichael had come to nothing. The UDA's leadership, perhaps naively, thought that because its membership was so much larger than the UVF's, it would simply transfer into electoral success. We were all guilty of naivety as we made our fledgling steps in politics; while the UDA may have had a huge number of members, the UVF had a significant network of grassroots support in loyalist areas from community workers and various community organisations such as those I had worked with in my day job. David Ervine's persona and charisma provided us with a broad appeal while Hughie Smyth and I, and even Gusty to an extent, had the ear of UVF men and UVF supporters on the ground. We were a genuinely fresh alternative to the stolid but stale politics of unionism's past. At that time, we also had the advantage of being regarded as the men who had been through the worst of the violence. Gary McMichael was well liked, and his father, John, had been a popular figure as a UDA commander before his death in 1987, but he didn't have the experience that we had. To put it bluntly, he wasn't a former combatant.

Northern Ireland finally had its first functioning government since the collapse of the Prior Assembly in 1986. Inevitably a huge number of those who had been elected were new to parliamentary politics. While I and others had some experience at local council level, we were now in the position of making decisions and passing legislation that would have a bearing on the lives of all the people of Northern Ireland, not just those in our small council areas. I suggested that newly appointed Members of the Legislative Assembly (MLAs) and staff should go on educational trips to institutions such as Westminster so that lessons could be learned about a functioning government and parliament. Unfortunately, there were many among the class of 1998 who felt that they knew best, and they weren't keen on taking advice from outside bodies. These people were arrogant, but they were also juvenile. I still remember when I made my maiden speech in the assembly during its first sitting on Monday, 14 September 1998; certain politicians, mainly from the DUP, kept talking over members when they were speaking and attempted to hector those they disagreed with, which was nearly everybody. It was clear that they wanted to make the assembly completely unworkable. I was on my feet, arguing that Sinn Féin had a legal right to be in the executive without IRA decommissioning: 'People should stop catcalling and let others speak. I did not catcall when other members were speaking. The public are watching, and they will recognise the childish behaviour of some members.'

Being in the Northern Ireland Assembly often brought me into close quarters with people I didn't agree with politically. More often than not, we tried to make things work, but it was within unionism that I found some of the most intransigent opponents of what we were trying to achieve. While the DUP was vocal about the fact that they didn't want Sinn Féin about the place, I was particularly critical of David Trimble's continuing insistence that an executive could not be formed until the IRA had decommissioned some of its weapons. He appeared to have forgotten how important the PUP and UDP had been to him when he was taking his first tentative steps as UUP leader in the early stages of the talks process. Ultimately, by publicly supporting him, the PUP and UDP provided Trimble with the political credibility he needed among those guys who had been at the front-end of the conflict. While the UVF and PIRA had been at loggerheads throughout the bloody years of the conflict, there was a large amount of dovetailing on socio-economic issues between the PUP and Sinn Féin that made our relationship work more flexibly than some people might have expected. I felt that decommissioning was something that could be addressed once we had a stable political framework.

The DUP seemed to hate us even more than Sinn Féin. They called us Mo Mowlam's pups in what was a crass attempt to make the loyalist people think that we were merely the Secretary of State's playthings. They were afraid that we were edging in on their vote. Paisley was yesterday's man during the early years of the assembly, but it didn't make him shy away from giving the PUP stick. One day I was getting into the lift and suddenly heard heavy footsteps hurrying along the corridor. 'Stop the lift, please!' The thundering tone and the Ballymena accent were unmistakable. I held the button to keep the doors open. As a breathless Paisley went to step into the lift, he looked up and realised that I was inside it. 'Go on!' he panted, 'I'll not be getting in a lift with a UVF murderer!' There was an awkward pause for a second before I responded: 'Well, it didn't worry you too much when you sent Tom McDowell to his death.'* As the doors to the lift slowly closed, Paisley's face dropped and for once he was speechless. Here was a man who had the led the loyalist people to heartache and death, and still, thirty years later, he hadn't changed his tune. He was a total hypocrite.

I think that one of the problems for Trimble and Paisley was that they regarded Mo Mowlam as being too close to the smaller

---

* Tom McDowell was a member of the UVF and the Ulster Protestant Volunteers. In October 1969 he died from injuries he had sustained when planting a bomb at a hydroelectric power station in Co. Donegal. Many people at the time believed his actions were inspired by Paisley's anti-republican rhetoric.

parties, as well as Sinn Féin. The PUP and the Women's Coalition had a good relationship. Often, Monica McWilliams, Pearl Sagar, Bronagh Hinds and David and I would have a catchup in the assembly canteen. Mo Mowlam was very down to earth, and she didn't see any problem in sitting with us and chatting. She obviously recognised the importance of minority voices in terms of making the political institutions work. Despite her bonhomie and frank attitude, or perhaps because of it, she rubbed David Trimble up the wrong way. Trimble could be quite stiff in his manner, but he was under immeasurable pressure from many UUP members who hadn't been totally sold on the agreement. Jeffrey Donaldson had famously walked out of the talks at the eleventh hour and would later defect to the DUP, as would Arlene Foster. Trimble had reassured his voters that he had a guarantee from Tony Blair that there would be legislative amendments to the way the assembly functioned if there was no movement on decommissioning within six months or so of the agreement. Of course, that famous piece of paper, which Eamonn Mallie had told us about as we had prepared to speak to the press on Good Friday, was completely worthless and a classic piece of Blair chicanery. So when Trimble perceived that Mo Mowlam was too cosy with Sinn Féin and the PUP, it must have pushed him over the edge when he walked into the canteen at Parliament Buildings or Castle Buildings and saw her having breakfast and a hearty laugh with people like myself, David and Hughie. Eventually Trimble must have made it clear that he could no longer tolerate Mo Mowlam, and in October 1999 she was replaced by Peter Mandelson. If Blair was prepared to remove Mo to keep Trimble happy, we were wondering what else he was capable of.

Trimble also took the PUP for granted; he needed us to help him through the peace process and into the assembly, but that didn't stop him referring to me as an 'uneducated man'. That breathtaking arrogance alienated a lot of people, and he proved to be an awkward and uneasy representative for unionism during what were historic times. Loyalists and unionists had become conditioned to being treated in this shoddy manner by politicians who only came out at election time to seek their votes. It's like a dog that is kicked by its owner and keeps coming back to get fed. Part of the problem was a class issue. The PUP and UDP might have been a fresh voice, but the unionist community have always seemed to resist voting for people who come with paramilitary baggage; this resistance has been fostered by middle-class unionists. There were accusations that I was uneducated; that I was a communist; that I was a socialist revolutionary. All these things were levelled at me. It didn't worry me. It was pure ignorance. It was just a ploy to make people think that they had to vote for doctors and lawyers, like they had always done. I wouldn't let the likes of Robert McCartney (a Queen's Counsel and the leader of the anti-agreement United Kingdom Unionist Party) put me down. He came from the Shankill as well, but there was a sense among the great and good that my degree was worthless because I achieved it after studying in prison. Trimble and McCartney must have thought that they were the only educated people around unionist and loyalist politics. Every time David and I stood up in the Stormont chamber and put forward our point of view, they got their regular reminder that they weren't.

At times I sympathised with David Trimble's intransigence over the issue of PIRA decommissioning. He had to sell the partnerships he had agreed upon to middle-class unionists who were vehemently opposed to the idea of Sinn Féin holding office, but the PUP analysis was that the alternative was even worse. We had to be forceful about what could happen in alternative circumstances; essentially, it was a form of disaster-planning. We felt that when power was devolved to the assembly, Sinn Féin should be allowed to form part of a power-sharing executive without PIRA decommissioning as a prerequisite. If the PIRA hadn't decommissioned by the originally agreed date of May 2000, then Sinn Féin could be excluded. Otherwise we were all engaged in a meaningless process of prevarication, and I felt that the two governments would become impatient and implement what would be an Anglo-Irish Agreement Mark Two. I slipped into 'bad cop' mode and had to deliver my interpretation of what the UVF's response to such an outcome could be. As Samuel Johnson once said, 'when a man knows he is to be hanged in a fortnight, it concentrates his mind wonderfully'. I told the press that if another Anglo-Irish deal was agreed above the heads of the local parties in Northern Ireland, then loyalists could mirror the tactics used by the IRA on the mainland in 1996 when Sinn Féin wasn't getting its way in the peace process. A betrayal of the Belfast Agreement would, I said:

> lead to a more sophisticated campaign by loyalists, who would attempt to cripple the Irish economy, attacking the tourism and agricultural sectors. It is very easy to attack bloodstock and it is very easy to attack tourists. I mean tourists can be got anywhere in any main street, in any city or rural area, in Dublin, and those things aren't hard to do. There would be a bigger threat from loyalism than there has been in the past.

Until the UUP relented on the issue of decommissioning, the assembly functioned only as a glorified talking shop with no powers. Trimble's intransigence was tantamount to tugging the tiger's tail, and I feared that not only would the republican tiger bite back but that the loyalist tiger could follow suit and devour the progress that had been made since 1994. This would be hugely frustrating for myself and David Ervine in particular.

Despite the headaches that always seemed to threaten the stability of the peace process, I was proud to be an MLA representing the people who had voted for me. Politics in Northern Ireland is, by its very nature wrung up in the constitutional question a lot of the time, but it was satisfying to be able to get things done for people. Unfortunately, as the year 2000 approached, I was about to be dragged into events on the street that most constitutional politicians would not have to contend with, and which would eventually tear the very fabric of the Shankill apart.

On 10 January 2000, Richard Jameson, the Mid-Ulster UVF commander, was shot dead outside his home by elements of the LVF. David Ervine summed up my feelings when he described the guys who killed Richard as a 'disparate group, masquerading as loyalists giving cloud cover to the nefarious trade in drug-dealing'.* Although Billy Wright had been dead for two years, his destructive legacy lived on among those who had followed him. Richard was a successful businessman and his death left a young family without a father. If the LVF wanted to wave a red flag at the UVF, then killing someone like Richard was the perfect way to do it. His murder surprised most people, but the killing of such a popular member of the UVF wasn't going to go unpunished by the organisation, and two teenagers who had been supporters of Wright were stabbed to death in Tandragee in an unsanctioned retaliatory attack.

All of this angered me; I was wondering what we were going to do. We couldn't revert to type. I thought long and hard about what had happened, and I remembered the time I had challenged Billy Wright about his agenda. Since the inception of Northern Ireland, there had always been certain individuals choreographing things to suit their own ends. This continued to be the case in

* Jim Cusack and Henry McDonald, *UVF: Endgame* (Dublin: Poolbeg, 2008), p. 385.

the recent conflict. Indeed, I believed, and I know David Ervine also believed, that the security services were pulling the strings of elements of the UVF on the Shore Road, and in Mount Vernon in particular. We both briefed journalists about our concerns, but they dismissed out of hand what we were saying. Later on, in 2007, David and I were vindicated to some degree when Dame Nuala O'Loan, the Police Ombudsman, published her 'Operation Ballast' report (full title: 'Operation Ballast: investigation into the circumstances surrounding the murder of Raymond McCord Jr').* It was demonstrated that elements within the RUC had been working with informers and encouraging them to join the UVF to get inside information on the organisation. My only surprise was that it was the RUC and not an organisation higher up the pecking order.

The obvious question would be why the organisation didn't notice what was going on under its nose. The thing about the guys who were being manipulated by the RUC was that they were clever and played their roles perfectly. By day they were doing positive work within the community by engaging young people and families and supporting charities, but by night they were carrying out murder with the knowledge of their police handlers.

Republicans talk about collusion in relation to the loyalist paramilitaries as if the UVF/RHC and UDA couldn't have done anything without the help of the security forces. There's a narrative that loyalist paramilitaries were wound up and pushed in the right direction by subversive agencies in the government who then cleared up after them. Let's take Mark Haddock as an example. Haddock was prominently mentioned in the 'Operation

* The Police Ombudsman for Northern Ireland released (2007) the findings of her three-and-a-half-year investigation into a series of complaints about police conduct in relation to the murder of Raymond McCord Junior in November 1997.

Ballast' report, but the reality behind the headline was that Mark Haddock was recruited by the RUC as an informer and was sent with instructions to join the UVF. Haddock successfully, and quickly, worked his way up the organisation, probably to the glee of his handlers. He was reported to have been the first to volunteer to do anything, so it's no surprise that he became popular in the UVF. Unlike most other volunteers who had joined the UVF for genuine reasons, Haddock was operating with impunity under the protection of certain people in the RUC. The RUC tactic was simple: get a lad when they're 16 or so, get them to join the UVF and get low-level information, and then hope that they climb the ladder and report back with more important high-level intelligence, all the while being paid for it.

There were certainly agendas at play in the background as we attempted to keep the PUP in the assembly. I continued to liaise with the IICD on the issue of UVF/RHC decommissioning, but the intermittent intra-loyalist killings made it an even more difficult task than it would have been before.

In May 2000, the UVF spotted the man who was alleged to have killed Richard Jameson in the Oldpark area. Although this guy escaped with his life, he was said to have gone to Tennent Street police station to give a statement; after that, Johnny Adair and some of his men in C Company of the UDA were alleged to have enabled his safe passage out of the area and back to Co. Tyrone, where he was from. In the eyes of the Shankill UVF, this was a provocation that was further exacerbated when, on 26 May, a guy I was friendly with, Martin Taylor, was killed by the LVF while working on a wall outside a house in the Silverstream area of North Belfast. Martin just happened to be in the wrong place at the wrong time, but there were suspicions that the UDA had assisted the LVF in his killing. People were now on the alert. The mood on the Shankill, which was already tense, threatened to boil over.

A few months passed. On Saturday, 19 August I was at Windsor Park watching Linfield grind out a disappointing draw with Omagh Town. Linfield had won the league by eighteen points the previous season and should have been beating a side like Omagh easily. Shortly after Glenn Ferguson had scored in the twenty-fifth minute to give the Blues the lead, I received a call on my mobile phone. All hell had broken loose on the Shankill, apparently. I raced out of the ground and sped back across the Westlink to the Shankill Road, where I was confronted with a scene of absolute carnage. Unlike previous occasions, when the IRA had struck at the heart of the Shankill, it was so-called loyalists who were responsible for what had occurred during the afternoon. Ever since his release from the Maze in September 1999, Johnny Adair had been driving up tensions within loyalism and resurrecting old alliances with anti-agreement loyalists. In the Shankill estate, where Adair lived, there was a new mural honouring Billy Wright.

On this particular Saturday, Adair and some of his cronies in C Company had staged a so-called 'day of culture' event in the Lower Shankill. Masked and armed UDA members, including Adair and his wife Gina, made speeches and fired shots into the sky from a rickety makeshift platform as the British Army watched from a strategically placed position on the top of the nearby Divis Flats. During a subsequent parade up the Shankill, later in the afternoon, an LVF flag was unfurled as the UDA walked past the Rex Bar. This was like a red rag to a bull, given the tensions that had existed since Billy Wright had gone rogue after the 1994 ceasefire. Beer glasses were thrown at the UDA members and their supporters, many of whom had come from hotbeds of anti-agreement sentiment in rural areas around Northern Ireland. Hand-to-hand fighting ensued before the UDA spirited weapons from the Lower Shankill and fired shots at the Rex and the people who had been forced to barricade themselves inside for safety.

These cheerleaders from the countryside had been giving me and others stick, but they quickly returned to their buses when things began to get hot and heavy. The locals were angry, and they realised that they were out of their depth.

I went to talk to the UVF, as well as the police. I told the police that the proverbial balloon had gone up and asked them why things had been allowed to develop the way they had throughout the afternoon. Surely, I asked them, there was enough intelligence to see this coming from a mile off.

That evening Adair and some of his C Company men decided to carry out a purge against UVF-linked families in the Lower Shankill and the Shankill estate. Gusty, who was fortunate to be in Groomsport at the time, had his house trashed by UDA hooligans. A bloody civil war threatened to erupt as brothers, UVF or UDA, fought each other and families were completely split apart. It didn't matter if a person was in the UVF or not; just being the father, mother, brother, sister, son or daughter of a UVF member was enough, in the eyes of C Company, to be condemned to a campaign of intimidation and violence. One guy who was in the UDA, and whose brothers were in the UVF, put his own mother out of the Shankill estate. The hatred ran deep and to the point of irrationality. The UDA raked the PUP office on the Shankill Road with gunfire, and in return the UDP office was blown up by the UVF.

An invisible border was created at Agnes Street, and the Lower Shankill became Johnny Adair's personal fiefdom. A couple of nights after the initial attack on the Rex, I led a large number of men down to what was now the border between Adair-land and the rest of the Shankill. It was a strange experience, and as I stood there in solidarity with my friends and colleagues, it almost brought me back to the bad old days when we would march en masse past Unity Flats to and from the Linfield matches. The difference now was that I was a 44-year-old elected member of

Northern Ireland's legislative assembly. Some people might argue that this wasn't the right kind of behaviour for an MLA to be engaging in, but we had to show that we would not be intimidated. I was a politician, yes; but sometimes you face intracommunal issues that can't be solved in the parliamentary chamber. I still had to show leadership on the street.

As a member of the PUP and a former UVF prisoner, I was a prime target for the Adair brigade. By this stage I was used to receiving death threats. I'd been the subject of about thirty-two of them altogether since I had been released from Long Kesh, and when I was elected as an MLA, the assembly had provided me with a mechanism for my car that would alert me if somebody had planted a device underneath it. Most of these death threats had come from republicans, but in the years surrounding the Belfast Agreement, I had begun to receive more from loyalists. I wasn't in the least bit worried about the threats from the LVF after I stood up against Billy Wright, so there was no way I was going to let the UDA on the Shankill get to me. This was my home, but it was inevitable that once things kicked off on that August weekend, I would become a scalp for UDA renegades. At this stage I was living in a flat on Tennent Street, around the corner from my family home in Ambleside Street. The house in Ambleside Street was fitted with steel doors, bulletproof glass, security cameras and alarms. This was a hazard of being both a prominent public and political figure and a former leading paramilitary.

One evening shortly after things had kicked off on the Shankill, the UDA arrived at Ambleside Street and threw a pipe bomb at the house. Fortunately, the device bounced off the living room window's reinforced glass. My wife's former father-in-law was in the house. He was a man in his nineties and had been incarcerated in a Japanese POW camp during the war. Other people didn't have the luxury of that kind of protection, and I was thankful, for my family's sake, that I was an MLA at the time. Little did the UDA know that I was just around the corner with flimsy DIY security grilles that were reminiscent of the sort of things people had in the 1970s.

The UDA began to up the ante and it was clear that Adair wanted me dead. On one occasion during the early days of the feud, I was being interviewed by the local television news on the Shankill Road. I was trying to appeal for calm, but little did I know that I was in Johnny Adair's crosshairs as I spoke to the journalist. It later transpired that Adair had phoned another UDA commander in the Woodvale and told him to 'Go and shoot that fucker right now, where he's standing.' Unaware of all of this, I later drove to a meeting in the Woodvale to talk about mediation. As I did so, the police waved our car over to the side of the road. They told me that they had information that my life was in immediate danger. Special Branch had been listening in on Adair's phone calls and were able to buffer his plans to have me killed. It was all well and good of the police to notify me of this threat, but I found it frustrating that they weren't doing more to take Adair's henchmen off the streets. Threats were being made against me, and my home was being attacked while I was living only yards from Tennent Street police station. John White, who was by now a close ally of Adair, had constant police protection on his home near Carrick.

I think I symbolised everything that Adair hated at that time. He was anti-agreement and despised the PUP's left-of-centre political outlook. Adair had developed his crude political views through his early involvement in the National Front, whereas I was, and still am, a socialist. He was also an egomaniac who wanted to be the supreme leader of loyalism in Northern Ireland, and sadly he had a degree of support for his anti-agreement rhetoric. He didn't have two brain cells to rub together, but I am convinced that he was being manipulated by dark forces. This is what we were dealing with at the time. I couldn't understand why he and others close to him were allowed to act with such impunity, so there had to be a hidden hand at work. Certainly, if it had been the 1970s, he wouldn't have been around for too long. More significant people than him had been killed as part of loyalist paramilitary internal housekeeping.

Another thing I detested about Adair was that he was a drug dealer, and he wasn't shy about it either. Before the feud, I was driving down the Crumlin Road early one Sunday morning when I saw young lads on scooters carrying out what was obviously a drug deal. Across the road sat a police Land Rover. I pulled in and asked the officers why these guys weren't being arrested for dealing. 'You know better than us, Mr Hutchinson; we can't touch him. It goes higher up than us.' I was disgusted. Here I was, as an MLA, trying to create a culture on the Shankill whereby young working-class Protestant boys would begin to engage with education. Despite all of my hard work in the assembly and on the streets, I was unable to do anything about these young lads who were dealing drugs and earning in a day what someone with a degree might hope to earn in a week. For me it was simple: if someone was involved in criminality and drug-dealing, then the police should have been interested in pursuing them. However, new role models had been created, different agendas were at play and my work had become increasingly difficult.

Whatever Adair was doing, it was nothing to do with loyalism. He masqueraded under the banner of the UDA, but he was dealing drugs and creating turf wars that were destroying loyalist communities. Another problem with Adair was that the media loved him. He made for an easy story and was always willing to meet with reporters to give his opinion. With his larger-than-life persona and cartoonish appearance, Adair seemed to appeal to what the public was titillated to imagine loyalism was all about. Basically, he was good copy and sold newspapers. He wasn't the first loyalist to find himself courted by the media, and he certainly won't be the last. The press should have taken more responsibility for the monster they were creating; they should have been aware of the dark mood emerging, and how the culture that was evolving around Adair and C Company was affecting people's whole way of life on the Shankill.

It wasn't long until the first blood was spilled in what would become a violent internecine feud. On Monday, 21 August, Jackie Coulter of the UDA and Jackie Mahood's brother Bobby, who was also a veteran UVF man, were sitting in a vehicle on the Crumlin Road discussing potential ways to end the nascent feuding. They were spotted by someone and Bobby was mistaken for Jackie. A call was made and a UVF gunman opened fire on them, killing Jackie Coulter outright, with Bobby Mahood dying in hospital a few hours later. It was a mess. While the UVF didn't claim responsibility, it was clear that they had been behind the shooting, and the PUP had to carry the can for it when the media came looking for an explanation.

I was finding it exceedingly difficult to comprehend why the Shankill was being torn asunder like this, and it was hard to see how it was ever going to end. Johnny Adair was lifted by the police on 22 August. Peter Mandelson, the Secretary of State, claimed rightly that the people of the Shankill were gripped by fear, and he was full of self-confidence when talking about Adair's arrest, stating that

> Now one of the principal sources of that fear – a man who with his associates has been inciting so much violence in recent days – has been removed. I think it is that action that opens the way to the community as a whole to come together and to promote the cause of peace and put this feuding behind them once and for all.

Mandelson was an extremely intelligent man, but he didn't understand how the street worked. I feared that Adair's arrest wouldn't end the bloodshed and stated that it would actually intensify it, telling the press that 'I'd expect attacks against our party and the UVF.'

I was sadly proved correct in this prediction. The UDA wanted vengeance for the killing of Coulter, and the next day a young lad by the name of Sam Rockett was killed in cold blood by the UDA as he visited his partner and baby in Summer Street off the Oldpark Road. He had been told to stay away from the area, which was overwhelmingly UDA affiliated, but like any young man with a family, he desperately wanted to see his partner and child. He was told by so-called friends that he would be safe to return. Sam was a popular guy, and he was friendly with my son. He was well liked in the PUP and among those in the UVF, and his involvement with the YCV appeared to have been enough to sign his death warrant.

At Sam's funeral, leaflets were distributed that described Johnny Adair as a 'drug baron, racketeer and Nazi'. I thought that just about summed him up perfectly. A few days later, I read, with a large degree of incredulity, that John White felt that I had 'hyped up the situation' in the Lower Shankill. Ironically, White also said that he didn't want to see 'ghettos' created. I certainly wasn't hyping up anything. After all, my family home had been attacked and people I knew had been killed. I responded to White in the *Irish Examiner*, stating that

> It has been very clear for a long time that two people have been dictating what goes on in the UFF on the Shankill. They have been building up a relationship with the LVF and other people, and you have to ask the question, why? Everyone knows it has nothing to do with Ulster and unionism. They have given loyalists a bad name. They have led loyalists into a cul-de-sac.

John White was right about one thing: there had been no truce between the UVF and UDA on the Shankill. And I knew that we would have to look to the UDA outside the Shankill to get some sort of resolution in motion. 'There is no chance of talks between rival groups on the Shankill,' I told the press. 'You've only got to look at C Company (of the UFF) on the lower Shankill, and you can see that there is nobody that the UVF could talk it out with. I think it can be resolved – but only by people from outside the area.'

Despite my life clearly being in danger, the police were constantly making strange decisions. Shortly after the feud started, I was travelling down the Crumlin Road in a car with other PUP members. We were heading to the Monkstown Social Club, which by now was the safest place for the PUP and UVF to meet. The police pulled us over and asked us to step out of the car. When they discovered that we were all wearing bulletproof jackets, they tried to arrest us on charges of UVF membership. It was totally crazy. I was an elected politician with a very real death threat hanging over me, and the police appeared more interested in collaring me than they did with sorting out C Company. By the time we arrived in Monkstown, I was absolutely furious.

Things were relatively quiet for the next two months or so, but there was a tangible feeling of threat, tension and hatred in the air. The febrile atmosphere simmered on until the end of October, when guns were once again produced. On 28 October, the UVF killed a local youth named David Greer who was involved in the UDA. The shooting occurred after a fight between UVF and UDA men and subsequent attacks on houses belonging to UVF men in Tigers Bay. The UVF in Mount Vernon arrived in the area and Greer was shot dead. The UVF had been criticising the UDA's inability to reign in C Company, and now guys in Mount Vernon were going rogue. The killing of Greer inflamed a situation that hadn't been stable since August. On 31 October, I received a phone call from my constituency office secretary, Frances Dunseith. She was in hysterics and told me that a PUP member called Bertie Rice, who had been in the office a short time before, had been shot. This was the UDA's revenge for the Greer killing. Bertie Rice was a 63-year-old who had returned with his wife from South Africa, where they had lived for a number of years. As he reached his front gate, he was accosted by UDA men; they chased him through his front door and shot him dead in front of his wife, Mary, in the house in Tigers Bay that they had called home again for only a short while. I was extremely upset. I had known Bertie through the UVF in the 1970s, but he was no longer involved in paramilitarism. Since returning from South Africa, he had been helping me in my constituency office on the Shore Road by dropping leaflets through people's doors.

Here was an elderly man who had recently returned home after emigrating, and who was trying to make a positive difference to the community he loved through an involvement in politics. He was a soft target, and his killing highlighted to me that nobody was safe and that we would have to end this feuding. The following night, Mark Quail, the son of a friend of mine, was shot dead in his home by the UDA. After the killings of Mark Quail and Bertie Rice, I knew it was inevitable that the UVF would have to respond. I told the *Irish Examiner*, 'My position is clear. Once someone kills somebody else, they are putting it up to the other organisation. Paramilitaries live in a macho world and their code is you live by the sword you die by the sword.' I didn't think there was any point in dressing it up. The fact was that we were in the middle of a shooting match between the UDA and the UVF.

Gary McMichael hit back and was critical of me, calling me an obstacle to finding a solution to the ongoing feud. The reality was that I was feeling raw and emotional, and I wasn't going to be inauthentic and hide my feelings. Politics calls for a certain level of diplomacy, but this had gone beyond politics. The instincts I had learned on the streets in the early 1970s kicked in, as I knew I had to be true to myself. Martin Taylor was dead, Sam Rockett was dead, and now an associate of mine was dead – as was a young man whose father I was friendly with. The feud had affected me directly. It had affected my friends and the community that I loved. I think the UVF recognised how emotionally tied up in the whole thing I had been, and during the early weeks of the feud, they encouraged me to go on a holiday to Normandy I had booked. Maybe they did think that I was inflaming the situation through my comments in the media, but I could only speak honestly as I felt and saw things around me.

Just a few hours after Mark's funeral, I attended the cremation of Bertie Rice at Roselawn. Two funerals in one day. Things had spiralled out of control in North Belfast, and the violence seemed like it would never end. It was all very bleak. David Ervine called for the attacks to stop, but I couldn't in all honesty condemn the UVF at the time; the UDA had been responsible for starting the feuding, and it was inevitable that UVF members would seek revenge for the killings. David had also received some threats and was quite entitled to call for calm, but he was slightly immune to the worst of the bloodshed, which hadn't crossed the Lagan into East Belfast. I hit back at Gary McMichael, stating that 'He should have got up off his backside and stopped Johnny Adair and John White taking us down this cul-de-sac.'

As I had predicted back in August, a solution to the internecine violence between the UVF and UDA could not be found in the Shankill or those areas nearby where people had been put out of their homes, involved in fights or killed. The Monkstown Social Club, where we had held meetings since the feud first erupted, was to prove pivotal in the weeks ahead as the UVF and UDA tried to bring an end to the bloodshed. A few weeks after the killings of late October and early November, a meeting was held in the

Monkstown Social Club which was attended by paramilitary and political representatives from those areas that had been worst affected by the feud violence. I attended and represented the PUP, and I was joined by two popular figures from East Antrim, Billy Greer and Rab Warnock. Norman Sayers and a few other members of UVF Brigade Staff joined us, while the UDA delegation included spokespeople such as Jackie McDonald and Tommy Kirkham. We debated issues that were causing tensions and rancour in North Belfast and Newtownabbey, including flags, murals, intimidation, bar fights and other matters. This led to a document that was drafted over the space of a year and provided the basis for the first UVF/UDA agreement, which was between 1st East Antrim UVF and South East Antrim UDA.

It was obvious that the people who met in Monkstown didn't want the violence to continue. We were adamant that, as well as causing heartache to the loyalist working class, it was a distraction from our ultimate aim, which was to progress loyalism politically.

***

In the months after the feud quietened down, I still felt the need to look over my shoulder. I was living like a fugitive, switching cars and houses and unable to tell anyone my plans. In a way it was like the early 1970s all over again. In March 2001 I was interviewed by Darwin Templeton for the *Belfast Telegraph* and was adamant that despite the continuing threats to my life, I wasn't going to hide behind the door. 'I spent 16 year in jail not going where I wanted, but I'm not a prisoner now,' I said. 'I don't want to die, but I'm not going to be a prisoner again.'

Despite the progress that had been made in bringing the UVF/UDA feud to an end, inter-communal problems would rear their head in 2001 and events that would be broadcast across the globe would bring shame upon loyalism in Northern Ireland.

As the school-term came to a close in June 2001, tensions erupted around Holy Cross Girls' Primary School in North Belfast. The Catholic school was situated in the loyalist Glenbryn estate in the Upper Ardoyne area, the site of many sectarian confrontations going back decades. Protestants in Ardoyne had been complaining for months about sectarian attacks being carried out on their homes; they claimed that they felt unsafe using local amenities, which were in the mainly Catholic part of Ardoyne. Flags were erected along Ardoyne Road by the guys from both sides of the divide to try and mark out territory.

In the middle of June, I received a phone call to tell me that a couple of men were using a stepladder to climb a lamppost and put up loyalist flags. As they did so, local republicans drove onto the kerb, and one of them got out of the car and kicked over the ladder, causing one of the guys to fall. This started a fight which exacerbated the bad feeling that existed in the area. The situation escalated very quickly, and large crowds gathered. Pupils and parents from Holy Cross were targeted by local residents, who threw stones and other debris. The following day, several hundred people from the republican side of Ardoyne Road emerged onto the street, which had by now been blocked off by the police. Troops were also deployed as loyalists began to hurl bricks. I arrived in the area, as did Gerry Kelly of Sinn Féin. We appealed for calm, but it soon became apparent that despite the fraught and violent atmosphere, the parents of the Holy Cross children were going to march them up to the school no matter what. Obviously, kids should be able to go to school without coming to any harm, but I had to question the motivations of the parents, who must have known that walking up the Ardoyne Road en masse with guys like Gerry Kelly and Eddie Copeland in the background was going to raise tensions and lead to local Protestants coming to the conclusion that republicans were trying to force a situation whereby they could portray themselves as the victims. Analogies were made with the struggles of African-Americans in Little Rock, Arkansas, and loyalists were depicted by the media as white supremacists.

By the time the kids were back at school in September, the world's media had fixed its gaze on Ardoyne, expecting something dramatic to happen.

On Wednesday, 5 September 2001, things came to a head for me with the Holy Cross saga. While I had been depressed by many of the actions of the protesting so-called loyalists over previous weeks, I was absolutely sickened when a blast bomb was thrown by loyalists. It landed at the police lines and missed the kids and their parents, though the explosion was loud and debris was flung all over the road. When asked for a comment by the *Irish Independent*, I stated, 'I was disgusted to be a loyalist this morning when I saw that happen and I won't change that statement. The people responsible should be ashamed of themselves. The terror on those children's faces was unbelievable. It totally sickened me to the pit of my stomach.' I went back up to the PUP office later that day and stated that this was now, in my opinion, a very dangerous situation where kids could end up getting hurt. David Ervine told me that I needed to go back up and help diffuse the situation. It was easy for him to say that, but I told David that there was no way I was going to tolerate that sort of thuggish behaviour, which put the lives of innocent children or police officers at risk.

After a long conversation with David, I decided I would return to Ardoyne to see if I could help calm things down. I had to ensure that I helped the local loyalists formulate a peaceful means of protesting. There is no doubt that they had legitimate grievances about intimidation and violence, but this was totally counterproductive and portrayed loyalism as backward and nasty in the eyes of the world. I later said, 'I still stand with this community to protect their rights and I will argue for them as an elected representative. We can't walk away from this; this thing needs to be finished in a structured way.'

A lot of the guys up in Glenbryn were from a UDA background, and a lot of them told me to my face that they didn't want me up there. Some even went as far as to threaten me, but I was an MLA for the area and a councillor for the Oldpark, and I felt that I had a mandate to be there. While the people who lived there wanted me to help them, I wasn't going to let any residual bad feeling from the UDA force me out of doing what I had been elected to do.

I had a feeling that people in the area were going to be offered something, and eventually the NIO suggested a bend in the road! This was totally ridiculous. A bend in the road might have stopped people from seeing each other, but it wouldn't allay fears of physical attack. The reality was that here we were, seven years on from the ceasefires, and it looked as though new peace walls needed to be built to prevent people murdering each other. Jane Kennedy, the direct rule security minister, suggested building a gate that would be closed at night-time, but this was just paying lip service to the idea of sectarian division rather than dealing with the violent realities on the interface at Ardoyne. I had a meeting with Jane during which I explained to her in no uncertain terms that her idea was rubbish. Like many other civil servants from England, she just didn't understand the complexities of the situation in Belfast.

Things took a slightly surreal turn when I was approached by David Ervine with a message from Gerry Adams. Adams thought that a good resolution to the Holy Cross issue would be for Gerry Kelly and me to embrace for the cameras. It was absolute nonsense, and not in my nature to be part of such a choreographed stunt. What would it have achieved other than to make us both look stupid. Adams again demonstrated to me that he was totally detached from reality. I told David in no uncertain terms that I would certainly not be hugging Gerry Kelly at any time. I've little doubt that the feeling was mutual.

On one occasion a republican activist who I knew of, but didn't know personally, came over to me in a threatening manner and stood toe-to-toe with me, with his head right up against my face. 'I'll blow your brains out,' he said. I stood my ground and didn't move or flinch. 'What's wrong, then, did you forget your gun?' He was incensed, and as he pushed his head further into my face I lost my footing and fell over. On seeing this, Gerry Kelly and other Sinn Féin members ran up the street and pulled this fella off from me and trailed him away.

It was clear, as time went on, that Sinn Féin and their numerous arms-length community bodies were intent on making political gain from the episode. People were being bussed in from other republican areas like West Belfast. Shortly after many of the parents had agreed to go into the school via the back entrance on the Crumlin Road, Sinn Féin interjected and told them they had to go up the road past the loyalist protestors. It was devious, it was cynical, it was manipulative, and with the crude reaction of some of the loyalist protestors, it was manna for the global press. It was a simple story of good versus evil. Once again Sinn Féin had outflanked loyalism on the propaganda front and this time young schoolgirls were the collateral.

***

I felt that raising the educational standards of the loyalist working class was an important investment for the future. With the emergence of the Troubles in the early 1970s, and the subsequent decline of traditional industries such as shipbuilding through de-industrialisation, young loyalist men in particular found their path to employment to be more complicated than that of their fathers. When violence had flared in the 1970s, education perhaps took a backseat as people looked to defend their communities against violent republicanism. As a politician, I was determined to make a difference and reverse the declining standard of educational achievement in areas like the Shankill. Unfortunately, I faced opposition in the form of an old paramilitary foe who had also moved into the political arena.

During his tenure as Minister of Education, I had some run-ins with Martin McGuinness. Whereas we were both previously commanders of paramilitary groupings (McGuinness was a one-time PIRA commander and leader), we were now parliamentary colleagues with a range of differences on certain issues. I was passionate about solving the issue of educational underachievement in the loyalist working class, but also more generally in Northern Irish society. I was particularly drawn to the successful Scandinavian model regarding early years intervention. I felt that the Scandinavians were right; that 4-year-old kids shouldn't be under pressure just to read and write, but should also be socialised and develop through play and interaction from an early age. This was a model that I knew would work in my constituency. Even if the minister didn't adopt it formally, surely he could find money from the departmental budget to run a pilot project and get an assessment of its success, or otherwise, in areas of socio-economic disadvantage like the Shankill. McGuinness flatly refused my request. I couldn't help but take it personally.

I had a feeling deep in my gut that he wouldn't adopt the idea because it was the PUP advocating for it – because it would help Protestants. If it had been suggested within Sinn Féin in relation to specific examples in Catholic working-class areas, I have no doubt he would have run with it immediately. When it became clear in the chamber that this intransigence was going to stymie my suggestion, I raced to Martin's Stormont office and entered without invitation. After his initial surprise, he became angry and asked some of his minders to remove me. I held on to the chair

I was sitting on, and they removed the chair with me on it into the corridor.

In the summer of 2002, my son and I took a trip out to South Korea and Japan to watch England play in the World Cup. In late June we were in Shizuoka for England's quarter-final tie against Brazil. After going 1–0 up with a goal by Michael Owen, England collapsed and lost 2–1 to a Brazil side that included Ronaldinho, Ronaldo and Roberto Carlos. When I got home, all my friends were phoning me and saying, 'I saw you on the telly, Hutchie; was that you when England scored?' I had been sitting in the front row of the second tier in the stadium, and when Owen scored, I was clearly visible on camera, celebrating. I thought nothing of it until shortly after the assembly reconvened in September, when we were at an event in Hillsborough. When I arrived, David came looking for me in a slightly panicked mood. 'Martin had his men round here, looking for you. What the hell have you done now?' 'I've no idea. Sure, I haven't seen him since before the summer recess. Come on with me and we'll go and see what he's after.' We made our way round to an office where McGuinness and his colleagues were sitting, chatting informally. 'Martin, I hear you were looking for me? What do you want?' McGuinness's face crumpled and he looked irritated: 'You, Billy. You started a row in my house!' I was immediately taken aback. I had never been near McGuinness's house, so I wasn't sure what was going on. 'You were at that England and Brazil game at the World Cup.' I stopped him: 'Whoa, Martin, are you preparing to admit to me that you were watching England?!' I knew then that he was bantering me. 'My wife was making tea and biscuits.' 'Oh, I see there's plenty of equality in your house, Martin!', I retorted only half-jokingly. 'Yeah, yeah – but when England scored, we saw you on the telly and we all jumped up and roared. Bernie dropped the tea and biscuits and came racing in and shouted at me, "What are you doing cheering for England, Martin?!"' We had a good laugh about that, but sadly I couldn't gel with him on the issues that mattered most to me.

Shortly after this, in early October 2002, the Northern Ireland Assembly collapsed when it was alleged that the PIRA was running a spy-ring in Parliament Buildings, gathering intelligence on various individuals from opposition parties. One of those arrested was the Sinn Féin assembly group administrator, Denis Donaldson.

There were other broader issues relating to Sinn Féin that had begun to concern me. It had been an open secret for quite a while that the Blair government was using the carrot of an amnesty for 'on the run' IRA members to encourage the Provos to move on decommissioning. I couldn't comprehend how Blair thought that this would go unnoticed by loyalists. If Provos were being given letters of comfort, then the whole edifice of what had been agreed in April 1998 could come apart at the seams. I stated at the time that there would be no point in the PUP trying to maintain support for the agreement if the government pursued this with the Provos. After the feud in 2000, things had become totally unstable within loyalism, with the UDP collapsing completely in the years that immediately followed. If loyalists saw that Sinn Féin and the Provos were being provided with special conditions, it would be difficult to keep the increasingly faint support for the agreement alive in loyalist areas. It became evident to many loyalists, myself included, that Blair had a clear strategy to demonise loyalism. Indeed, he had stated that he would personally deal with Sinn Féin and allow the Police Service of Northern Ireland (PSNI) Chief Constable to deal with loyalists. We were being marginalised on purpose while Blair charmed the republicans.

Sinn Féin appeared to be enjoying different back-door deals and special treatment while loyalists like myself and the PUP were being lumped in with criminal elements who I didn't regard as having anything to do with loyalism. Never once did I see

Sinn Féin pushed into the same box as the so-called dissident republican factions, even after the Northern Bank robbery and the murder of Markets man Robert McCartney. People just seemed to turn a blind eye to the bad behaviour of the Provos in order to keep Sinn Féin in the political process. All our hard work and all our sacrifices were rapidly disappearing down the drain. We were being marginalised so that Blair, guided by his spin-doctor and advisor Alistair Campbell, could deal with those he wanted to, which was now Trimble and Sinn Féin.

Without a functioning assembly, I occupied myself with Belfast City Council matters and stuck to my rigid daily running routine. One early morning in August 2003, I was jogging along Cambrai Street, as I usually did. I had been told a few days previously by some people on the Shankill to keep an eye out for a white Vauxhall Cavalier, which had been acting suspiciously. It had been spotted in and around the area, and its occupants had been trailing flags off people's houses before returning back into Ardoyne. On this particular morning, I was finishing off my run, heading down Cambrai Street, when this car appeared beside me and stopped. A guy jumped out and apprehended me, grabbing me by my T-shirt. I struggled, and fortunately for me the T-shirt ripped, and I was able to get a few feet away. As I did so, a fella in the back of the car opened the door and produced a gun. I instinctively kicked against the car door, which caught his hand, forcing him to drop the gun. All I could hear was the voice shouting, 'Fucking bastard! My hand!' I ran to the gate of O'Hara's bakery, where luckily the security man was on the other side. He immediately opened the gate and let me in until the police came. If it hadn't been for the security man, I'd have been a goner for definite. When the police arrived, I told them who had attacked me, naming one of the guys as the son of a prominent veteran member of the PIRA in Ardoyne. He was allegedly *persona non grata* among the rank and file of the Provos at this stage, but nonetheless, he was still a member. Sinn Féin and the security services denied that this had been an attempt on my life, but by this stage I had become so used to my life being under very real threat that I had to treat it as an occupational hazard. The point I made to republicans was that even if Sinn Féin were denying the PIRA was involved, this guy still fell under the remit and rules of their Green Book. I could only pass on the information.

***

After a year of stasis, elections were finally called on 26 November 2003 to revive the assembly. Since I had first been elected to the assembly in the optimistic afterglow of April and May 1998, I was hamstrung by issues that were untypical of those that other MLAs had to deal with. The loyalist feud and the issues at Holy Cross were not standard political issues, and I had to respond to them in a way that ensured a resolution for those involved without turning my back on the people who I had known for so many years. Middle-class unionists wouldn't have been able to understand the culture of the loyalist feuding. It was something that I didn't particularly want to have to deal with, but when it kicked off, I had to. I couldn't just wash my hands of the loyalist people who had elected me, whether they were UVF supporters or not. For the casual voter who gave me a tick on the ballot paper in June 1998, the optics in 2000 and 2001 was perhaps not as appealing. Obviously, looking back, I wish those events hadn't occurred. On the other hand, what else could I do? I couldn't betray myself or where I had come from.

It came as no surprise to me when the results came through and I had lost my seat. The Women's Coalition lost its MLAs, but thankfully David managed to hold on to his seat. The DUP made significant gains, and shortly after the election Arlene Foster,

Norah Beare and Jeffrey Donaldson all defected from the UUP to increase the DUP's representation. Paisley was now in charge of the largest party in the assembly. All his protesting and yelling about betrayal and sell-out had worked as he shifted Trimble into second place. The political extremes of the DUP and Sinn Féin were now the two largest parties. The moderates who had been involved in the Belfast Agreement had been pushed to one side. Perhaps, if they could find an accommodation, the DUP and Sinn Féin would move things forward? I had to draw positives from somewhere.

CHAPTER 12

A Huge Task Ahead

On 8 January 2007, I received a call from Mark Ervine, David's son. Mark is a fantastic artist, who has done a lot of good cross-community work. At first I couldn't quite absorb what he was telling me. 'My dad is dead, Billy.' I couldn't find any words. I had known David for just over thirty-two years. Given my choices in life, I was used to hearing about people I knew well dying or being killed, but being told that David had died just didn't seem real. It seemed as if he would always be there. He was my friend, my political colleague and confidante, and an articulate voice for the loyalist community.

It transpired that David had suffered a brain haemorrhage, heart attack and stroke; he was only 53 years old. A few days before his death, I took a call from him, and he appeared to be extremely stressed out. I told him he needed to get things in perspective and not to allow politics and the circus that often surrounded it to overbear him. It wasn't the first time I had warned David that he would give himself a heart attack if he wasn't careful. I thought back to a previous occasion when he had just been put on some new medication for his heart and had been advised to cut down on the drink. I was dropping him home to East Belfast when he said to me, 'Hutchie, can you just drop me off at the Longfellow.' The Longfellow is a bar off the Ravenhill Road, where David was well known and well liked. 'David, are you wise? You've just been told to cut down on the pints and the minute you get in there everyone will be over to you asking you to sort out their constituency problems. You need to learn how to relax.' His response summed him up: 'But that's how I relax, Hutchie. I love helping my people.' David was a very sociable person who was loved by people across the board. That is why he did so well in politics. He was a popular guy and his premature death left a gaping void in loyalist politics.

I had lost my Belfast City Council seat in May 2005, and between that and my earlier defeat in the assembly elections of November 2003, I had gone back to community development work. It's what I had done after I had been released from Long Kesh, and I felt like the proverbial duck taking to water again. I enjoyed being involved in politics and was proud to represent the PUP, but the truth was that after my defeat in the 2003 election, nobody lifted the phone to talk to me or keep me in the loop. I'm not the kind of person who goes chasing after people, and although it was slightly disappointing to be cut somewhat adrift of the PUP's assembly team, I was ensconced in a new position as director of the Mount Vernon Community Development Forum in North Belfast. I was also still the interlocutor between the UVF and the IICD.

People thought I was mad to take the job in Mount Vernon, and all the usual stereotypes came out, with people saying to me, 'They eat their babies down there' or 'They're tout-ridden.' Some people in Mount Vernon were equally as suspicious at first, thinking that I had been sent on a spying mission by the Shankill UVF, given all the turbulence with the organisation in the estate. I came to love the people of Mount Vernon, but there was a hole in my life where politics had once been.

The political landscape in Northern Ireland, which had shifted dramatically at the end of 2003, was changing immeasurably. On 26 March 2007, the unthinkable happened as negotiations between the DUP and Sinn Féin resulted in the announcement of a new assembly and executive. The announcement was made by Ian Paisley and Gerry Adams. Few people would have taken bets on that partnership happening back in 1998. The UVF was also edging toward some kind of progress as the decade wore on. Just over a month after the historic agreement between Paisley and Adams, in early May, the UVF/RHC announced the end of its campaign. As he had in October 1994, Gusty Spence addressed the media at Fernhill House. In doing so, he stated, on behalf of the UVF, that 'We welcome recent developments in securing stable, durable, democratic structures in Northern Ireland and accept as significant, support by the mainstream republican movement of the constitutional status quo.' The UVF felt that the Union was safe but wouldn't give guarantees over weaponry being decommissioned.

Although the UVF announcement was welcomed in most quarters, there was scepticism over the fact that weapons were being 'put beyond reach' rather than being destroyed. This issue continued to be a delicate one for the organisation. I knew, through my work as interlocutor with the IICD, that while the UVF was happy to end its campaign, it didn't want to leave itself in the position of being impotent if things went awry. After all, violent republican campaigns had emerged generation after generation throughout history. The UVF was wary about leaving the loyalist people open to attack with no defence within reach.

In Gusty's statement, the UVF had declared that it was adopting a 'non-military, civilianised role'. Like the issue of decommissioning, this was a delicate matter that had to be navigated carefully. I had been involved for some time, along with my old running partner William Mitchell and Alternatives Restorative Justice, in setting up a civilianisation programme for former UVF/RHC combatants. The outworking of this was done by an organisation called Action for Community Transformation (ACT), directed by William, and it was intended to give guys who had been involved in the conflict the chance to get involved in community development work.

A formal process of disarmament, demobilisation, and reintegration (DDR) had never taken place in Northern Ireland after the 1994 ceasefires. While Sinn Féin had several former PIRA members in its ranks who had gone on to be elected to the assembly, loyalist paramilitaries had no similar representation on the political stage. It was up to the grassroots of loyalism to try and address this through conflict transformation initiatives such as ACT.

A week after the UVF announced the end of its campaign, Ian Paisley met the Taoiseach Bertie Ahern on the site of the Battle of the Boyne. The previous month he had shaken Ahern's hand outside Farmleigh House in Dublin. I remember seeing this on the television and feeling the hairs stand up on the back of my neck. It wasn't the presence of Ahern that annoyed me, nor the fact that the DUP was sharing power with Sinn Féin; after all, it was necessary for the extremes to meet in the middle. Rather it was the hypocrisy of Paisley himself. After all the thundering and bluster about the threat from the Irish Republic and the IRA, here he was doing everything he had criticised myself and other unionists and loyalists for doing for years before him. What was different now, I asked myself. Why had all those lives been lost in the years of the Troubles?

Around this time, I remember seeing a news item on the television about the Free Presbyterians and their discontentment with Paisley's Damascene conversion. One elderly lady, who had followed Paisley in his religious and political guises since the 1960s, was talking about how she felt utterly betrayed – how her whole worldview had been brought into question. In the past I would have easily dismissed her as a relic and a bigot, but for some reason this lady's dejection struck a nerve with me. I didn't agree with her religious or political convictions, but I could understand her sense of betrayal. It must be a devastating experience to live your life by the ideals and doctrine of another person, with no room for individual thought or expression, only to then see that person do the opposite of almost everything they had preached to you about. It must have felt personal.

Shortly after all of this happened in Northern Ireland, I was invited out to Finland by the Finnish government to engage in a workshop with armed groups from Iraq and speak about universal issues such as radicalisation, disarmament, ceasefires and how to wind down a conflict. I was at the airport waiting to embark on my flight to Helsinki, chatting to some Finnish diplomats, when I spotted Martin McGuinness along with Jeffrey Donaldson, who had defected from the UUP to the DUP in the early '00s. I had been to Finland before, and the diplomats were telling me that I was on the US government's anti-terrorism list for speaking to these groups from Iraq. I was brought across diplomatic lines and was able to get out to Finland to do the work I had been scheduled to do. After the first day of the workshop, I noticed that McGuinness was also staying in the hotel – but that he was part of a group of politicians from various places and we were being kept away from them.

The next morning, as usual, I went out early for a fifteen-mile run around a nearby forest. As I came back into the hotel, I heard a familiar voice; I knew the Derry accent straight away: 'Billy, are you not going to say hello?' I turned around and saw Martin McGuinness, now the deputy First Minister of Northern Ireland. He had been out for a walk and was coming into the lobby behind me. 'Alright, Martin. Where's the other "chuckle brother"? I thought you went everywhere together these days?' McGuinness started to approach me, holding up his hands: 'Look, Billy, Ian Paisley is the most misunderstood man in Irish history.' I was shocked to hear McGuinness say this, and immediately hit back, 'How dare you say that?' He was obviously hoping to start a conversation about this: 'Look, look, Billy.' I started to walk off. 'Don't you dare tell me he was misunderstood. He was the biggest recruiting sergeant your guys ever had! The heartache and misery that Paisley caused in the loyalist community was massive.' 'Let me explain, Billy,' he replied. I walked a few steps back toward McGuinness and looked him straight in the face. 'I don't want to hear it! I don't know what it would be like for Catholics, seeing you so cosy with Paisley, but I'll tell you my point of view. I had no time for the man, never did; but there were plenty of young fellas ended up in Long Kesh who would never have been there if it hadn't been for Paisley's sectarian rhetoric.' I walked off before he could explain.

People might ask was I not curious about what McGuinness was going to say to justify his new friendship with Paisley, but to be honest I wasn't. It was good that they were working together for a better Northern Ireland, but I didn't want to hear soundbites to dress it all up. I'm not that sort of person. If Paisley had given the same public support to some of the violent actions that he had advocated in private over the years, he would have been the UVF's brigadier.

***

In June 2009 my work with the IICD came to a conclusion after twelve long years when the UVF/RHC announced that it would decommission its weapons. It had been a long process, with careful steps taken to ensure that things were done in the right way and for the right reasons. My role as interlocutor was to work with the commissioners and report progress. For a number of years, this consisted of discussions about how the process would work. I had contacts in the UVF that worked hard throughout the process. Together we explored the modalities, such as armaments safely for preparation of decommissioning, who could be present and how could this be done under the legislation. An important question was what would happen if I, for example, was travelling in a car with a number of guns to be decommissioned and it was intercepted by the police – how would this be explained and what protection was there for the people in the UVF involved in this delicate process? The IICD provided me, as interlocutor, with a letter that could be shown to the police or army to give us safe passage if I, and others, were stopped with a carful of weapons to be presented to the IICD commissioners. As a former life sentence prisoner, I will always be on license, so if I was intercepted with weapons without that letter from the IICD, I could be automatically thrown back into jail.

The process of decommissioning had been planned for earlier in the year but had to be suspended when, in March, two sappers, Patrick Azimkar and Mark Quinsey, and a policeman, Stephen Carroll, were shot dead by dissident republicans. It was to the credit of the UVF and RHC leadership that we had got to this point so soon after the outrage that surrounded those killings. The UVF/RHC had also learned lessons from the PIRA's decommissioning announcement in 2005. We examined the way in which the press had been given access to the independent witnesses who were there to verify the decommissioning process. Once they spoke to the press, they opened the process to scrutiny and society was able to pick it apart. The process was never to be a political one. In my opinion, the PIRA got it wrong when they embedded PR as part of their decommissioning process. So, it was crucial for the UVF/RHC to have the right independent witnesses to verify what was taking place. It was also important not to do a PR job on the actual mechanics of decommissioning the weaponry, as it wouldn't be right. The optics would be bad for victims. People would rip it to pieces on moral and legal grounds, because it would be outside the legislation which was designed to allow the process to work safely and in such a way that it would not be an open house to prying eyes. The UVF/RHC chose Chris Hudson and Rev. Gary Mason, an East Belfast Methodist minister, to oversee the decommissioning of their arsenal.

A press event was held at the East Belfast Methodist Mission off the Newtownards Road, where a statement was read by a representative of the UVF. One line in the statement regarding the UVF's decision to decommission its weaponry stuck out for me: 'We have done so to further augment the establishment of accountable democratic governance in this region of the UK, to remove the pretext that loyalist weaponry is an obstacle to the development of our communities and to compound our legacy of integrity to the peace process.' The UVF leadership was putting the loyalist people first in the hope that they would be brought into the political process – a process from which they had felt alienated since the post-agreement period of the late 1990s.

On 4 September 2009, the IICD published a progress report on decommissioning by loyalist paramilitary groups. While the UDA, which had also been present at the event in East Belfast in June, were still carrying out the process of decommissioning, the September report by the IICD included the following statement:

> Ulster Volunteer Force/Red Hand Commando
> 2. In verbal reports to both governments in June we said that we had overseen a decommissioning event in which substantial quantities of firearms, ammunition, explosives and explosive devices belonging to the Ulster Volunteer Force and the Red Hand Commando had been decommissioned.
>
> 3. The UVF and RHC representatives told us that some of their arms had been lost over the years through seizure by the security services, deterioration or damage, or the death

> of those responsible for them. They said that the arms decommissioned under our supervision in June comprised all that was under the control of both organizations.*

I felt that with this announcement by the UVF and the subsequent progress report by the IICD should have given the PUP the impetus and energy to drive forward and attempt to play a more significant role in the new political dispensation. Like David, Gusty and I had all proved to Bill Flynn and his Irish American friends in the early and mid-1990s, there was more to unionism and loyalism than the messages espoused by the DUP and UUP. I was sad to see that after David's untimely death, the PUP had begun to swing in a different direction to the party which had been involved in the peace negotiations of the late 1990s when people like Eddie Kinner and Billy Mitchell, who had been through the Long Kesh experience, drove the party forward as a genuine left-leaning alternative to mainstream unionism. I think that David was perhaps surrounded by one or two people with self-interest at heart, rather than the interests of the loyalist people. To put it bluntly, I believe some individuals saw the PUP as a stepping-stone to greater things. David retained his Stormont seat between 2003 and his death in 2007 because he was able to appeal to some UVF supporters, grassroots loyalists and middle-class floating voters in East Belfast. Even some middle-class Catholics – the constituency we had been careful to take into account way back in the early 1980s – had given David support. He was an everyman. In terms of the grassroots side of things on the Shankill, Hughie Smyth was still doing a fantastic job in the Court ward on Belfast City Council and

---

* 'Report of the Independent International Commission on Decommissioning (IICD) – [A progress report on decommissioning by loyalist paramilitary groups]', 4 September 2009 (Belfast: IICD, 2009).

would continue to do so until he died in May 2014. Elsewhere, as the decade came to a close, other people appeared to be getting itchy feet.

When a former RHC member named Bobby Moffett was shot dead by the UVF on the Shankill in broad daylight in late May 2010, Dawn Purvis resigned as leader of the PUP. While the killing was wrong and out of step with what we had worked so hard for back in the late 1990s – and what had been announced by the UVF in June 2009 – I did wonder why this killing in particular had proved to be the final straw.

While I had been involved in the PUP, my motivation had always been to try and prevent killings from happening. I'm not saying I could have prevented Moffett being killed, as I didn't know all the details across what had happened. But a large part of what the PUP was about was influencing the UVF and RHC, and trying to use our political will and analysis to decommission mindsets that could lead to this sort of bloodshed.

Brian Ervine, David's brother, tried in vain to steer the PUP ship back into steadier waters, but the brand had become confused. No one was exactly sure what the PUP was anymore; it was suffering from an identity crisis. When David, Gusty, Hughie and I were working toward the agreement in 1998, people understood who we were and what we were hoping to achieve. By 2011, the PUP was almost dead in the water. The party had been sunk in the assembly elections and was running on a huge deficit of £57,000. On 15 October, I was elected as the PUP's fourth leader in eighteen months at the annual party conference. I was honoured to be installed as the leader of the party – a party that I had seen grow from the small informal seeds of political debate between UVF/RHC prisoners in Compound 21 of Long Kesh; a party that had moved through to the pinnacle of parliamentary representation from 1998 onwards. I was also under little illusion as to the huge task that lay ahead.

When I became leader, I felt that we could find common ground with other parties and stakeholders whose constituencies were being devastated by the economic downturn. Despite this desire to proceed on an anti-austerity ticket, constitutional matters overtook the party when, on 3 December 2012, a new anti-unionist cadre of Sinn Féin councillors in Belfast City Council pushed to have the Union flag removed from above City Hall. An Alliance Party amendment to the issue brought a compromise of sorts when it was decided that the flag should only be flown on certain designated days.

Loyalists and unionists were up in arms when the vote went through. People might ask why loyalists were so upset over a flag. In my experience of growing up in, and working with, socially and economically disadvantaged communities, the flag isn't the centre of the world. Mothers and fathers in loyalist working-class areas strive to work and feed their kids. They are at the mercy of large companies who operate zero-hour contracts. So, when you take the flag away, people who already feel like 'white trash' are left with nothing. People's culture gives them a sense of belonging and identity where the labour market has failed them.

When I arrived at City Hall on that December night, I saw hundreds of loyalists and unionists protesting at Donegall Square South. It wasn't just a case of mob rule or loyalist thuggery – I was approached by several middle-class Protestants who told me that they were disgusted at what had happened. People were becoming frustrated by Sinn Féin's gimmickry, and I was adamant that they were acting outside the spirit of the Belfast Agreement. Like the pressure groups that had been set up in the 1990s to disrupt Orange marches, this was another attempt to erode loyalist identity and culture. The whole thing was choreographed to ensure that any protests that occurred would look extremely bad, given that it was three weeks before Christmas and the continental market, which was pitched at the front of City Hall, would inevitably suffer disruption if loyalists descended on the city centre in protest.

I took a conscious decision as leader of the PUP to support the protest and to ensure, as best as I could, that nobody ended up with a criminal record. History had demonstrated to me that when people come out onto the streets and there is no strategy or organising behind what they are doing, then things can get out of hand. Protests can be easily infiltrated and made to look bad, and civil disobedience, if not planned out, can lead to the police being heavy-handed. In the end, both of those things happened. In the days and weeks that followed, young loyalists came out onto the streets and vented their frustration through rioting. Young men were being arrested by the PSNI and charged with 'flying the Union flag provocatively'. Criminal records, which would never be expunged, were affecting the future opportunities of a new generation of young loyalists.

To my dismay, Jim Dowson, a prominent figure in the far-right from Scotland, edged his way into a pivotal position in the flag protests. Having people like Dowson speaking at public rallies was a bad look for loyalism, and his politics represented everything I stood against. I didn't want him around, and I didn't trust him.

Willie Frazer was another person who was passionate about the flag being flown at City Hall. Willie had suffered immeasurably at the hands of the PIRA over the years, and I was worried that he might be prone to being used by the wrong people. In the heat of the moment, people were being pulled in different directions and strange alliances were being formed, sometimes with people who had never been heard of before. I saw my role as being on the ground, trying to calm things and giving people sensible advice based on my years of experience.

Around this time, the PUP saw an influx of new members. I saw an opportunity. Some of these people were rough around the edges, but I felt that if we got them into the party, we could work with them and show them how to proceed politically, with a positive vision of the future. A few people went on to become articulate proponents of progressive loyalism, and I hoped that maybe the transition from protest to politics would galvanise the fortunes of the PUP. I wanted to take people on a journey, and to bring them to a point where they could buy into the politics that David and I had espoused, which was both proudly loyalist and progressive.

This initially worked and the PUP made gains in the 2014 local council elections, but we couldn't make inroads into the Northern Ireland Assembly, where our voice would perhaps be heard louder.

One of the problems about this period was that the flag protests encompassed a coalition of disaffected people who called themselves loyalists. Very many of them, particularly those who were involved in the far-right had nothing in common with the PUP that I had joined when I came out of Long Kesh. Those people would not have been welcome in a party which espoused a woman's right to choose and which explicitly stated that you couldn't be a loyalist and a racist. I am a proud socialist, and always have been. I want to progress society, but some of these people from the right-wing were perhaps harking back to the old days of division. While Sinn Féin had been cynical in their ploy to have the flying of the flag changed, I couldn't abide those who were using the loyalist people as fodder for their own extreme political rhetoric. The PUP was accused of mimicking the flag-waving loyalists and unionists that we had spent so many years criticising. Any negative criticism of the flag protests inevitably bled into the reputation of the party.

The flag protests brought to bear something which had been a problem for the loyalist people for almost a generation. The term 'loyalist' had become a derogatory byword for criminality and negativity since the days of Tony Blair's time as prime minister.

When he wanted to have the Belfast Agreement pushed through to bolster his reputation and legacy, he decided to support the Ulster Unionists, the SDLP and Sinn Féin (and later the DUP). Blair quite blatantly said he would look after republicans and the chief constable could look after loyalists, so he created that whole notion – that's where it started. From then right up to the flag protests and the present day, there has been a lingering bad taste in the mouth of many loyalists. The flag was a symbolic issue that galvanised loyalists to protest, but there was so much else going on that people were angry about. There was anger over a perceived disproportionate use of the Historical Enquiries Team (a body formed to investigate cold case murders from during the conflict) to target loyalists, and the tabloid media was constantly lambasting loyalists and ignoring any good news stories that emanated from our community. The flag became something that people found common anger over, but there were many other issues eating away at loyalism. There was deep-rooted disillusionment, and people sensed that they had been left behind by a political process and a new economic reality that they felt they had no stake in. There is a huge task ahead to ensure that the loyalist people feel part of society and the mainstream political process and the decision-making that goes on at Stormont and Westminster.

***

In May 2014 my old friend and comrade Hughie Smyth died after being in ill health for some time. Hughie had been the PUP councillor for the Court ward, and I replaced him when he stood down due to his health problems. Hughie was a loyalist legend, and his presence in Belfast City Council had ensured that a thread of socialist-minded loyalism had run through Belfast politics since the early 1970s, when he had first been elected as an independent loyalist councillor. He was a pioneer of working-class politics and a staunch and proud unionist who had made a monumental contribution to the political process in Northern Ireland over the course of the previous forty years. Hughie had been there in the 1970s when things often seemed bleak. He injected humour into stressful situations that arose during intense political negotiations in the 1990s, and he was a good friend and comrade to have. I was honoured to take his place on Belfast City Council, though saddened by the circumstances. In a subsequent election, I retained the seat and continue to fight, like Hughie, for the betterment of working-class loyalists in Belfast. There have been many challenges to society and the people and city I represent in recent times, with Brexit, Covid-19 and an ongoing transition from a troubled past to a peaceful future all ensuring that I am kept extremely busy. But this is the life I have chosen. This is my life in loyalism.

Epilogue

In April 2018, there was a lot of coverage in the media about the twentieth anniversary of the Belfast Agreement. I looked back on 1998 with a sense of regret. I've never wanted to change the world; there are very few people capable of doing that. I have just wanted to make a difference, and I think the PUP and loyalism did make a positive difference in the 1990s. In 2018 you wouldn't have guessed the pivotal role that we played in the Agreement from the commentaries about the era in which it came to fruition. It was, I feel, a revisionist attempt to redraw loyalism as a criminal constituency, ignoring all of the positive work that had been done in the 1990s. That suits the narrative of loyalism equalling criminality. In the 1990s, when the PUP and loyalism was making positive strides towards peace, the media chose to focus on these negative individuals who sought to ruin the process. This continued into the year 2000 and beyond. These individuals were caricatures who then became the byword for loyalism. There is very little written about the positive contributions that David Ervine made, that Hughie Smyth made, that Jim McDonald and Billy Mitchell and I made. There are countless others who cannot be named. We came through the worst of the Troubles and tried to learn from the past and make a difference.

I am now in my 60s. I have lived a long and eventful life where others have not been so fortunate. When I look at old photographs from PUP meetings, or group photographs from Long Kesh, I am shocked to find that I am often one of the only people still alive. People ask me what David would make of the current malaise we have in local politics. Well, I know he would be frustrated. He did want to change the world and was of the belief that he could. That determination is probably what cost him his life. He put himself under undue pressure and his death was a massive blow to loyalism. Those who say things would be different if David were still alive are right, but credit must be given to the men named above. The lesser known figures in the background who worked tirelessly alongside myself and David to make the progress that we did in the 1990s.

As Northern Ireland approaches its centenary in 2021, it is our opportunity to talk about unionism in a positive way. We have to promote Northern Ireland as an integral part of the Union. There are a number of hugely positive aspects to being in the UK. It is a diverse tapestry of different ethnicities, faiths and political outlooks living across a range of nations which have a proud and shared history of military service, industrial endeavour, free speech and above all, the NHS. I hope that in the future young loyalists can focus on the positive aspects of being British and make their own political decisions. The years since the 1998 agreement have not been perfect, and there is much to improve, but life in Northern Ireland is broadly much better and ultimately more peaceful than during the Troubles period, when people, myself included, felt compelled to find our answers down the barrel of a gun. In those dark days and fearful, bloody nights of the early 1970s, I was of the genuine belief that the working-class community of the Shankill where I lived was going to be decimated by the republican movement. Along with others, I decided to take action, which I take full responsibility for. Many people were calling for such action. They felt that the police and the army could not protect them. They looked to young men like me. I felt proud to call myself an Ulster Volunteer, but I want people to understand that if it had not been for the toxic atmosphere created in society here, young men like myself would never have seen the inside of a prison.

This toxic atmosphere had been created by the so-called 'better class' of unionist whose sectarian attitudes and lack of generosity had kept Catholics disenfranchised and working-class Protestants in their place. We were the men and women who toiled in factories, shipyards, mills and ropeworks to make the rich even richer. They tried to tell us that they knew what was best for us. These big-house unionists would not entertain the notion of alternative voices from within the Protestant community, and they tried to discredit and destroy anyone who sought to guide working-class loyalists in a different direction.

Outsiders and those from the republican community liked to claim that we were pampered and privileged. Those same people wouldn't dare call workers in the shipyards of England or Scotland at the time 'privileged'. What privilege is there in being used as expendable labour and sectarian muscle by those supposedly genteel men and women whose own children would be paid through school and sent to university rather than forced to stand outside the shipyard gate, begging for work. What privilege is there for those living in fear when news of another IRA bombing in a loyalist area came through on the wireless.

What happened in the early 1970s when young men like me joined the loyalist paramilitaries was the beginning of a voyage where we would begin to discover our own political voices. The civil rights campaign of the late 1960s, while commendable, wasn't of benefit to loyalists like me and those in my community. While there was a demand for equity, justice and fair treatment, there was also a sense that republicans had encroached on the civil rights movement for their own nefarious objectives which ran in complete opposition to those of me and the people I lived among. In these circumstances there was no way we could buy into such a campaign. It would run contrary to our very way of life.

I, and many young loyalists of my age, felt that we had to stand up to the Provos. The state had tied the hands of the police and the military, so someone had to provide resistance to republican violence.

When I was eventually incarcerated for my involvement with the UVF, I was able to engage in dialogue with my fellow comrades, who also found themselves looking at long, often indeterminate sentences for their loyalty to Ulster. This dialogue was different to that which we engaged in on the outside. Under the guidance and influence of Gusty Spence, we were able to vocalise ideas that would perhaps have caused physical fights on the streets of the Shankill if we had dared air them there before our imprisonment. But we were all in the same boat and had seen that violence was not the answer to the problems that besieged Northern Ireland. We didn't suddenly become pacifists, and we certainly did not renounce our allegiance to the UVF, but we increasingly understood that dialogue was an enriching way out of the cul-de-sac which violence had brought us to.

I have used that experience of incarceration, when I spent all of my twenties and nearly half of my thirties in Long Kesh, to try and make society a better place. I have dissuaded others from using violence while constantly living under the threat of death myself.

During the Troubles I often heard loyalists say that they wouldn't be the generation to fail Ulster in her time of need. I certainly felt that way in the 1970s, and through my political career and community work, the mantra is still the same. I will never fail the people I represent. The people who elected me, and the people whose lives I aim to make better. Those are the motivations for me to keep going when I get up in the morning.

I would like to think that the next generation will continue to live normally, without the backdrop of violence in their lives. I hope, in telling my story, that I have contributed to a better understanding of the Troubles and the role that young loyalists played in it so that we must never repeat those violent years. Loyalists must be confident in telling their stories so that revisionists can never be allowed to rewrite the past.

APPENDICES

RESULTS OF 12 MIN RUN TEST

#	NAME	LAPS	+ METRES	DIST RUN	SPEED METRES/MIN	"X" (−150m/min)	ESTIMATED VO_2 MAX
1.	W. MITCHELL	11	230	3640	303.33	153.33	60.59
2.	W. HUTCHINSON	11	13	3423	285.25	135.25	57.37

Running statistics from my time in Long Kesh. (See overleaf for further details.) 'Running provided me with a canvas of space and time to get lost in my own thoughts ... It had become an obsession and a form of self-discipline.'

3-7-85 2:00 pm 1x4x200m (1:6)
1x4x100m

1.	29:09	1.	12:99
2.	28:97	2.	13:11
3.	28:88	3	13:13
4.	29:45	4.	13:01
Ave	29:09	Ave	13:08

Am pleased with these speed endurance units. Detect that his natural speed will suffice if added to the proper endurance workouts. Have to eradicate mental barrier of feeling less strong than he actually is with a few pre-competitive, motivational strength units.

4-7-85 6:00pm Football Pitch
1 mile Form Assessment 5:02:31

Started too fast – relaxed too much in middle phase but picked up quite a bit over last 400m. Considering the time was just 5 secs outside his best and was executed comfortably, we're both pleased at this particular time. Will start tapering training units to coincide with increase in competition.

5-7-85 2:00pm 3x800m (1:2)

1. 2:23:68
2. 2:19:77
3. 2:24:80

Working again to approximate new racing speed. Will have a few easy days of relaxed continuous running then a 24 day microcycle of build-up and competitiveness to include time trials + races.

9-7-85 2:00pm 1 mile time trial 4:53:53
A very good time trial today coming early in his season. Had a good few days of resting since the 4th's run which left him feeling stronger + mentally better prepared. Ran with a pacemaker which he outkicked easily over last 200. Splits of
75:79 75:62 73:41 68:71

PETITION FROM PRISONER OR YOC INMATE

NAME William Hutchinson PRISON/YOC ______
BLOCK/WING, ETC Compound 21 PRISON/YOC NO 260

To the Secretary of State for Northern Ireland

Sir,

I am petitioning you because I am being denied access to education facilities which I am need of to complete a course with the open university. My complaint is with not being allowed access to Compound 19 which is a study centre. The reason I need access to the centre is to use the video facilities for the television programmes related to my course. I have been informed by the prison education that I may not use the study centre until September and that I will be denied access to the video because it is prohibited from entering the compound.

This unavailability of the video facilities is a great inconvenience to me as the course (D202 Urban change and conflict) I am studying concentrates its comparative material in the television programmes. Too quote the course guide 'the programmes are important because they provide crucial material to back up the arguments of the course and help you critically assess them'. Another reason they cause me an

Inmate's Signature Wm Hutchinson Date 8th July 1985

109

'Education was also a form of resistance. Though the UVF/RHC leadership in Long Kesh was amenable and supportive of volunteers seeking to pursue education and knowledge, the prison system would often create obstacles ... On many occasions I was forced to petition the governor for access to educational facilities so that I and others could continue our Open University education.'

inconvenience are that the programmes are also necessary for tutor marked assignments and the final exam which I will have to take on the 12th October 1985. My next programme is due to go out on Sunday 14th July 1985, which is shortly therefore I would like to have this matter cleared up one way or the other before then.

I have been informed that the reason for the denial of education facilities is due to a shortage of staff. If this is the true reason I can understand the closure of study centre, but I cannot understand the archaic attitude towards the admittance of the video facilities to the compound for my use.

Inmate's Signature Wm Hutchinson Date 8th July 1985

110

Personal

15 February 1985.

Mr. William Hutchinson
25 Jersey Street
Belfast 13
Northern Ireland.

Dear William,

Many thanks for your letter of 18 January. Forgive the delay in replying but I have been exceptionally busy, not least over my imminent departure on leave which I think I mentioned to you in my last letter.

I didn't thank your document was superficial as you put it. I thought it had the bones of a good appeal which perahps may need to be published if the NIO initiative goes nowhere. I agree that you should adapt a wait and see, with the caveat that you should document clearly as you did in your letter to date, what is acually done by the civil servants. The only additional point I would make at the moment is that it may be polite to emphasis, not least note, that with life sentences, any release is revocable at any time. It is not likely to happen of course, and it could be argued that this should not be emphasised, but it may prove a useful arguement that short of an amnesty, release will be release on licence. In particular cases I also think it would be important to have outside people, family friends etc, at least make efforts to demonstrate that employment opportunities are available. Equally evidence that the family is still involved with the prisoner and together would be important. Of course this sadly will not apply to all cases, but where it does there seems no reason why it shouldn't be brought out. In that regard I enclose a note I made of a radio interview given by Nicholas Scott the relevant Minister. The issue was LSPS but it may give you some ideas.

Finally, I would suggest (and would be happy to help organise) that the Committee for the Administration of Justice in Northern Ireland, a non sectarian, and non political group, that has some leverage with the civil servants, might be asked to run a conference/seminar, say in October next on the whole subject of release of LSPS. This would be a forum for your document, and update, and a useful publicity focus too. Perhaps you could let me have your reactions.

12/1/1985

But I'm afraid in terms of doing anything I must sign off until I return in October. Nevertheless,,I would be optimistic that fxom your initiative if it is sustained and the tone of your approach which is balanced and factual is maintained that we could make progress before Christmas.

Keep ypuyour spirits and I look forward to meeting with you perhaps in the autumn.

Yours sincerely,

C.K. Boyle

My correspondence with the human rights lawyer, Kevin Boyle, while in Long Kesh. 'Communicating with Kevin Boyle was important. We may have come from different sides of the sectarian divide, and experienced the early Troubles in very different ways, but I knew there was no point in existing in an echo chamber. Prison, with its access to education, had ironically broadened my horizons.'